"This is the story that could not happen—but it did. Two young men reared as Muslims find Jesus as their Savior and provide the most enlightening insights into the world of Islam that I have read anywhere. A great story, a fabulous read, and an arresting assessment."
—PAIGE PATTERSON, PRESIDENT
SOUTHWESTERN BAPTIST THEOLOGICAL SEMINARY
FORT WORTH, TEXAS

"*Unveiling Islam* . . . is must reading for all who take the Great Commission to heart. When Christians and Muslims both know that difference as revealed in this book, both will want to really know the God of the Bible. Critically important."
—ZIG ZIGLAR, AUTHOR/MOTIVATIONAL SPEAKER

"[The Caners are] articulate and authoritative, and [have] an excellent grasp of the politics, theology, beliefs, and thinking of a majority of Muslims."
—VICTOR OLADOKUN, HOST AND PRODUCER,
TURNING POINT, CBN INTERNATIONAL

"This is a crucially important book, written by former Muslims who share, in a loving fashion, the real differences between Islam and biblical Christianity and give information concerning this religion about which all Americans need to be informed."
—JAMES MERRITT, HOST OF *TOUCHING LIVES*
PAST PRESIDENT, SOUTHERN BAPTIST CONVENTION

"This book by the Caner brothers, both esteemed professors, is not only a phenomenal work of scholars, but the shared knowledge of former Muslims. It is more than interesting reading, in light of current events it is *must* reading. There is no other work like it. This book is strong without being strident, factual without being stale, profound without being impractical. It is indeed the best on the subject."
—BAILEY SMITH, PRESIDENT AND CEO
BAILEY SMITH MINISTRIES

"Don't expect to curl up with this book and have a cozy read. Instead, once you've been exposed to the challenges of Muslim teachings and their desperate spiritual needs, it will drive you to your knees in prayer. As well, you'll eventually be up on your feet, going to share the gospel with a Muslim friend! Read this book; it is packed full of pertinent and important information!"

—R. PHILLIP ROBERTS, PRESIDENT
MIDWESTERN BAPTIST THEOLOGICAL SEMINARY
KANSAS CITY, MISSOURI

"The writing is personal and accessible; the research is extensive. Ergun and Emir Caner have produced a timely and valuable work for all who wish to understand the relationship between Islam and Christianity."

—GARY LEDBETTER, EDITOR
THE SOUTHERN BAPTIST TEXAN

UNVEILING
ISLAM

AN INSIDER'S LOOK AT
MUSLIM LIFE AND BELIEFS

UNVEILING
ISLAM

UPDATED AND EXPANDED EDITION

ERGUN MEHMET CANER
EMIR FETHI CANER

Kregel
Publications

To
Maria Eleonora Lindberg.
Revelation 14:13

CONTENTS

FOREWORD

HOW COULD THERE be A more timely and critically important book in the world of Christian publishing than *Unveiling Islam*? In the aftermath of the horrific terrorist attacks of September 11, 2001, Christians have searched for a trustworthy guide to the unfamiliar and suddenly threatening world of Islam. God, in His gracious providence, has provided precisely such an invaluable guide. The Caners have written the riveting, inspiring, and heart-rending story of Islam and their own conversion to saving faith in Jesus Christ.

Ergun and Emir Caner are trophies of God's grace—once devout followers of Allah, now of Jesus of Nazareth. Their story is both a compelling example of God's love and a sobering and informative trip through the world of Islam.

Unveiling Islam is exactly what its subtitle describes; it is an insider's look at Muslim life and beliefs. It is a bonus that this vivid analysis of Islam is by former insiders who are now Christians. The Caners have provided us with an invaluable perspective that will do much to inform, challenge, and inspire Christians.

Perhaps *Unveiling Islam*'s most compelling aspect is the "human face" that it puts on the conflict between the religion of Islam and the personal relationship with Jesus Christ that is the foundation and essence of Christianity. The Caners' compelling story reminds us of the severe, often bloody, persecution faced today by fellow

11

Christians around the world, who have come to understand that all faiths are *not* the same, but that Jesus is "*the* way, *the* truth, and *the* life" (John 14:6).

—RICHARD LAND, PRESIDENT
THE ETHICS & RELIGIOUS LIBERTY COMMISSION
SOUTHERN BAPTIST CONVENTION

PREFACE

A MAN OF GRANITE

HE SEEMED CARVED out of granite. Broad-shouldered, legs rippling with muscles, he prowled the soccer field like a tiger. Nimbly he maneuvered with his teammates on that rough little field in Galion, Ohio. Then he turned to give us a wink. At forty-five years old, he ran, played, and kicked like a man half his age. His jet-black hair was offset by bronzed olive skin. Clean-shaven and quick to smile for the three boys standing on the sidelines, he was more than our favorite soccer player. He was our father. He was our hero.

Of course, we never called it *soccer*. We called it *football*. For hours our father would kick the ball back and forth to us and regale us with stories of games gone by—games played in Turkey, Germany, and other countries. With his thick accent, he would sing Turkish songs in a loud and boisterous voice, as we butchered the words he was teaching us.

But of all the memories of our father, this one pristine day sticks out in Ergun Caner's memory: Our father's yellow car, saturated in the smoke of Pall Mall and Chesterfield cigarettes; that nose, which hovered elegantly beyond his face; those strong, rough hands that engulfed his soda; that laugh; the drive home to our duplex in Whitehall, Ohio—every moment remains seared in Ergun's memory. It was 1978. Four years later our father would disown his three sons. Twenty-one years later we would see our hero one last time.

Acar Mehmet Caner

Many authors state that their book is a "labor of love." That's not the case with us, Ergun and Emir Caner. This has been an arduous and sometimes painful exercise of unspoken memories that are never far below the surface. Neither is this a "Mommy Dearest" exposé of a "bad father" or a betrayal of family secrets. Our father was a wonderful, sincere, mountain of a man. He was in every way our hero—intelligent, warm, loving, handsome, determined, hard working, and funny. It gave him no pleasure to disown or disinherit his sons. It broke his heart. Yet it was all he could do, given his beliefs and the teachings of Islam. On the August day in 1999 when our father succumbed to cancer, the stark reality of religious systems and our relationship with Jesus Christ as our Savior came into sharp focus.

As you begin this investigation into Islam, its teachings, and its adherents, we want you to see the human side of religion—where faith often means the total rejection of culture, ethnicity, family, and friends. To find heaven's glory in Jesus Christ, we Caner brothers lost our father—our earthly hero—as have millions of others worldwide.

Since September 11, 2001, we have spoken nationwide in hundreds of assemblies, colleges, universities, churches, conventions, and conferences. Often, reporters are puzzled about our disinheritance. Implied are the questions, "Why would switching your religion mean the loss of family? Doesn't religion enhance the family? Isn't your nuclear family the most important thing?"

These questions betray a postmodern and Americanized bias. For the other 95 percent of the world's population, conversion to Jesus Christ often means disowning, disinheritance, expulsion, arrest, and even death. In the world that does not embrace the "beliefs don't matter" mentality, the American attitude seems inane. At this moment, for the sake of the gospel of Jesus Christ, men and women are being bullwhipped into submission, tortured, imprisoned, beaten, battered, and broken. Homes are being burned, families are executed, and other lives lost through hateful revenge. If you believe that torture and murder because of belief in Jesus Christ is a thing of the past, then you are tragically mistaken. Across our globe, the blood of Christians runs down cobblestone streets, dirt paths, paved alleys, and concrete prison floors.

The media's questions also belie a mistaken assumption that "All religions are the same. Getting to God, if there is one, is like getting to Chicago. You can get there by plane, train, or automobile. It doesn't matter what path you take (or religion you follow), as long as you get there."

This attitude reflects the "Oprahization" of American culture.

To those of that syncretistic persuasion, may we state clearly that we did not "switch religions." The blood of Jesus Christ saved us. What happened to us was not an act of a religious person; rather, it was God's gracious act of redemption.

We are not particularly religious men. If you were to look at either of us, you would not immediately assume that we have served as preachers, evangelists, and pastors for a combined thirty years. You wouldn't guess that we are now both professors of theology and church history. We don't fulfill the caricature of the clip-on tie, white-socks-with-a-bad-suit preacher. Ergun Caner has shaved his head bald for years, wears a goatee, and is prone to an African-American style of preaching. Emir Caner plays basketball and tennis regularly, looks like a college fraternity pledge, and has memorized virtually every date in church history. Neither of us fits the "religious" profile, but we are clothed in the righteousness of Christ. Christianity is not about religion; it is about a relationship with the Savior.

It must be understood that orthodox, biblical Christianity assumes the existence of truth. Truth implies the existence of error, and mutually exclusive claims of truth cannot both be correct. Such is the case with Islam and Christianity. Either Islam is correct in the assumption that "there is only One God, Allah, and Muhammad is His prophet," or Christianity is correct when Jesus says, "I am the way, the truth, and the life. No one comes to the Father except through Me" (John 14:6). They cannot both be correct.

Often in public debates and forums, Muslims have risen to ask us the tangential and poignant question, "Was it not you who disowned your father when you turned your back on the teachings of the Qur'an?" Perhaps they are correct. Neither Ergun, Emir, nor Erdem (Mark) Caner desired to break our relationship with our father, but we were aware of the consequences of following Jesus Christ. Perhaps in those terms we did, in fact, turn from our father. But to receive eternal life through Jesus Christ our Lord, one often experiences painful destruction of relationships. Some of you who read this book have experienced such rejection. We understand your journey.

Salvation Comes to the Caner Brothers

Our father, Acar, met Mother in Sweden, where he was attending university. After falling in love, getting married, and having their first two sons, Ergun and Erdem, in Stockholm, Father and Mother moved to America, the land of opportunity. Emir was born after we arrived in Ohio.

The marriage was doomed from the beginning, a clash of cultures. Our mother was an only child, raised in Stockholm and educated all over Europe. By the time she was twenty, she had attended the Sorbonne in Paris, and had traveled the world. Father was from heartier stock. As the youngest child in his family, he had earned everything he owned and was steeped in Islamic culture. Their assumptions about marriage clearly clashed.

The divorce, which was finalized in America, was painful. As in most divorces, the children became the human "ropes" in a tug-of-war, torn between parents. A pattern developed of weekend visits between Columbus and Gahanna, in central Ohio. Yet even the wrenching experience of divorce could not prepare us for our father's disavowal.

Entering high school, Ergun was a typical young man, except that he was a devout Muslim. Even through the divorce, our parents had maintained our rearing in the mosque. Each weekend, we would travel to Broad Street in Columbus, Ohio, where our father had helped found the Islamic Foundation. The mosque in Toledo was too far a drive, so the Foundation Center was established. Father did the call to prayer on occasion.

We did our *rakats* (daily prayers); we celebrated Ramadan. We read the Qur'an and Hadith regularly. In every way, we were devout, serious Muslims. But our devotion was not an act of love, but of fear. No Muslim has eternal security. Every Muslim fears the scales of justice, which weigh his good deeds against his bad deeds. We were taught that Christianity and Islam were antithetical, stemming from a centuries-old conflict dating back to the Crusades, when Muslims were slaughtered by the thousands.

This history, however, did not stop Jerry Tackett. Ergun's best friend in high school, Jerry was the son of a preacher, and an active member at Stelzer Road Baptist Church. Jerry didn't know all of the history. He simply told Ergun that Jesus loved him, and invited him to church for revival services. At Stelzer Road Baptist, the environment was so different from what Ergun had expected. People were warm. They didn't mock when he stumbled through the hymns. They loved him in spite of his reticence—they literally loved him to the Cross.

After hearing about the saving grace of Jesus Christ, it became evident to Ergun that Islam was wrong about one seminal thing: there was no way that Jesus could have been a prophet, as Islam taught. Jesus was arrested and imprisoned on a dual indictment—the Romans held Him for insurrection, and the Jewish leaders convicted Him of blasphemy, that is, claiming to be God. Islam, in order to resolve the matter of the Resurrection, teaches that Judas, not Jesus, was crucified, allowing Jesus to appear three days later. Yet even that bit of misinformation doesn't confront the larger issue of Jesus' deity. Even extrabiblical history notes that Jesus claimed to be God, an act of blasphemy, which was a capital offense.

To borrow a motif from the Christian philosopher C. S. Lewis, if Jesus claimed to be God, He couldn't have been a prophet.[1] He could have been insane, like those who wander the streets assuming they are divine. But if He were insane, He couldn't have been one of Allah's prophets. He could have been a fraud, deceiving people, but, again, an impostor and charlatan couldn't have been a prophet of Allah. Ergun faced one other option: Jesus was who He said He was: Immanuel—God with us.

On that particular night in the revival services, the conviction of the Holy Spirit was palpable. On the next day, a Friday, Ergun returned to the Islamic Foundation Center a new creature, freed from the scales of fear by grace and the atonement of Jesus. He assumed that other Muslims also wanted to be free of fear. That was not the case.

Ergun's brothers, however, listened. Erdem accepted Christ in the basement of their home. Ergun then invited Emir to a revival service the following year. There, for the first time in his life, Emir heard that God loved him and desired to have a personal relationship with him. Though he had been to church before, this was the first time he could recall hearing a preacher speak openly and honestly about the exclusivity of the gospel. Only through the blood of Jesus, spilt on the cross, can someone be saved. Yet the preacher also spoke compassionately about God's desire to save everyone. Although there was only one way, the path was open for all who would believe. On November 4, 1982, Emir was born again.

In 1982, Ergun surrendered to the gospel ministry. It was the last time he saw our father for seventeen years. Acar disowned his sons, although it could have been worse: according to hadith 9.57, all three of us brothers should have been killed.

Tragedies and Commitments

Seventeen years later, we Caner brothers were reunited with our father, four days before he died. His second wife had convinced him to see us, and we flew in from all over the country, hoping. By this time, Erdem was married with a son, Anthony, was a successful stockbroker, and had remained active in his church. Emir had completed his Ph.D. and was teaching at Southeastern Seminary in North Carolina. Ergun had married Jill Morris in 1994, and had a four-month-old son, Braxton Paige. Ergun and Emir had pastored and preached, and completed their education, with Ergun's Th.D. dissertation alone left to complete.

Yet as we three brothers entered our father's house, our minds returned to that long-ago day on the soccer field. We were the three sons of Acar Mehmet Caner, our hero. In our culture, it is an important rite of passage to lay your son in your father's hands. As Ergun did so, tears filled his eyes. Seventeen years after expulsion, Ergun and his father met one last time.

All throughout the time together, we shared in small talk. Ergun was introduced to his two half-sisters, whom he had never met. Other men from the mosque were in the home, some of whom had taught us brothers in our youth. We all avoided the inevitable and obvious: our father was dying; it was only a matter of time.

We would love to complete the story with a deathbed conversion, but that was not the case. Our mother made her profession of faith in 1991, and our grandmother did the same in 1995. But our father never accepted Christ as Lord. As far as we know, he entered a Christless eternity.

As these words are written, tears spring afresh.

If the events of September 11 have spurred a national debate, some of the topics discussed are not new for us. Since 1982, we have preached and taught about Islam, sharing our hearts' desire for salvation among the 1.2 billion Muslim people who need Jesus. After allowing us to preach in their churches, pastors would graciously pat us on our backs and tell us how fascinating this world religion seems.

After thousands of people were incinerated in the World Trade Center bombings, people began to listen.

But please do not assume this is a diatribe filled with invective against a world religion. We want Christians to understand Islam more clearly and to present Christ more effectively. We want the former because it is our history, and it is our past. We want the latter because we wish we'd had the opportunity to do so for our father . . . our hero.

Notes

1. C. S. Lewis, *Mere Christianity* (New York: Harper Collins, 2001), 52.

ACKNOWLEDGMENTS

SEVERAL GUIDES ALONG our Christian pilgrimage have made our ministries and this book possible:

- Mark Erdem Caner, the wisest of brothers
- Jerry Tackett, who led Ergun to faith in Jesus Christ
- Clarence Miller, who led Emir to faith, baptized us, and allowed us to preach our first sermons at Stelzer Road Baptist Church, Columbus, Ohio
- Brian Grable, who discipled Ergun without knowing it
- Roger Williams, who taught Ergun how to be a pastor
- David Eppling, the consummate example of a pastor and friend
- Jim and Monica Hunt, who have walked with us throughout our spiritual lives
- Drs. Paige and Dorothy Patterson, who gave intellectual and spiritual tools for ministry and were like parents
- Dr. Mac Brunson, Ergun's pastor and friend
- Dr. Richard Wells, Criswell College, and Southeastern Baptist Theological Seminary, which allowed us the time to complete this book
- All who have allowed us to stand in their pulpits to preach the inerrant Word of God and Christ alone as Lord and Savior

- Ergun's wife, Jill: You are more than just the mother of our son, Braxton; you are my heart. *Jag älskar dig.*
- Emir's wife, Hana: My greatest source of strength and inspiration. *Miluji te.*

INTRODUCTION

CHILLING WORDS IN A
FRIGHTENING WORLD

THE FLICKERING IMAGE on the screen is surreal. With effervescent glee, Sheikh Osama bin Laden reposes after a meal hosted by an ally in Qandahar, Afghanistan. He hints broadly of his central role in planning and implementing the airliner hijackings and attacks that had shocked the world. Considering the fate of one of the willing martyrs of that operation, Bin Laden quotes the Hadith:[1]

I was ordered to fight the people until they say there is no God but Allah, and his prophet Muhammad.

Some people may ask: Why do you want to fight us?

There is an association between those who say: I believe in one god and Muhammad is his prophet, and those who don't [. . . inaudible . . .]

Those who do not follow the true fiqh [jurisprudence]. The fiqh of Muhammad, the real fiqh. They are just accepting what is being said at face value.

He happily recounts indications that the bombing had increased awareness of Islam worldwide, and was possibly one of the greatest events in Islamic "evangelism" in recent days:

Those youth who conducted the operations did not accept any fiqh in the popular terms, but they accepted the fiqh that the prophet Muhammad brought. Those young men [. . . inaudible . . .] said in deeds, in New York and Washington, speeches that overshadowed all other speeches made everywhere else in the world. The speeches are understood by both Arabs and non-Arabs—even by Chinese. It is above all the media said. Some of them said that in Holland, at one of the centers, the number of people who accepted Islam during the days that followed the operations were more than the people who accepted Islam in the last eleven years. I heard someone on Islamic radio who owns a school in America say: "We don't have time to keep up with the demands of those who are asking about Islamic books to learn about Islam." This event made people think [about true Islam] which benefited Islam greatly.

He speaks of his estimation of casualties and the time lapse between the two impacts, both of which gave him great pleasure:

[. . . inaudible . . .] we calculated in advance the number of casualties from the enemy, who would be killed based on the position of the tower. We calculated that the floors that would be hit would be three or four floors. I was the most optimistic of them all [. . . inaudible . . .] due to my experience in this field, I was thinking that the fire from the gas in the plane would melt the iron structure of the building and collapse the area where the plane hit and all the floors above it only. This is all that we had hoped for.

The difference between the first and the second plane hitting the towers was twenty minutes. And the difference between the first plane and the plane that hit the Pentagon was one hour.[2]

He speaks of his purpose to "pull America out of its caves" and concludes the videotaped session with a chilling poem:

> I witness that against the sharp blade
> They always faced difficulties and stood together. . . .
> When the darkness comes upon us and we are bit by a
> Sharp tooth, I say . . .
> "Our homes are flooded with blood and the tyrant
> Is freely wandering in our homes." . . .
> And from the battlefield vanished
> The brightness of swords and the horses . . .
> And over weeping sounds now
> We hear the beats of drums and rhythm. . . .
> They are storming his forts
> And shouting: "We will not stop our raids
> Until you free our lands."

People in those nations that lost citizens on September 11, 2001, and especially people in the United States, heard the voice of terrorism. For many, especially in the media, the tape seemed irrefutable proof that Bin Laden was a leading conspirator in the acts. Bin Laden's Islamic defenders, who had spent three months in front of cameras screaming for proof, were silenced. For those not familiar with the Qur'an and Hadith, the tape was a shock. For those of us who know these foundations of Muslim faith, it was sad validation.

During the first months following the bombings we, the authors, were thrust onto the front lines of a war of competing words and images. Raised to follow Islam and to heed every word of the Qur'an and Hadith, suddenly we were called upon to dispel myths and rumors, especially concerning Islamic theology and the idea of jihad.

At first, our loudest detractors tended to be Christians, who did not believe that we understood the protocols of jihad and the beliefs regarding an Islamic martyr's eternity.

That was before the Bin Laden tape became public.

Bin Laden told of the "waves" of jihad of which we had spoken. He cited the Hadith copiously. He declared that the bombing was a blow for the *fatwa* (a declaration of jihad) that had been signed two years before as a virtual declaration of war on the West. He spoke of the universal call to jihad and the obligation to fight.

After the videotapes were released, our lives, and the lives of our families, became a blur of media interviews, sermons, and lectures in packed auditoriums, after which we hurried to respond to innumerable e-mail messages. Days at a time became a time loop of airports, cramped flights, conferences, and return flights. Nor could we drop our work responsibilities: Emir was teaching a full load at Southeastern Baptist Theological Seminary in Wake Forest, North Carolina, and Ergun was teaching a full load at Criswell College in Dallas, Texas.

In our "spare time" we were writing this book. Though we had been discussing such a project with Kregel Publications for some time, the tragedy suddenly set things on a fast track. All those involved with editing and publishing this work felt we needed to be in print as expeditiously as possible. Thus, every night, after our wives and children went to bed, we typed . . . and typed . . . and edited . . . and typed some more.

This book is not an academic exercise, but an easily understood panorama of Islam, explaining motives, beliefs, and history. It is meant to guide and encourage every person who wants to be a more effective witness to Muslims.

Thus, the book you now hold is unique, written by two professors of theology and church history, who happen to be brothers and former Muslims. We've organized a lot of information into a package that people without previous knowledge of Islam will be able to unwrap. Arabic terms are defined (see appendix D). The book is comprehensive yet concise, explicitly addressing evangelical Christians who share our desire to reach 1.2 billion Muslims with the gospel of Jesus Christ.

A few caveats: First, remember that this is a guide with sources, not a systematic theology of Islam. We have, however, included numerous endnotes and suggestions for further reading.

Second, Arabic terms are expressed in the English alphabet and in transliteration, rather than in Arabic. If transliterations vary from those in other sources, that is because there are few hard rules and standards for transliterating Arabic. At best, phonetic spelling is imprecise. Third, the conversational style of writing is deliberate, the literary equivalent of a classroom lecture—precise but not pedantic.

As this book first went to press, our assessment of Islamic affairs was confirmed once more. On Tuesday, December 18, 2001, world media broadcast a shocking address from Jerusalem by Palestinian Authority Chairman Yasser Arafat. He told of a Palestinian youngster who had been killed in a Gaza Strip gun battle with Israeli forces. Speaking passionately about his struggle against Israel, Arafat called upon Palestinians to regard the youth as an example of a Palestinian Muslim martyr. Arafat said he was willing to sacrifice seventy Palestinians to ensure the death of one Israeli. The speech was broadcast several times on Palestinian radio:

> We will defend the Holy Land with our blood and with our spirit. We do not only wear uniforms; we are all military. We are all martyrs in paradise.[3]

At that point, as reported by the *World Tribune*, the crowd began to chant that millions of Palestinians were prepared to march as martyrs to Jerusalem.[4]

These chilling words represent a viewpoint that is more prevalent than most non-Muslims are willing to believe.

In the second sura, or chapter, of the Qur'an (Al-Baqarah), two verses stand in marked contrast to one another. First, Allah encourages the Muslim to "fight them until there is no persecution and the religion is Allah's" (2:193). But then Allah tells Muhammad not to impose Islam by force, because "there is no compulsion in religion" (2:256).

May the Muslim world be guided by leaders who are willing to follow the latter admonition. And may our churches be filled with a bold and gracious witness to the returning Christ, "which in his times he shall show, who is the blessed and only Potentate, the King of kings, and Lord of lords" (1 Tim. 6:15 KJV).

Notes

1. All transcript quotations come from the video released in December 2001 by the United States government. Transcript and annotations independently prepared by George Michael, translator, Diplomatic Language Services; and Dr. Kassem M. Wahba, Arabic language program coordinator, School of Advanced International Studies, Johns Hopkins University. Michael and Wahba collaborated on their translation and compared it with government translations. There were no inconsistencies in the translations.
2. From the second session on the tape, with an indeterminate time lapse.
3. "Arafat's Call to Sacrifice: 'We Are All Martyrs in Paradise'" *World Tribune,* December 19, 2001, A1, available at http://www.world tribune.com/worldtribune/WTARC/2001/me_palestinians_12_19 .html.
4. Ibid.

1

SECURITY, POLITICS, AND JIHAD

GOD LOVES YOU! This is the brash claim of Christianity. The key, in fact, to winning people to a saving faith in Jesus Christ as Savior is based upon this claim. Yet in the Qur'an, no such statement is to be found. Whereas the Bible teaches that God hates sin and is angry with sinners, (e.g., Prov. 6:16-19; Jer. 4:4; Rom. 1:18; James 4:4), Islamic scripture affirms that Allah *hates* sinners: "For Allah loves not transgressors" (sura 2:190).[1]

The Bible says:

For God so loved the world that He gave His only begotten Son, that whoever believes in Him should not perish but have everlasting life. (John 3:16)

But God demonstrates His own love toward us, in that while we were still sinners, Christ died for us. (Rom. 5:8)

These things I have written to you who believe in the name of the Son of God, that you may know that you have eternal life. (1 John 5:13)

The Qur'an says:

And spend of your substance in the cause of Allah, and make not your own hands contribute to destruction, but do good; For Allah loves those who do good. (sura 2:195)

Say: "If you do love Allah, follow me: Allah will love you and forgive you your sins: For Allah is Oft-forgiving, Most Merciful." (sura 3:31)

Say: "Obey Allah and His Messenger": But if they turn back, Allah loves not those who reject Faith. (sura 3:32)

The greatest difference between the two faiths is the *personal quality of God.*

Allah sent prophets and messengers to proclaim the truth. In Christianity, God the Father sent His Son to *be* the truth, to die for sin, and to reconcile men and women to Him. In Islam, it is hoped that salvation is earned through one's good works (sura 3:31). One must love Allah in order for Allah to love that person in return. In Christianity, God loved people first in order to secure their salvation.

There is no security for the believer of Islam. One is left wanting and waiting for the will of Allah to be accomplished. Good works can only give one hope for heaven, but never the guarantee of such. Since God is removed from the equation, the question of whether one is admitted to heaven is left unanswered until the Day of Judgment. For the Christian, judgment came on the cross, an event rejected by Muhammad and Islam.

Fatalism, the Heart of Islamic Insecurity

We sent not a messenger except (to teach) in the language of his (own) people, in order to make (things) clear to them. So Allah leads astray those whom He pleases and guides whom He pleases and He is Exalted in power, full of wisdom. (sura 14:4)

Allah is exalted and pleased as he sends people to hell: this is the fatalistic claim of Islam. Fatalism is a belief that events are fixed in advance for all time in such a manner that human beings are powerless to change them. In this case, Allah will send to heaven whomever he pleases, and send to hell whomever he pleases.

No wonder there is no security in Islam. One can be the most faithful of all believers in Allah and still rightly be sent to hell. Paradoxically, someone can be the worst person in the world and hypothetically still go to Paradise. One needs to look no further than Islam's founder, Muhammad, to see the anxiety and insecurity that such a view produces.

The Insecure Messenger

Muhammad said: "By Allah, though I am the Apostle of Allah, yet I do not know what Allah will do to me." (hadith 5.266)

Muhammad questioned his own salvation, even though he was the greatest of prophets, the apostle of Allah himself. Therefore, how could Muslims have any real sense of security when the one who gave them their faith (or as the Muslim says, *restored* the truth to them) was himself apprehensive?

The Muslim is commanded in the Qur'an to "Obey Allah and His Messenger" (sura 3:32) and to follow his "exemplar example." As a result, the more devoutly one understands the Qur'an and follows the exemplar, the less certain one will be of reaching Paradise. Further, the more sensitive one is to his or her moral failures, the more spiritually anxious one must become.

The Insecure Believer

Every man's fate we have fastened on his neck; on the day of Judgement [sic] we shall bring out for him a scroll which he will see spread open." (sura 17:13)

Although this statement seems relatively straightforward, a

devout Muslim knows better than to presume upon good works alone. Doing so would malign and abuse the sovereignty of Allah. One of the most famous oft-used phrases in the Muslim world, "*En sh'Allah . . .*" ("If God wills"), illustrates the complexity of this union. And although Muslims can never be sure of their destiny, they can be assured about many of the things that will keep them from enjoying the pleasures of Paradise.

> As to those who reject Faith. It is the same to them whether you warn them or do not warn them; they will not believe. Allah has set a seal on their hearts and on their hearing. And on their eyes is a veil; Great is the chastisement they [incur]. (sura 2:6–7)

"Allah loves not those who reject Faith" (sura 3:32). The Muslim can be totally sure that Allah will never restore a believer who has rejected the teachings and faith of Islam. This is why so many Muslims quickly disown children who have converted to another religion, especially Christianity. Why love them when almighty Allah will never love them? Furthermore, the worst person in the world, in fact, is the Muslim who turns his or her back on belief in Allah. Indeed, one has a greater chance of earning heaven if one never knows the creed, "There is no god but Allah. Muhammad is the messenger of Allah."

> Muhammad said: "The deceased person is being tortured in the grave not for a great thing to avoid, it is for being soiled with his urine." (hadith 2.460)

The Muslim is instructed to fast, pray, worship, give money to the poor, and make a pilgrimage to Mecca. Yet, apparently all of these things cannot keep someone out of hell if they have soiled themselves with urine.[2]

Believers in Allah must worry, too, about who is speaking about them. According to the Hadith, "The deceased is punished because of the weeping of his relatives" (2.375). Relatives then must not be carried away in their grief or their deceased loved one will be punished. Moreover, if a person speaks badly about another person, "hell has been affirmed" to the one who is being despised (hadith 2.448).

Throughout Muslim thought, hell always seems much nearer than Paradise. People are continually reminded of Allah's wrath and the slippery slope toward eternal punishment. If someone has a fever, for example, Muhammad believed that the "fever is from the heat of hell" (hadith 7.619). Consequently, the Qur'an has much to say about who Allah does *not* love:

- For Allah loves not transgressors. (sura 2:190)
- For [Allah] loves not any ungrateful sinner. (sura 2:276)
- For Allah loves not those who do wrong. (sura 3:57)
- For Allah loves not the arrogant, the vainglorious. (sura 4:36)[3]

Politics and Eternal Security

Any religion built upon a foundation of salvation by personal righteousness is based upon the follower's loving God before God will love the follower. Allah must be enticed to love the individual by some demonstration of his or her faithfulness toward him (sura 4:54). In return for showing this love, however, Muslims expect something in return. Their obedience earns prosperity (sura 24:51–55).

Here is the profound weakness of a religion in which there is no genuine connection between God and human beings. Allah guides people into the truth through his messenger Muhammad, but one should never anticipate speaking to Allah personally or relationally. Love is never part of the equation—the religion depends upon a sense of duty and a desire for payback.

The Islamic world counts the blessings of Allah in a variety of ways. The faithful Muslim will be victorious politically: those in influence earned an "inheritance of power, as He granted it to those before them" (24:55). According to one Muslim scholar, people obedient to the Qur'an inherit authority "in order that they may maintain Allah's Law."[4]

Inheriting and maintaining authority is an important theme in the Muslim's relationship to Allah. Just as the individual expects prosperity from the arrangement, so does Allah expect to give prosperity, giving it to those who will enforce his law. No wonder the victorious Muslim warriors were so quick to coerce a conquered people to embrace Islam, or at the least submit to its law.

Prosperity extends to other areas of life as well. Muslims believe as long as they are faithful to Allah they will live in peace and security instead of suffering persecution at the hands of oppressors. They will not have to practice faith in secret. It is paradoxical, however, that to earn this religious freedom Muslims believe they must deny religious freedom to others. Saudi Arabia is a good example of this paradox in action.

The key is that prosperity is understood as integrating politics and religion. The Islamic theology of prosperity is vitally important to a symbiotic relationship with Allah. Thus, politics and religion are inextricably linked. When Allah gives success, he expects his faithful to expand his kingdom politically and spiritually. Political success is intrinsic to eternal security, although no guarantee of it.

> O you who believe! Take not My enemies and yours as friends (or protectors),—offering them (your love), even though they have rejected the Truth that has come to you, and have (on the contrary) driven out the Messenger and yourselves (from your homes), (simply) because you believe in Allah your Lord! If you have come out to strive in My Way and to seek My Good Pleasure, showing friendship unto them in secret: for I know full well all that you conceal and all that you reveal. And any of you that does this has strayed from the Straight Path. (sura 60:1)

Eternal security is further based on a Muslim's hatred toward enemies of Allah. Muhammad gave the above command as future guidance to all believers, and it still applies. Muslims must not trust others who seek to harm the cause of Allah. The worst thing the enemies of Allah can do is persuade Muslims to "reject the Truth" (sura 60:2).

Therefore, the Muslim is called to hate enemies of Islam in order to achieve more hope of Paradise. Nor may a Muslim covertly love people although seeming to hate them outwardly. If he or she does so, Allah will judge him or her nonetheless. In the end, the Muslim, both externally and internally, must passionately hate those who stand against the expansion of Allah's cause.

Jihad and Eternal Security

And if you are slain or die in the way of Allah, forgiveness and mercy from Allah are far better than all they could amass. (sura 3:157)

The Prophet said, "The person who participates in [holy battles] in Allah's cause and nothing compels him to do so except belief in Allah and His Apostles, will be recompensed by Allah either with a reward, or booty [if he survives] or will be admitted to Paradise [if he is killed in the battle as a martyr]. (hadith 1.35)

Talking heads on television continually pass along the politically correct notion that jihad means "internal struggle for piety" and not military engagement. Yet it does not require a cleric's teaching to see that the Qur'an promises Paradise more certainly to those who die in battle for Islam than it promises salvation to anyone else.

The Hadith makes it transparent that jihad has as its primary characteristic a bloody struggle involving military battles. Allah's apostle said, "There is no Hijra [i.e., migration from Mecca to Medina] after the Conquest [of Mecca], but jihad and good intention remain; and if you are called [by the Muslim ruler] for fighting, go forth immediately" (52.42).

The promise of eternal security is the ultimate motive behind the passion for Allah in the eager young Muslim warrior. He follows the footsteps of the messenger Muhammad, who fought for the cause of Allah. He is obeying the noble words of the Qur'an and Hadith, which legitimize his use of the sword. And if he is killed in battle, he achieves the desire of his heart—Allah's guarantee of a spot at the highest level of Paradise.

The Search for a Personal God

Young Timothy grew up in Egypt, the son of devout Muslims. Studying the Qur'an and worshiping within the mystical Sufi sect of Islam, Timothy desired to have a closer, more intimate relationship with Allah. At the age of fourteen he began preaching Islam publicly on the first Monday of every lunar month.

Eager to win others to the faith, Timothy began writing to a Christian in the United States. John wrote back to Timothy diligently for two years. Then Timothy was shocked when John visited him in Egypt. Timothy later recounted, "I became jealous of John's intimacy with God and increased my recitations of the Qur'an."

After incredible soul searching, God manifested Himself to Timothy:

> One night Christ appeared to me in a dream and said with a tender sweet voice, "I love you!" I saw how obstinately I had resisted Him all these years and said to Him in tears, "I love You, too! I know You! You are eternal for ever and ever." I woke up with tears all over my face filled with abundant joy, believing that Christ Himself touched both my mind and my heart, and I yielded. I was filled with great passion for Christ, jumping up and down, singing praises to His name and talking to Him day and night. I would not even sleep without God's inerrant Word, the Bible, next to my chest.[5]

Timothy had found what he had been searching for his entire life: an intimate, personal relationship with God. Love secured him eternally. Yet it did not come without cost. Timothy's refusal to hide his faith almost cost him his life. Persecuted and imprisoned, Timothy took refuge in the love of Christ. Finally he was sentenced to death by the authorities. Yet Timothy escaped and emigrated to the United States. Now, years later, Timothy holds to the Bible's greatest promise—salvation. He concludes his testimony:

> Please don't let me rush your salvation, Lord, in the midst of trouble, but please give me patience so I can endure hardships as a soldier of the cross of Christ! Lord, may *Your love* consume me to such an extent that the doing of Your will would be the real bread of my life.[6]

Notes

1. Most quotations from the Qur'an used in this volume are from the well-accepted English interpretation by Mohammed Marmaduke Pickthall. While the text cites the Qur'an text, it is to be understood that only the Arabic text is accepted as the actual Qur'an. All other translations are regarded as interpretations of the Scripture given to Muhammad.

2. It is ironic that Muhammad also stipulated that drinking camel's urine would make the sick man healthy. "The prophet ordered them to follow his camels, and drink their milk and urine, so they followed the camels and drank their milk and urine until their bodies became healthy" (hadith 7.590).

3. For further discussion, see Tom Terry, "Does Allah Love Me?" at http://www.thomasterry.com/index.php?option=com_content&view =article&id=51&Itemid=77.

4. Mushaf Al-Madinah An-Nabawiyah, trans. and commentator, *The Holy Qur'an* (Saudi Arabia: King Fahd Printing Complex, 1956), 1024.

5. Timothy Abraham, "In the Valley of Tears," at http://www.answering -islam.org/Testimonies/ibrahim.html.

6. Ibid. Timothy and the authors have become very good friends. It is a privilege to use his testimony for this work.

2

MUHAMMAD: THE MILITANT
MESSENGER

And they sang a new song, saying: "You are worthy to take
the scroll, And to open its seals; For You were slain, And have
redeemed us to God by Your blood Out of every tribe and
tongue and people and nation." (Revelation 5:9)

We have truly sent thee as a witness, as a bringer of Glad Tidings,
and as a Warner; In order that you (O men) may believe in Allah
and His Messenger, that you may assist and honor him, And
celebrate His praises morning and evening. (sura 48:8-9)

LEADERS COMMAND OBEDIENCE. Any major religion must first be seen
through the eyes of its founder. In both Christianity and Islam,
the founders demand respect and submission. Both Christ and
Muhammad told their followers to listen to their words and look
at their lives as a model for pleasing God. Paul tells Christians in
Philippians 2:5, "Let this mind be in you which was also in Christ
Jesus." In the Qur'an, the prophet explains, "You have indeed in
the Messenger of Allah an *excellent exemplar* for him who hopes

in Allah and the Final Day, and who remembers Allah much" (sura 33:21).

Exemplars need not be followed precisely and exactly in either religion. But disciples must be able to trust the leader's commands and teachings. The first criterion for evaluating the worth of Islam or Christianity is to determine whether Muhammad and Jesus Christ are worthy models.

Since Muslims and non-Muslims have written vastly divergent biographies of Muhammad, primary source information is most reliable. One of our best readily available sources is the Hadith, the oral tradition that Muslims have closely guarded almost from the days of the prophet's life.

The Life

Birth, Childhood, and Tragedy

Traditional Christianity and Islam teach that Jesus was born of the Virgin Mary. The origin of Muhammad is more complex and less fortunate than Christ's childhood with Joseph and Mary. Born about A.D. 570 in Mecca, Muhammad was part of a tribe whose duty was to keep the Kaaba, a stone used for various offerings to pagan deities. Muhammad's father, Abdullah, died before his birth and his mother, Amina, died when Muhammad was only six years old. A grandfather, Abd al-Muttalib, took care of the young boy for two years; then he too died. Finally, Muhammad's uncle, Abu Talib, became custodian. With all of the calamities that befell Muhammad, he lived a normal childhood, except that he never participated in the pagan activities of Meccan life.

The Love of His Life

O Prophet! Say to thy Consorts (wives[1]) If it be that you desire the life of this world, and its glitter,—then come! I will provide for your enjoyment and set you free in a handsome manner. (sura 33:28)

As a young man, Muhammad gained the patronage of a

wealthy widow, Khadija, and conducted a successful caravan trade to Syria. Eventually he married Khadija, who was fifteen years his senior. The marriage proved to be fulfilling for both, although their two sons died in infancy. They also had four daughters, two of whom married future caliphs, spiritual and political leaders of Islam.

When Muhammad was fifty, Khadija died. For twenty-five years, Muhammad had known one woman, who was the love of his life and his greatest supporter. Muhammad was, in fact, an exception in his culture; most men of high status took numerous wives. Only later did Muhammad have eleven other women as wives and concubines, the youngest of whom was nine when they consummated their marriage.

The First Revelation: Divine or Demonic?

Say: "I am not an innovation among the messengers, nor do I know what will be done with me or with you. I follow but that which is revealed to me by inspiration; I am but a Warner open and clear." (sura 46:9)

Because of his financially comfortable marriage, Muhammad enjoyed fifteen years' leisure to meditate. When he was forty years old, he believed the angel Gabriel called him as the last and most authoritative prophet. The most accepted account relates,

When it was the night on which God honoured him with his mission and showed mercy on His servants thereby, Gabriel brought him the command of God. "He came to me," said the Apostle of God, "while I was asleep, with a coverlet of brocade whereon was some writing, and said, 'Read!' I said, 'What shall I read?' He pressed me with it so tightly that I thought it was death; then he let me go and said, 'Read!' I said, 'What shall I read?' He pressed me with it again so that I thought it was death; then he let me go and said 'Read!' I said, 'What shall I read?' He pressed me with it the third time so that I thought it was death and said 'Read!' I said, 'What then shall I read?' —and this I said only to deliver myself from him, lest he should do the same to me again. He said: 'Read in the name of thy Lord who created, who created man of blood coagulated. Read! Thy Lord is the most beneficent, Who taught by the pen, Taught that which they knew not unto men' [96:1–5]. So I read it, and he departed from me. And I awoke from my sleep, and it was as though these words were written on my heart."[2]

Muhammad's "call" creates difficulties. The future prophet expresses skepticism of the encounter, although he sees in his vision one of God's archangels. Why would the greatest of the prophets doubt the validity of his own defining vision? Two possible reasons can be cited: Either Muhammad was too weak or naive to understand the prophecy, or Allah did not reveal himself clearly enough or did not understand the man's weaknesses.

Muhammad was deathly afraid of the source of the revelation, believing at first that he was possessed by an evil spirit, or jinn. He told his trusted wife what he had experienced. The account, passed down through the Hadith of Sahih al-Bukhari, explains:

Then Allah's Apostle returned with the Inspiration and with his heart beating severely. Then he went to Khadija bint Khuwailid and said, "Cover me! Cover me!" They covered him till his fear was over and after that he told her everything that had happened and said, "I fear that something may happen to me." Khadija replied, "Never! By Allah, Allah will never disgrace you. You keep good relations with your kith and kin, help the poor and the destitute, serve your guests generously and assist the deserving calamity-afflicted ones." (hadith 1.1.3)

To those who would imitate the faith of the founder of the religion, Muhammad's doubts are troubling, for what major prophet doubts the source of his prophetic revelation? The Bible's prophets occasionally wonder how God will vindicate His words, but there is never any doubt that He had spoken. Certainly no major prophet in the Bible attributes God's revelation to demons, as Muhammad believed that he was demon possessed after Allah's revelation.

Finally, Islamic theology asserts that women are intellectually inferior to men. One hadith explains, "The Prophet said, 'Isn't the witness of a woman equal to half of that of a man?' The women said, 'Yes.' He said, 'This is because of the deficiency of a woman's mind'" (hadith 3.826). Yet, it was Khadija who confirmed Muhammad's revelations.

It must be noted that Muhammad received his first vision during the month of Ramadan, the holy month of Islam where Muslims fast from eating, drinking, sexual intercourse, and other activities. Therefore, to attack the vision of Muhammad is to attack the holiest of months on the Islamic calendar.

More Revelations

> They will call thee a liar. They will persecute thee; they will banish thee, and they will fight against thee. (Waraqa to Muhammad)

After the first revelation, the voice of Allah was silent for about three years. The prophet became despondent, doubting that Allah was pleased with his conduct and obedience. Even his faithful wife Khadija asked, "Does it not seem that your Lord is displeased with you?" Muhammad sought solace at his favorite retreat—Mount Hira. Here, the prophet experienced the dark night of his soul, even contemplating jumping off the mountain and ending his life. According to one Muslim biographer, however, peace came to the prophet through the words of Allah:

> By the forenoon, and by the night as it spreads its wings over the world in peace, your Lord has not forsaken you; nor is He displeased with you. Surely, the end shall be better for you than the beginning. Your Lord will soon give you of His bounty and you will be well pleased. Did He not find you an orphan and

give you shelter? Did He not find you erring and guide you to the truth? . . . The bounty of your Lord, always proclaim.[3]

Muhammad's call was finally confirmed after obsessive soul-searching. Given his mental state, the obvious question arises as to whether that call can be trusted. Remember that the tortured prophet repeatedly believed himself to be demon possessed. What suddenly convinced him that he now received what he so desperately wanted—the authentic voice of God?

First, his wife's desire must be evaluated. She reassured her husband that he would be "the Prophet of this nation."

Second, the confirmation of the revelations can be questioned. Muhammad's wives believed the visions were authentic because of the uncontrollable convulsions of Muhammad. Aishah, the youngest wife, rationalized,

> Thinking that something ominous was about to happen, everyone in the room was frightened except me, for I did not fear a thing, knowing that I was innocent and that God would not be unjust to me. As for my parents, when the Prophet recovered from his convulsion, they looked pale enough to die before the gossip was proven true. After Muhammad recovered, he sat up and began to wipe his forehead where beads of perspiration had gathered. He said, "Glad tidings! O Aishah, God has sent down proof of your innocence."[4]

Third, later revelations became more and more eccentric. At one point Muhammad claimed to speak to the dead. Questioned about the incident by his novice disciples, the prophet replied, "[The dead] hear me no less than you do, except that they are unable to answer me." Muhammad not only claimed to communicate with the dead; he prayed for the dead at the cemetery of Baqi al Gharqad. Muslim scholars do not explain away this phenomenon. Rather, they believe that he was a psychic, endowed with heightened perception and sensitivity. One commentator says that communication between the living and the dead is an "indubitable fact."[5]

Muhammad oscillated between revelations from Satan and Allah.
The most famous of these visions resulted in the so-called "Satanic
Verses." Muhammad revealed to his followers the words of Allah:

> Did you consider al-hat and al-Uzza
> And al-Manat, the third, the other?
> Those are the swans exalted;
> Their intercession is expected;
> Their likes are not neglected.[6]

This revelation, commanding them to allow intercession to
certain idols, shocked Muhammad's disciples. Recognizing the theological discrepancy and the concession to paganism, Muhammad
withdrew his revelation, explaining that Satan had deceived him
into writing the verses. The angel Gabriel came to the prophet
and declared, "God cancels what Satan interjects." As expected,
Muhammad quickly received a substitute revelation that canceled
the last three lines (verses).

Fourth, Muhammad felt the need to improve on the words
of Allah, since he changed Allah's wisdom for his own on several
occasions:

> On a number of occasions [his scribe] had, with the Prophet's
> consent, changed the closing words of verses. For example,
> when the Prophet had said, "And God is mighty and wise"
> [*'aziz, hakim*], 'Abdollah b. Abi Sarh suggested writing down
> "knowing and wise" [*'alim, hakim*], and the Prophet answered
> that there was no objection. Having observed a succession of
> changes of this type, 'Abdollah renounced Islam on the ground
> that the revelations, if from God, could not be changed at the
> prompting of a scribe such as himself. After his apostasy he
> went to Mecca and joined the Qorayshites.[7]

Almost fourteen hundred years later, the curious seeker must
ask the same question as the scribe 'Abdollah: How can a mere
messenger of Allah have the right, power, or arrogance to change

the very words of God? Even if the source were God himself, the Qur'an cannot be trusted, since its human author was careless and inconsiderate with the revelation.

Consider that 'Abdollah joined the Qorayshites, who devoted themselves to worship of the moon god. For 'Abdollah, the polytheistic theology Muhammad was fighting against had become more convincing than the new monotheism.

Persecution and Attempted Assassination

When Muhammad proclaimed to the Meccans that their goddesses were mere myths and that Allah was the only true god, he was quickly subjected to persecution. Shortly thereafter, his wife Khadija died, and his greatest benefactor, Abu Talib, also passed away. Without their protection, not even his own tribesmen would intercede for the prophet. The assault upon Muhammad began with verbal sparring and expressions of indignation. People accused the self-proclaimed prophet of being a lunatic, a liar, and demon possessed. No longer safe from physical harm in Mecca, Muhammad had to seek refuge elsewhere.

Before he left Mecca, Muhammad claimed to have been translated into the realm of heaven, passing first through the land around Jerusalem. Here he met all of the major prophets, including Moses and Jesus. Allah used this fantastic journey to explain to his prophet the daily prayers of Islamic worship. This was the final straw for many in Mecca. They wanted this fanciful prophet out of their sight. Two years later in 621, however, a dozen men from Medina secretly accepted the faith of Islam at the annual pilgrimage to Kaaba. The following year, the group added adherents who were zealously committed to their leader, committed enough to die for their leader as they would for their own families.

This gradually growing sect infuriated Mecca's leaders. To stamp out this new religion, they devised a plan to assassinate Muhammad, believing that eradicating the prophet would end the newly invented faith. This decision, however, became the chronological and theological starting point for the Islamic faith. Muslims today begin their lunar calendar with the flight (Hijra) of Muhammad out of

Mecca. Muslims consider Allah's protection of Muhammad during this persecution to be a confirmation of their faith.

Muhammad and his best friend Abu Bakr eluded the assassins and arrived safely in Medina on September 24, 622. Here, the new band of believers in Allah was well received in an area that had a strong tradition of Jewish monotheism. The prophet quickly acclimated himself to the cultural customs of Judaism. Following the example of the Jews, Muslims faced Jerusalem (not Mecca) while praying to Allah, and Muslims, too, retained the Jewish Day of Atonement as a day of fasting in the Islamic community.

Muhammad quickly united a factionally divided region. He taught the citizens to live in peace and protect each other from foreign enemies. The Jews, however, quickly noticed the contradictions between the Hebrew Scriptures and the Qur'an and rejected Muhammad's message and authority. The Qur'an is vituperative in its assessment of the Jews:

> Fight those who believe not in Allah nor the Last Day, nor hold that forbidden which has been forbidden by Allah and His Messenger, nor acknowledge the Religion of Truth, from among the People of the Book [Jews and Christians], until they pay compensation with willing submission, and feel themselves subdued. (sura 9:29)

> Strongest among men in enmity to the Believers [Muslims] will you find the Jews and Pagans. (sura 5:82a)

> Those who disbelieve, among the People of the Book and among the Polytheists, will be in hell-fire, to dwell therein [for aye]. They are the worst of creatures. (sura 98:6)

The Legacy

Jihad

Muhammad had unified the region, yet lost the ability to make a living. He could no longer sustain his family financially by the caravan trade. Therefore, the Muslims began raiding caravans for financial gain. They felt justified, since their enemies had expelled them from their homes; they were fighters in the cause of Allah. Not all the new believers were willing to take up the sword to seek power and theocratic rule. Through the warrior-prophet Muhammad, Allah announced incentives for those who fought in the cause of Allah:

Not equal are those Believers who sit [at home], except those who are disabled. And those who strive and fight [jihad] in the cause of Allah with their goods and their persons. Allah has granted a grade higher to those who strive and fight with their goods and persons than to those who sit [at home]. Unto all [in Faith] has Allah promised good: But those who strive and fight has He distinguished above those who sit [at home] by a great reward.—Ranks specially bestowed by Him and Forgiveness and Mercy. For Allah is oft-forgiving. Most Merciful. (sura 4:95–96)

Those who have left their homes, and were driven out therefrom, and suffered harm in My Cause, and fought and were slain,—Verily, I will blot out from them their iniquities, and admit them into Gardens with rivers flowing beneath;—A reward from Allah and from Allah is the best of rewards. (sura 3:195)

Muhammad himself gave the example for jihad (fighting; holy war). There was no governmental call for warfare, only individual desire that led to the greatest rewards in heaven. Ethical values seemed to play little or no role. Whatever the Muslims did was justified, since their cause was just. Muslims believed that they received forgiveness for all their sins only by fighting in jihad. Is it any wonder, then, that holy war continues to be a prophetic call?

Muhammad gave his prescription for victory, now recorded in the Qur'an, thereby giving it eternal significance:

Fighting is prescribed upon you, and you dislike it. But it is possible that you dislike a thing which is good for you, and that

you love a thing which is bad for you. But Allah knows and you
know not. . . . Tumult and oppression are worse than slaughter.
Nor will they cease fighting you until they turn you back from
your faith if they can. (sura 2:216–17)

The Military Expeditions of Muhammad

But when the forbidden months are past, then fight and slay
the pagans wherever you find them, and seize them, beleaguer
them, and lie in wait for them, in every stratagem of war. (sura
9:5)

When considering whom to fight, the Muslim receives an
unequivocal answer in sura 9:29, "Fight those who believe not
in Allah nor the Last Day." This admonition only ends when the
enemies are "subdued" and will pay continual compensation for
Islamic protection. This tribute program eternally unites Islam with
the state. Thus, the safety of any non-Muslim rests in the hands
of the same militant Muslim who is promised heaven for slaying
the unbeliever. The Hadith explains that no Muslim who kills an
infidel deserves death.

The greatest difference between Jesus Christ as God and Savior
and Muhammad as prophet of Allah, comes at this point. Jesus
Christ shed His own blood on the cross so that people could come
to God. Muhammad shed other people's blood so that his constitu-
ents could have political power throughout the Arabian Peninsula.
Further, since Muhammad is held to be the "excellent exemplar
for him who hopes in Allah and the Final Day" (sura 33:21), we
need to look no further for explanation of violent acts within Islam
than at the character of its founder. Was Muhammad a man of
peace who shed other people's blood only as a last resort? When he
killed others, were his acts part of war or for personal vengeance?
The answers to such questions tarnish the ethical integrity of the
Islamic worldview.

An important battle for the prophet occurred at Badr in
March 624. Muhammad had led three hundred men against a

large caravan of merchants enroute to Mecca. The booty won by the raiders was said to be worth the equivalent of fifty thousand dollars today—a needed infusion of wealth to carry forward their military task. In response, the Meccans sent 950 troops to challenge the Muslims. Their encounter was a brief and convincing victory for the Muslims, who lost fourteen men. The Meccans lost forty-five men, and another seventy were taken as prisoners. The prophet attributed the victory to the power of Allah. To draw more men to fight for the cause of Islam, Muhammad revealed Allah's words to the messenger: "O Apostle! Rouse the Believers to the fight, if there are twenty among you . . . they will vanquish two hundred; if a hundred, they will vanquish a thousand of the unbelievers" (sura 8:65).

Yet, in victory, Muhammad committed an act of cruelty that demonstrates his need for vengeance. Among the prisoners sent to his camp was a Persian poet named Uqbah ibn Abu Muayt. This lyricist asserted that his folktales were more pleasant to listen to than the Qur'an. When the warrior-prophet ordered him executed, the man exclaimed, "O Muhammad, if you kill me, who will take care for my children?" The prophet replied, "Hell's fire." Other prisoners were more fortunate than this poet. Many were set free without condition if they had large families. Some were released on condition that they teach others how to read and write. It seemed that the actions of the warrior were erratic, depending upon his mood and his perception of the prisoner's vice.

Clearly Muhammad was progressing and gaining confidence. He and his followers would no longer tolerate insubordination toward and ridicule of Muhammad or the name of Allah. Anyone found insulting the name or cause of Allah was dealt with swiftly. One example is the woman poet Asma, who satirized the prophet continually. One night Umayr ibn 'Awf, a military leader among the Muslims, attacked the poet while she was nursing one of her seven children. Although nearly blind, ibn 'Awf did not let his disability impede his zeal. Tearing the child from her hands, the militant slaughtered the mother joyfully. He then returned to camp and told Muhammad what he had done. Muslim scholars find solace in this event because the tribe in which she belonged, Banu Khutmah, converted to Islam.

Muhammad's troubles with the Jewish community can be most clearly seen through the struggle with a Meccan lyricist named Ka'b. The son of an Arab father and Jewish mother, Ka'b persuasively criticized the effectiveness and character of the prophet. Muhammad fought back both intellectually and militarily. He hired a talented poet named Hassan ben Thabit to sing his praises and acts. Then he told his followers to eliminate the antagonist. Ka'b was enticed from his home one night and slaughtered. One of the crusaders, Abu Na'ilah, seized Ka'b by his hair, pulled him down to the ground, and said to his friends, "Kill the enemy of God!" Ka'b was struck with a sword.

Although the Muslims seemed invincible, they soon learned that evangelization by the sword was not easy. At the Battle of Uhud, for instance, the Meccans had not forgotten about the travesty of previous battles. The Meccans also knew the terrain far better than did the Muslims. The battle that ensued was vicious. One Muslim warrior was particularly noticed for his ferocity: "By God, he was killing men, sparing no one like a huge mad camel." The Muslim forces used the battle cry "*Allah Akbar*—God is Great!" Hassan ben Thabit, the poet of Muhammad, cried, "We scattered them like fawns." Neither women nor animals were spared. Thabit further wrote, "We attacked them thrusting, slaying, chastising. . . . Had not the Harithite woman seized their standard, we would have got them all to market and sold them like goats."

But the battle turned when the Muslim archers defied Muhammad's orders and assisted their beleaguered friends near them. The Muslims were flanked by the storming Meccans and surrounded. The women of Mecca then joined the forces, encouraging their valiant men with tambourines. One woman, caught up in the height of war, cut out the entrails of a fallen Muslim and draped them around her body. Muhammad and the rest of the Muslims retreated to higher ground. The Meccans, recognizing that triumph was in their hands, believed the god Hubal was victorious. Muhammad shouted back at his adversaries, "God is most high and glorious! Our dead are in Paradise, yours are in Hell!" The Muslims were defeated and had to regroup.

In 627, an Arab confederacy force of ten thousand fought the Muslims of Medina. The Meccans were discouraged by their inability to cross a deep ditch before the Muslim fortification, so they retreated, leaving the remaining Jews of Medina without protection. Muhammad, seeing the opening to exterminate the Jewish tribe, accused the Jews of plotting with the Meccans. Eight hundred Jewish men were beheaded on the edge of a trench, a procedure that occupied the entire day and went on far into the night.

Some may claim that those who fought for the cross of Christ committed similar crimes against humanity during the Crusades and in other military expeditions. But at issue is not what followers do in wartime that besmirches the supposed honor of Muhammad or Allah or Christ. Both sides have committed grave offenses. Indeed, war itself demonstrates the extent of human sinfulness. At issue is the worthiness of the leader. Jesus did not command the murderous crusaders. Muslim apologists do not present a powerful argument for Muhammad's worthiness when they equate his penchant for bloodshed to the Christian armies, who disobeyed Scripture.

Muhammad's personal failures likewise are serious matters. Although Muslims consider Muhammad a mere man, they ascribe to him a most noble character, which Muslims are called to emulate. Too often they do. It is no wonder that some Muslims are willing to die for their faith and that others feel no ethical restraint against killing for Allah and his prophet. Clearly Jesus was a far superior prophet of peace and mercy. Muhammad was ruthless in war, not considering ethical ramifications when he was caught up in the height of savagery. The only life Jesus Christ voluntarily gave up was His own. His character offers continuous, unassailable compassion. Muhammad was both erratic and hostile to those who would not follow him.

After eradicating the Jews at Medina, Muhammad quickly progressed to his final goal: the conquest of Mecca. Desiring to rule his hometown and believing it to be the holy city for Islam, the prophet set his sights on his enemies. Events that led to the battle are shown in the chart below.

The Years of Success

Year

627 Muhammad subdues allies of Meccans/Qoraysh.
Muhammad sets out with 1,400 followers on pilgrimage to Mecca.

628 Muhammad and Meccan leaders sign a ten-year peace treaty granting the prophet permission for pilgrimages. Finally Muhammad is considered an equal adversary and not a renegade bandit. Muhammad fights the Jews for Khaybar. He does not believe he can control Arabia without exterminating them. The Jews surrender on condition of survival and annual recompense.
He marries Sufia, a Jewish woman.

630 The Qoraysh break the truce, killing several allies of Muhammad. Outraged at the broken truce, he prepares 10,000 men to march on Mecca, slaughtering any who resist. The prophet enters with little resistance. His rival Abu Sufyan converts immediately to Islam. Images of pagan gods are destroyed and the Kaaba established as the center of Islam. Only four people are executed, one a woman poet who wrote satirical lyrics about Muhammad.

Muhammad was outraged at the breaking of the truce. He prepared ten thousand men to march on the city of Mecca and to slaughter anyone who resisted. Yet once there, the prophet seemed not inclined to shed unnecessary blood. Muhammad entered the city with little resistance, and his greatest rival Abu Sufyan converted immediately to Islam. Images of the pagans gods were quickly destroyed and the Kaaba established as the center of Islam. Only four people were executed, including a female poet, who had committed the capital crime of composing satirical lyrics against the prophet.

In the overall pattern of his life, the prophet was merciful and forgiving, even sharing equally in the booty obtained in war. But he also was a murderer, guilty of crimes against humanity.

As we analyze the military life of Muhammad, several observations are necessary. First, Muhammad was less cruel than many other warriors in the Arabian Peninsula. Second, Muhammad's desire was to see his fellow tribesmen convert to Islam, in his eyes the true religion and the only way to Paradise. Third, Muhammad was an incredible tactician on the field of battle.

Yet criticisms quickly emerge. First, Muhammad had no sympathy for his critics. Second, he made no distinction between combatants and noncombatant women and children. Third, the generous mercy shown toward his own tribe at Mecca was not repeated elsewhere. Jews and members of other tribes were shown no such kindness. Fourth, Muhammad allowed his leaders to use barbarous tactics to subdue the enemy. Fifth, it is significant that he seldom gained conversions except through coercion. Muhammad's goal was complete control of the Arabian Peninsula. To that end, he enforced conversion of all people groups to Islam. If the stubbornness of large populations of Jews or Christians made that impractical, the people had to agree to be submissive to Islam and its adherents and to pay tribute for their protection.

What explanations do Muslim historians and theologians give for these conclusions? Muhammad Haykal, a noted defender of the Islamic faith, answers, "Is it equivalent to any part, however infinitesimal, of the slaughter that took place in the first or second World War? Is it at all comparable to the events of the French Revolution, or the many other revolutions which have taken place among the Christian nations of Europe?"[8] Again, this parallel is weak. First, the World Wars were not fought in the cause of religion, but for the sake of a just world peace. Second, most Europeans went to war in response to attacks against their own sovereignty; they did not instigate war as did Muhammad. Their goal was not conquest, but freedom and survival. Third, Muslims continually generalize all activities by Europeans or Westerners as representative of Christian ethics. But Muslims see no irony in their generalization when they accuse Westerners of assuming that all terrorists are Muslim. If the comparison were truly equivalent,

Westerners would be justified in saying that suicide bombers represent Islam.

Faced with explaining the actions by the warrior-prophet, Haykal arrogantly asserts that, even if all charges against Muhammad are true, he could still "refute them with the simple argument that the great stand above the law." By this reasoning, Muhammad, although only a prophet of Allah and his messenger, is beyond the pale of human rights and responsibilities due to his "greatness." He could kill whom he wanted when he wanted. He could marry more than four women, though Islamic law at the time forbade it.

The irony is that Muslim scholars proclaim Muhammad as someone to be heard and also followed. Haykal concludes, "[Muhammad's] life constitutes the *highest* ideal, the *perfect* example, and the concrete instance of his Lord's command."[9] Need one wonder where militant Muslims get their inspiration and provocation?

The greatest danger to Christians and Jews has come when they have been subdued and forced to submit within an Islamic society. In such a setting, there is no concept of religious pluralism or liberty. The Qur'anic mandate is that anyone found guilty of "spreading mischief in the land" (sura 5:32), a thoroughly subjective judgment, is subject to one of four punishments:

> The punishment of those who wage war against Allah and His Messenger, and strive with might and main for mischief through the land is: execution, or crucifixion, or the cutting off of hands, and feet from opposite sides, or exile from the land: That is their disgrace in this world, and a heavy punishment is theirs in the Hereafter. (sura 5:33)

Muslim countries widely differ, however, in regard to the definition of "treason" against Allah and the Islamic state. In the perfect example of Muhammad, the criteria extend beyond violent uprising to verbal insurrection. Missionaries are criminals guilty of treason under this interpretation.

Polygamous Prophet

Men are the protectors and maintainers of women, because Allah has given the one more than the other, and because they support them from their means. Therefore the righteous women are devoutly obedient, and guard in [the husband's] absence what Allah would have them guard. As to those women on whose part you fear disloyalty and ill-conduct, admonish them [first], [next], refuse to share their beds, [and last] beat them. (sura 4:34)[10]

Muhammad's wives boasted that he was a great husband, although he advocated wife beating—albeit as a last resort. He believed that those who beat their wives are not the "best among Muslims," hardly a condemnation of the practice. While married to Khadija, his first wife, Muhammad went against the status quo of polygamy, remaining monogamous for twenty-five years. Yet, after the Battle of Uhud, he expanded his household, likely for political alliances. In all, he married eleven women and took two others as concubines (see "The Wives of Muhammad" on p. 56).

Muhammad was a complex figure. His standards of fidelity and kindness in marriage far exceeded the marriage ethics of his day among pagan tribes of the Arabian Peninsula. On the other hand, his allowing wife beating does not fit twenty-first-century standards, except in Muslim societies. His polygamy is acceptable conduct in the context of history, whether Christian or pagan. But if the standard is the one set in Genesis 2:24, his lifestyle was sinful and should not be emulated. Examples of polygamy are found in the pages of the Bible, but the practice is never advocated by Scripture. Conversely, the Qur'an says explicitly that a man may take more than one wife. In the final analysis, Muhammad improved the conditions of women in his own day, but those improvements are inadequate in terms of the twenty-first century. Islam does not uphold the importance of wives, and it does not protect women from the abuses found in conservative Islamic societies today.

The Wives of Muhammad

Name of Wife	Approximate Year of Marriage	Woman's Age at Marriage
Khadija	595	40
Sawda	620	30(?)
Aishah	623	9
Hafsah	625	18
Um Salama	626	29
Zaynab	626	30
Juweiriyeh	627	20
Zaynab bint Jahsh	627	38
Rayhana (Jewish)	627	(?)
Maryam (Christian)	628	(?)
Um Habeeba	628	35
Sufia	628	17
Maimoona	629	27

What view did Muhammad have of his wives? He once expressed the thought, "Be kind to women sprung from your rib. If you try to straighten out a rib, you will break it. Accept women as they are, with all their curvatures." Muhammad enjoyed spending time with his wives: "I love little children and women and sweet scent." But, he explained, "None of these can give me the happiness I find in prayer." This explains why Muhammad spent many nights standing in prayer with swollen feet instead of in bed with one of his numerous wives.

Muhammad maintained a simple lifestyle, even after he was successful financially. He built mud brick apartments for his wives and once told Aishah that she should not discard any clothes that could be patched. After a jealous dispute among the wives, Muhammad abandoned them for one month in order to meditate.

He pondered whether he should divorce any or all of them because of their attitudes. From his lonesome journey, he brought back a revelation from Allah:

> O Prophet, say to thy wives: if you desire the life of this world and its vanities, come—I will provide for you generously, and send you out into the world splendidly arrayed. But if you desire God and the Prophet and Paradise, then conduct yourselves as you should. For those who do, God has prepared a mighty reward.[11]

Muhammad's marriages can be separated into three categories: amorous, diplomatic, and tribal relationships. His first marriage to Khadija was clearly one of mutual devotion, love, and duty. Diplomatic relationships include Um Salama, a widow whose husband died at Uhud. Muhammad knew that she came from his original enemy's tribe, Makhzum, and he desired to be reconciled with that clan by converting them to Islam.

Tribal relationships included those who were in some way related to Muhammad. The most famous of these tribal marriages was his eighth wife, Zaynab bint Jahsh. Zaynab was Muhammad's cousin through his mother, and a marriage was arranged between Zaynab and Muhammad's adopted son, Zaid. This marriage turned out to be unfruitful and miserable. Indeed, historians suggest that Zaynab intended to marry Muhammad all along. Muhammad was troubled by the proposition of marrying his daughter-in-law, although he rationalized that his son was only adopted, not truly his own. Therefore, Muhammad received revelation from Allah:

> Behold! You did say to one who had received the grace of Allah and your favor: "Retain in wedlock your wife, and fear Allah." But you did hide in your heart that which Allah was about to make manifest: you did fear the people, but it is more fitting that you should fear Allah. Then when Zaid had dissolved (his marriage) with her we joined her in marriage to you: in order that (in future) there may be no difficulty to the Believers in (the

matter of) marriage with the wives of their adopted sons, when
the latter have dissolved (their marriage) with them. And Allah's
command must be fulfilled. (sura 33:37)

Consequently, this wedding must take place to destroy the pagan
taboo of marrying one who was related by adoption. Muhammad
asserted that he was protecting and providing for Zaid through the
marriage. Sura 33:37 also reveals much about Islamic marriage.
Mutual incompatibility is sufficient reason to dissolve the marriage.
As one Qur'anic commentator writes, "But marriages are made on
earth, not in heaven, and it is no part of Allah's Plan to torture
people in a bond which should be a source of happiness, but actually is a source of misery."[12]

Generally, women are afforded rights but not equality with
men. The Qur'an states, "Women shall have rights similar to the
rights against them, according to what is equitable; but men have
a degree over them, and Allah is Exalted in Power" (sura 2:228).
Although some commentators see this advantage as economic, once
again the Islamic scriptures are ambiguous, leaving interpretation
to the reader. Notice also that men may divorce women, but wives
do not have such explicit rights in the Qur'an.

The most questionable of the marriages of Muhammad was
with young Aishah. Muhammad betrothed her when she was just
six and consummated the marriage when she was nine. She was,
in fact, the only virgin the prophet ever married. Aishah became
a fiercely loyal supporter of Muhammad, but she was also a very
jealous wife. When Allah revealed to Muhammad the right to
"take to yourself any you wish" (sura 33:51), the young woman
replied, "It seems to me that your Lord hastens to satisfy your
desire." Ultimately, she loved Muhammad fiercely and served him
even after his death. She passed down more than two thousand
ahadith (traditions), served as an advisor to Muslim leaders, and
daily visited the grave of her late husband. Muhammad died in
her lap, evidence of her superiority over the other wives. She was
only eighteen.

How a prophet of noble character could wed someone so young, even in the culture of the day, remains a mystery. Many gloss over this act. Perhaps Muhammad did not at first love Aishah but wanted to strengthen ties to her tribe. It seems implausible to suggest, however, that Muhammad wanted to solidify the emerging Islamic community by marrying a nine-year-old. Muslim scholar Haykal argues, "It is contrary to logic to claim that he could have fallen in love with her while she was at this tender age." But this does not answer the echoing problem: How could any man consummate a marriage with a nine year-old? This question usually is ignored.

Centralizing Islam: Muhammad and Mecca

When Muhammad conquered Mecca, he went straight to the Kaaba, circled it seven times on his camel, and then demanded the door be opened. When he entered the sanctuary of the hallowed stone, he took out a wooden dove idol and scattered its decaying material on the ground. After removing 360 idols, Muhammad declared, "The truth has come and falsehood has passed away." He erased pictures from the walls, even those depicting Christ and the Virgin Mary. When the Kaaba was empty he spoke to the tribe:

> There is no God but God
> Nothing exists beside Him;
> He has made good His promise to His servant;
> He has put to flight His enemies.
> Quraysh! God now takes from you your idols
> And your ancestral haughtiness is no more,
> For man springs from Adam,
> And Adam sprang from dust.[13]

The center of Islam was now and forever established. Muhammad demanded that all Muslims make a pilgrimage to the Kaaba, and to this day, the Kaaba stone is the focal point of the Islamic faith. Millions come each year to pray around it.

After this monumental event, things changed rapidly. Many women began veiling their faces like the wives of the prophet. In 631, also known as the "year of delegations," the tribes of Arabia sent representatives to Mecca to submit to Allah and his messenger. Muhammad sent missionaries across the peninsula to convert many to the new faith. His goal was now firmly established—spiritually and governmentally, Muhammad owned Arabia. Intertribal fighting was subdued and the community solidified under the name of Allah as faith replaced blood as the closest tie. So Islamic life remains to this day.

Death Through the Eyes of Muhammad

> Every soul shall have a taste of death: and only on the Day of Judgment shall you be paid your full recompense. One who is saved far from the Fire and admitted to the Garden will have succeeded: For the life of this world is but goods and chattels of deception. (sura 3:185)

In February 632, the messenger of Allah unknowingly made his final pilgrimage from his home in Medina to Mecca. Here, he spoke his final words to his followers:

> O believers hearken unto my words as I know not whether another year will be permitted unto me to be among you. Your lives and possessions are sacred and inviolable [and so you must observe] the one toward the other, until you appear before the Lord, as this day and month is sacred for all; and remember you will have to present yourselves to the Lord who will demand that you give an account of your deeds. . . . Listen to my words and hearken well. Know you that all Muslims are brothers. You are all one brotherhood; and no man shall take aught from his brother unless it is freely given to him. Shun injustice. And let those here assembled inform those who are not of the same who when told afterwards may remember better than those who now hear it.[14]

Muhammad went back to his home in Medina, where he spent his last days with his beloved Aishah. Gathering his closest friends and family, he spoke to them intimately: "I have made lawful only that which God so commanded in His Book." He then spoke to his daughter Fatima and aunt Safiyah and explained, "You both work that which will gain you acceptance with the Lord; for verily I have no power to save you in any wise." On June 8, 632, Muhammad died. He was buried at his home, where later Muslims erected a mosque. His faithful companion Abu Bakr addressed his followers, "O Muslims! If any of you have been worshiping Muhammad, then let me tell you that Muhammad is dead. But if you really do worship God, then you know that God is living and will never die!"

What, then, was Muhammad's view of death? The Qur'an frequently refers to the deaths of both believers in Allah and of unbelievers. For the unbeliever, the picture is grim to say the least:

> If you could see, when the angels take the souls of the Unbelievers [at death], [How] they smite their faces and their backs, [saying]: "Taste the chastisement of the blazing Fire-This is because of [the deeds] which your [own] hands sent forth. For Allah is never unjust to His servants." (sura 8:50-51)

> In gulp will he sip it, but never will he be near swallowing it down his throat; Death will come to him from every quarter, yet will he not die; and in front of him will be a chastisement unrelenting. (sura 14:17)

Obviously, the believer in Allah has a much more pleasant destiny in the afterlife:

> To the righteous [when] it is said, "What is it that your Lord has revealed?" they say, "All that is good." To those who do good, there is good in this world, and the Home of the Hereafter is even better and excellent indeed is the Home of the righteous,— Gardens of Eternity which they will enter: beneath them flow (pleasant) rivers: they will have therein all that they wish: thus does Allah reward the righteous. (sura 16:30-31)

In the mind of Muhammad, God foreordains both death and

the afterlife. Yet God also looks at the works of the person. The Qur'an determines, "Every man's fate we have fastened on his own neck" (sura 17:13). Therefore, Muhammad depended on his own good works, along with Allah's mercy, to earn heaven. The Muslim has no concept of original sin, the Christian insistence that men and women are born sinful. Instead, sin comes from ignorance and pride. Muhammad saw Allah as utterly removed from creation by his holiness, but paradoxically Allah does not seem to be overly concerned by unholiness on judgment day. Allah demands only that the good outweighs the bad on the scales.

A Modern Hero?

Is Muhammad someone to be followed as the perfect example of obedience to God? The answer must be a resounding no. How can we trust his revelations and visions when he expressed doubt that they were revelations and sometimes thought himself to be demon possessed? Muhammad's own foster mother, Halima, admitted that she thought he was "possessed by the devil."

Also, how can we believe revelations from God when Muhammad himself either changed or modified them? His carelessness with the very words of Allah, words that he did not feel himself obliged to follow, casts a shadow on his trustworthiness.

Morally, the actions of Muhammad sometimes seem reprehensible. He killed critics for speaking their minds, ordered the severe beating of a woman to retrieve information from her, and had sexual relations with a child of nine. He was a ruthless general and raided caravans merely for financial gain to expand his movement. He even broke the rules of engagement when he fought during a sacred month. Nonetheless, he is praised as the most beloved prophet. Described by one Muslim scholar,

> Mohammad is the most favored of mankind, the most honored of all apostles, the prophet of mercy, the head or Imam of the faithful, the bearer of banner of praise, the intercessor, the holder of high position, the possessor of the River of Paradise, under whose banner the sons of Adam

will be on the Day of Judgment. He is the best of prophets, and his nation is the best of nations . . . and his creed is the noblest of all creeds.[15]

Any honest account of Muhammad's life can be summed up in the words *complexity*, *expediency*, and *depravity*. By any measure, the life on earth of Jesus Christ, the Son of God, far exceeds Muhammad's in integrity, grace, and wisdom.

Jesus never took another life. He did not demean women nor exploit young girls for social gain. Christ was the picture of true love. He came and was rejected, and while we were yet sinners, Christ died for us (Rom. 5:8). Muhammad came to shed blood and slaughter those who disagreed with him. Christ came to seek and save those who were lost (Luke 19:10).

Muhammad unified a country, indeed much of the world, by focusing on a stone in Mecca. Jesus Christ unifies sinners under His own death and resurrection. No one questions the influence of both individuals, but the character of their influence is as different as the difference between peace and war.

To discuss Muhammad's life is one thing, to emulate his life is quite another. Muhammad commanded in the Qur'an, "Fight and slay the Pagans wherever you find them" (sura 9:5). This passage allows either of two interpretations: It is *descriptive*, explaining how Muhammad fought the pagan tribes of the Arabian Peninsula in the seventh century. Or it is *prescriptive*, demanding that believers carry on the fight until Allah is completely victorious. Followers of Muhammad have taken this message *prescriptively*. And in a world searching for peace, following the life of this warrior brings about bloodshed.

Notes

1. According to Fahd in the *Holy Qur'an*, the Consorts (of Purity) refer to the wives of the holy Prophet. These were extraordinary women who had special duties and responsibilities due to their marriage to Muhammad.

2. Ibn Ishaq, Sirat Rasul Allah, *The Life of Muhammad*, trans. A. Guillaume (New York: Oxford University Press, 1980), 106.

3. Muhammad H. Haykal, *Life of Muhammad* (Plainfield, IN: American Trust Publications, 1976), 80.
4. Ibid., 337.
5. Ibid., 496.
6. Quoted in Norman Geisler and Abdul Saleeb, *Answering Islam: The Crescent in Light of the Cross* (Grand Rapids: Baker, 1993), 193.
7. Ali Dashti, *Twenty Three Years: A Study of the Prophetic Career of Mohammad* (London: George Allen & Unwin, 1985), 98.
8. Haykal, *Life of Muhammad*, 238.
9. Ibid., 298. Emphasis added. See also Geisler and Saleeb, *Answering Islam*, 176.
10. It must be noted that some translators use the phrase "beat them lightly," although such is not indicated in the text. Once again, the ambiguous text has led to much injustice.
11. Haykal, *Life of Muhammad*, 154.
12. Fahd, *Holy Qur'an*, 1254 (footnote 3723).
13. Betty Kelen, *Muhammad: The Messenger of God* (e-reads, 1975), 207.
14. Caesar E. Farah, *Islam, Beliefs and Observances* (Hauppauge, NY: Barrons Educational Services, 2000), 58. Words in translation have been emended for clarity as necessary.
15. Quoted in Geisler and Saleeb, *Answering Islam*, 84.

3

THE STORY OF ISLAM:
A TRAIL OF BLOOD

Collective Amnesia

A RECENT SURVEY by the Gallup polling organization asked teens raised in the United States to answer three of the most basic questions about American history:[1]

- *In what year did Christopher Columbus discover America?* Only 42 percent named the year 1492, while 22 percent gave the wrong answer and 36 percent could give none.
- *In what war was the issue of states' rights a major issue?* To this question, 39 percent were able to name the American Civil War, while 18 percent gave an incorrect guess. The other 43 percent couldn't give any answer.
- *In what year did the United States declare its independence?* Only one in four teens knew that the Declaration of Independence from England was signed in 1776, despite an annual national holiday devoted to that fact. Some 19 percent missed the correct answer, while an astounding 56 percent couldn't even frame an answer.

What Americans don't know about their own history is minuscule compared to what they don't know about Eastern history, especially the history of the Islamic world. So Westerners do not recognize that tragedies today grow out of fourteen hundred years of struggle between two religious and political giants—Islam and Christianity (see "Events in the Islam-Christian Struggle").

Bernard Lewis, Professor Emeritus of Near Eastern Studies at Princeton University, has offered this overview of "attacks and counterattacks, jihads and crusades, conquests and reconquests":

> For the first thousand years Islam was advancing, Christendom [was] in retreat and under threat. The new faith conquered the old Christian lands of the Levant [Palestine] and North Africa, and invaded Europe, ruling for a while in Sicily. . . . For the past three hundred years, since the failure of the second Turkish siege of Vienna in 1683 and the rise of the European colonial empires in Asia and Africa, Islam has been on the defensive, and the Christian and post-Christian civilization of Europe and her daughters has brought the whole world, including Islam, within its orbit.[2]

Lewis's article appeared in *Atlantic Monthly* magazine in September 1990, exactly eleven years before the attacks on the World Trade Centers and the Pentagon. During those years Muslims fulfilled Lewis's expectation and returned in unprecedented numbers to their root proposition that the world lives in either the House of Islam or the House of Unbelief. From the Muslim standpoint, said Lewis, "The greater part of the world is still outside Islam, and even inside the Islamic lands, according to the view of the Muslim radicals, the faith of Islam has been undermined and the law of Islam has been abrogated. The obligation of holy war therefore begins at home and continues abroad, against the same infidel enemy."[3]

As Islam reverts back toward the model that guided its first millennium, unbelievers of any race, creed, or background are fair game to the Muslim warrior. In the new crusades, the West is engaged in a battle that is political in process but religious in essence.

Events in the Islam-Christian Struggle

691	Dome of the Rock Mosque erected in Jerusalem
715	Great Mosque erected in Damascus
732	Battle of Tours checks Islam's advance across Europe
1095–1291	Crusades define bitter relations between Christianity and Islam for future centuries
1453	Ottoman Turks conquer the Byzantine Empire
1492	Roman Catholic Christianity enforced once more in Spain
1914–1918	Ottoman rulers make a fatal miscalculation in joining the Empire's fortunes with those of Kaiser Wilhelm.

The Four Horsemen of Muhammad (632–661)

Abu Bakr (632–34): Securing the Religion

When Muhammad died in 632, Islam entered its most vulnerable period. Abu Bakr, a father-in-law to Muhammad and one of the first converts, was named caliph (deputy successor) to Muhammad. This intimate companion of Muhammad knew how to carry out offensive war (jihad), achieving three main goals:

1. Islam secured the Arabian Peninsula from chaotic revolt and firmly fixed its lasting heritage.
2. Muhammad's message was eternally preserved through the first written version of the Qur'an.
3. Conquest fulfilled Muhammad's command: "No two religions are to exist in the Arab Peninsula."[4]

Umar (634–644): The Apostle Paul of Islam

With their base secure, followers of Islam expanded the kingdom. The second caliph, Umar, extended the Muslim Empire through conquest of Syria (634), Iraq (636), Egypt (639), and Persia (642). Jerusalem also submitted to Muslim control.[5]

A political genius, Umar masterfully administered this growing territory. Most Muslims still venerate him as the most just of the caliphs. Setting the example of mercy toward non-Muslims, Umar defined the protections given to Christians:

> The protection is for their lives and properties, their churches and crosses, their sick and healthy and for all their co-religionists. Their churches shall not be used for habitation, nor shall they be demolished, nor shall any injury be done to them or to their compounds, or to their crosses, nor shall their properties be injured in any way. There shall be no compulsion for these people in the matter of religion, nor shall any of them suffer any injury on account of religion. . . . Whatever is written herein is under the covenant of God and the responsibility of His Messenger, of the Caliphs and of the believers, and shall hold good as long as they pay Jizya [the tax for their defense] imposed on them.[6]

These rights were given to non-Muslims after their surrender. Only after peace (defined as Islamic rule) was established could unbelievers be protected. John Kelsay, an ethicist who is an expert on the values of war, explains:

> The way of heedlessness and the way of submission are seen as institutionalized in the existence of Islamic and non-Islamic political entities. The former may be described as the territory of Islam (*dar al-islam*); the latter is the territory of war (*dar al-harb*). The territory of Islam signifies a political entity that acknowledges the supremacy of Islamic values. . . . The territory of Islam is theoretically the territory of peace and justice. . . . More concretely, the Sunni theorists thought of jihad as the form of Islamic action at the intersection of the territory of Islam and the territory of war.[7]

Therefore, jihad (holy war) is completed only when the entire world is placed under the submission of Allah and when his laws reign supreme.

The laws of mercy written by Umar were not as compassionate as they seem. A contemporary chronicler of Umar, Ibn Timmiya, noted the restrictions enacted within these "acts of mercy":

- Christians have no right to build new places of worship.
- Christians have no right to remodel a church in conquered lands.
- Muslims could confiscate places of worship in towns taken by storm.
- Muslims could destroy every church in the conquered land.

When the chronicler asked the merciful Umar what should happen to those who violated the rules, he asserted, "Anyone who violates such terms will be unprotected. And it will be permissible for the Muslims to treat them as rebels or dissenters namely, it is permissible to kill them."[8]

Uthman (644–56) and Ali (656–61): Civil War

In 644, Uthman, a Persian slave, murdered Umar. As the third successor to Muhammad, Uthman was seen as a selfish ruler only concerned with his own kin. By the end of his tenure, Muslims were badly divided. Rebels killed the caliph Uthman in his own home while he was reading the Qur'an. (Uthman codified the Qur'an into its final form. Modern editions still bear his name.) Hatred for him was so intense that his body was left unburied for days, a great sin in the Qur'an. He was finally buried in his bloodstained clothes, a symbolic recognition of his martyrdom.[9]

Ali bin Abu Taleb, Uthman's son-in-law and a cousin of Muhammad, took control of the kingdom. Aishah, the widow of Muhammad, fought bitterly against Ali and his tribesmen. Muslim fought against Muslim in two major battles that ended without a victor. In 661, Ali was assassinated, and since that time, Islam has been divided between Ali's followers, the Shiites, and traditional Muslims, the Sunnis.

The Blessed Fruit of Jihad (661–1095)

After Ali's death, as internal strife subsided, Islam gained a larger vision—conquest of the known world. Through 732, that goal seemed within reach. Expansion swallowed Cyprus (647), Tunisia and Kabul in modern Afghanistan (670), the island of Rhodes (672), Constantinople (677), North Africa (700), Spain (711), the Chinese Turkestan border (715), and Morocco (722). By the end of its first century, Islam stretched to the western borders of China and the southern borders of France. North Africa was dominated completely.

Meanwhile, Damascus, Syria, became capital of the Islamic world. Islam's wealth and conquests grew, virtually unhindered, and two great edifices were constructed. First, the Dome of the Rock was built in Jerusalem on the Jewish Temple Mount in 691 to demonstrate the superiority of Islam over Judaism. Second, in 715 the Great Mosque of Damascus replaced the Cathedral Church of St. John to demonstrate the superiority of Islam over corrupt Christianity.[10]

The Turning Point at Tours

The Battle of Tours is among the most important battles ever fought. Islam had advanced through North Africa and Spain. If it conquered France, it would easily defeat Italy, the center of Western Christianity. Charles Martel (The Hammer) halted this invasion at Tours:

> For almost seven days the two armies watched one another, waiting anxiously the moment for joining the struggle. Finally they made ready for combat. And in the shock of the battle the men of the North . . . stood, one close to another, forming as it were a bulwark of ice; and with great blows of their swords they hewed down the Arabs. Drawn up in a band around their chief, the people of the Austrasians carried all before them. Their tireless hands drove their swords down to the breasts [of the foe].[11]

Islam was defeated—but only for a time. Muslims then pointed their swords east in the cause of Allah.

Baghdad Rises to Preeminence

At the Battle of Tours, the Islamic advance west was brought to a standstill. The defeat resulted in much internal strife, and Muslim leaders decided that Baghdad suited their needs for a capital better than did Damascus. The emphasis shifted toward an internal expansion of Islamic theology, law, and science.

Baghdad flourished in wealth and scientific learning, and as a gateway for commerce and culture. Inventions included the clock pendulum, the magnetic compass, and algebra. Baghdad had an unmatched library that housed writings from Aristotle and Plato. In medicine, Muslims were the first to use anesthesia in surgery, the first to discover that epidemics spread through contact and by air, developed the first ambulatory hospital (carried on a camel's back), and separated pharmacology from medicine.[12]

The energy of Muslim militancy was directed toward intellectual discovery. One of the earliest Islamic historical works, Ibn Ishaq's *Life of the Messenger of God*, was an invaluable biography of Muhammad. Literature was further enhanced as Muslims learned the art of papermaking from the Chinese. The Islamic diet improved with the introduction of plums, artichokes, cauliflower, celery, squash, pumpkins, and eggplant. This period is now regarded as Islam's golden age.

Cairo Surges in Prominence

Impressive though these intellectual endeavors were, Islam's political goals suffered. Land holdings stagnated for three centuries, and some regions were declaring independent rule. New dynasties arose to challenge Baghdad's sovereignty. The Fatimid Dynasty, centered in Cairo, captured North Africa, Palestine, and much of Syria. Their presence was limited, however, since others in those regions would not support them. The Fatamid Dynasty was ultimately unable to rule the heart of Islam in the Middle East.

Although Cairo is home to the oldest university in the world, al-Azhar University, the history of Islam remembers Cairo for the sixth caliph of the Fatamid dynasty, al-Hakim (996–1021), who declared himself the incarnation of God. His violent persecution of Christians and destruction of Roman Catholic holy sites encouraged the start of one of history's darkest hours, the Crusades. When al-Hakim vanished without a trace, a mythology grew around his whereabouts.

The Crusades (1095-1291)

The Crusades arose because Christians adopted the Islamic doctrine of jihad, that is, holy war, and moved it to the center of their universe. Two centuries before the first official crusade, Pope Leo IV (847-55) promised the forgiveness of sin to anyone who fought against the infidels. Thus, Leo implanted Christian jihad firmly into Western Christian thinking.[13] John VIII (872-82) and other popes reassured believers in Christ of their eternal security if they were slain in warfare.

In 1064-65, seven thousand Christians were ambushed on the way to worship in Jerusalem:

> They suddenly fell into the hands of the Arabs who leaped on them like famished wolves on long awaited prey. They slaughtered the first pilgrims pitiably, tearing them to pieces. At first our people tried to fight back, but they were quickly forced, as poor men, to take refuge in the village. After they had fled, who can explain in words how many men were killed there, how many types of death there were, or how much calamity and grief there was?[14]

Now Christians had a reason to put their militant faith into practice. The combined church and state imbibed in spiritual fury. The Crusaders were now ready to match Muslims in brutality.

Herald of the Crusades

"*Deus Volt!*" (God wills it!) was the battle cry of Pope Urban II (1088-99) and the Roman Catholic Church. The Western Church was struggling under the withdrawal of Eastern Christians in 1054. A crusade to reclaim much of the eastern landscape might help reunite Rome and Constantinople.

In the initial warfare, Christians were victorious at Antioch and Jerusalem, where the population was almost wiped out. Jews were caught in the middle, and Christians were especially brutal in killing Jews and destroying synagogues.

Christians believed the slaughter showed God's approval: He had laid waste the pagan enemy, allowing the Christians to recapture the treasured sites of the Holy Land. Such thinking led Bernard of Clairvaux (1090–1153), a Western Christian mystic, to develop a theology that life's highest and most honorable calling was to be a warrior-priest. Bernard thus elevated the office of soldier while lowering the office of priest. Even Bernard's persuasion, though, could not prepare soldier-priests for what they would face in the military genius of Saladin.

After reuniting the chaotic factions within Islam and declaring jihad, Saladin recaptured Jerusalem in 1187. He could not prevail against the large force besieging Acre, however, and in the end, Richard the Lionheart brought the 2,700 Muslim prisoners outside the city walls and slaughtered them one by one into the night. The blood of Christians had flowed at the hands of the infidels, and now Christians gave thanks for this revenge.

Results of the Crusades

In an era of scientific, literary, and intellectual advances, especially in the Islamic world, the Crusades mark the brutality and ruthlessness of both sides. In due course, Muslims won the vast majority of battles over the two centuries of wars. Islam was strengthened and Christianity became weakened. From a Christian point of view the Crusades

- failed to achieve a united Church;
- demonstrated far more Christian concern for booty and possession of special places than for spiritual renewal;
- emphasized victory by the sword over evangelization.

For many Muslims, the Crusades have never ended. For many Christians, they became the past that would haunt the future.

The Front Lines Move East (1298–1515)

During the Crusades, a Mongolian by the name of Genghis Kahn (1162–1227) began carving out a new empire. In 1258 even Baghdad was laid to waste. To this day, agriculture is hindered by the environmental savagery of the Mongols, who sowed salt in the fields. The Mongols, enemies of Islam, moved as far west as Egypt, where they were held in check by the Muslim alliance.

It was not the sword, however, that ultimately, defeated the Mongols, but Islam itself. Many of the Mongol warriors were converted, and by the fourteenth century one Mongol leader heralded Islam as the established religion of the Mongolian Empire. Other rulers were enemies of Islam, but Muslims survived their greatest threat. These setbacks, however, left Islam in intellectual decline: Muslim scholars were deported or killed; cultural centers were looted and destroyed.[15]

Islam would need time to heal its wounds, but the core of Islam remained intact, preparing itself to rise again.

Islam Restored to Splendor (1515–1919)

While Christianity saw the revival of Protestantism, Islam saw the emergence of Turks as heroes of the faith. As Christianity was splintering due to theological differences, Islam was reunified by political necessity.

Two history-changing events in the fifteenth century contributed to this new vigor—the capture of Constantinople and the loss of Spain. First, in 1453, the Islamic Ottomans defeated the Christian Byzantine Empire in Constantinople and expanded into the Balkan Peninsula. Constantinople was renamed Istanbul and inaugurated as the new capital of the Ottoman Empire. A contemporary account of the battle for Constantinople demonstrates the importance of jihad:

> At this came the essential role of the leader in the battle as the sultan stood and spoke to his soldiers taking example from the messenger of Allah (s.a.w.) during the battle of Uhud giving an example of bravery in a few words, saying: "my sons, here

I am ready for death in the path of Allah, so whoever desires martyrdom, let him follow me." Then the Muslims followed their leader like the flood from the dam tearing down the obstacles of Kufr until they entered the city and raised therein the word of monotheism. . . . In this manner fell the city of Heracle [Constantinople] which stood stubbornly in front of the Muslims for eight centuries. [Ahmad, authenticated by Al Albany][16]

Ferdinand of Aragon and Isabella of Castille ended Muslim domination in Spain and the Iberian Peninsula and reestablished Roman Christianity in Spain in 1492. All of Western Europe was again part of Christendom. Although deprived of the logistical base of Spain, the Turks persisted in the desire to rule Europe. Attacking from the east and south, they twice laid siege to Vienna. Little wonder that Christians likened the Turks to a devilish horde.

At its height, the Ottoman Empire stretched to Poland in the north, to Baghdad in the east, to the tip of the Arabian Peninsula in the south, and to Morocco in the west. Jerusalem, Mecca, Cairo, Tunis, and Belgrade were all under Turkish rule. The Ottoman Empire declined, however, because of internal strife and as a result of the advance of western European colonialism.

In the eighteenth century, Russia established itself as protector of the Christian Balkans against the Turks. Russia and Turkey fought a series of wars that stretched from the seventeenth to the twentieth centuries. Russia's greatest success came in a land and sea conflict that spanned 1768-74, in the end defeating the Turkish army and decimating their naval fleet. The Russo-Turkish wars gave Bulgaria, Romania, and Serbia complete freedom from the sultan.

The ultimate demise of the Ottoman Empire came when the Turks sided with Germany in World War I (1914-18). In 1923, the Conference of Lausanne drew the modern borders through the once vast Muslim stronghold.

After one thousand years of unprecedented expansion, Islam was now dormant. Over those centuries their record of domination even in Europe had been impressive. Arabs, Moors, and/

or Ottomans had controlled Spain for eight hundred years, Portugal for six hundred years, Greece and Bulgaria for five hundred years, Romania and Serbia for four hundred years, Sicily for three hundred years, and Hungary for one hundred fifty years. J. Dominguez notes, "Italy, Austria, Bosnia, Croatia, Wallachia, Albania, Moldavia, Armenia, Georgia, Poland, the Ukraine, and eastern and southern Russia were all battlefields where Islam conquered or was conquered in violent conflicts marked by cruelty, bloodlust, and a fearful loss of life, spread over considerably more than a thousand years."[17]

Islam on the Defensive

As the Ottoman Empire declined, Islam faced a worldview unknown to their psyche, one before which they adopted a stance of defensive survival. Islam's heroes had always arisen to advance its cause, but from the eighteenth through the twentieth centuries, Muslims cynically adapted as survivors, not conquerors. Meanwhile, they waited for a new golden age of supremacy.

The colonization of Asian and African lands was particularly abhorrent to Muslims. Colonial powers, attending the Berlin Conference of 1884, divided Africa among themselves in tyrannical fashion, although 80 percent of the continent remained under African rule. Great Britain took most of Muslim North Africa, while France took the west and equatorial plain. Italy took Somalia and Ethiopia, and Belgium settled for the Congo. Many modern national boundaries were laid during this conference.

In the hearts of Muslims, though, a worse European crime was the sending of Christian missionaries. In the minds of the Muslims, colonialism and missions were identified as interwoven elements of Western corruption. They still are. Missionaries are viewed, in fact, with greater disdain than colonialists due to the eternal nature of their mission. Consider, for instance, David Livingstone (1813–1873), who arrived in Africa in the 1840s. Although considered a hero to many Christians, to Muslims he is one of the most detested Europeans in history.

The final insult of colonialism came when Britain guaranteed a

Jewish homeland in Palestine, a promise fulfilled after World War
II. Muslims no longer ruled one of Islam's most revered cities.

Arabs placed the blame for all of these offenses squarely on the
Europeans and their American allies.

Conclusion

Several conclusions must be drawn from the fourteen hundred
years of shared Muslim-Christian history:

- With the notable exception of the Crusades, Muslims
  have initiated almost all wars, due largely to the philosophy of jihad.
- War is not a sidebar of history for Islam; it is the main
  vehicle for religious expansion. It is the Muslim duty to
  bring world peace via the sword.
- Conservative Muslims see Western culture as destructive
  to Islamic traditions and beliefs.
- While modern people are familiar only with the defensive Islam of the last three hundred years, the religion
  has never forgotten the previous one thousand years
  of conquest in the cause of Allah. It is this traditional
  conquering Islam that has reemerged.

Today, a cultural, political, theological, and social struggle ensues
for the soul of the Muslim. As Bernard Lewis explains, a threefold defeat occurred in regard to Muslim ideals: first Islam lost domination;
second, through the invasion of foreigners and their ideas, Muslim
authority was undermined in their own countries; third, the social
challenge of modernism encouraged the emancipation of women
and the rebellion of children. "It was also natural that this [Muslim]
rage should be directed primarily against the millennial enemy and
should draw its strength from ancient beliefs and loyalties."[18]

Many faithful Muslims believe they have no choice but to go
on the offensive. The more intense their belief that the West has
degraded Islamic values, the greater the risk of their violent reaction.
For example, a number of circumstances exist:

- The National Salvation Front and the Armed Islamic Group hope to overthrow moderate leaders in Algeria.
- In 1996, the tradition-oriented Islamic Welfare Party became the largest political group in Turkey's Parliament.
- Since U.S. liberation of Kuwait from the Iraqis in the Gulf War, Kuwait has outlawed non-Islamic education and any Christian proselytizing.
- The Brunei government, under a cloak of religious freedom, is pressuring Christian schools to replace Christian religion classes with Islamic instruction. Christian gatherings of more than five people are now illegal.
- All Mauritanian citizens must be Sunni Muslims. Attempting to leave the faith is a crime.
- Although the Bangladesh constitution guarantees religious freedom, a 1998 amendment established Islam as the state religion.
- Kenya's Islamic leaders have declared jihad against the African Inland Church and World Vision International.
- In 1992, Tanzania's government banned all religious preaching outside of churches.[19]

These are but a few cases of the rise of Islamic militancy. Islam is emerging as a power to be respected and to be reckoned with.

Learning from the Past

In 1524, Anabaptist Balthasar Hubmaier (1480–1528), in his book *On Heretics and Those Who Burn Them*, argued for total religious liberty.[20] Hubmaier presented a model attitude for modern Christians in regard to Muslims. He wrote that a Turkish Muslim "cannot be overcome by our doing, neither by sword nor by fire, but alone with patience and supplication, whereby we patiently await divine judgment."[21] Hubmaier went against the vindictive political system of his day and eventually was put to death for his views, including his sympathy toward the Turk.

Consider, then, the tradition of Hubmaier. It is the duty of the believer in Jesus Christ to persuade Muslims compassionately, wait for them patiently, and pray for them earnestly.

Notes

1. George Gallup and Alec Gallup, "American Teens Need a History Lesson," May 5, 2000, http://www.gallup.com/poll/releases/pr000505.asp (accessed December 17, 2001; site no longer available).
2. Bernard Lewis, "The Roots of Muslim Rage," *The Atlantic Monthly* 266.3 (September 1990): 47–60.
3. Ibid., 49.
4. Ibid. "Offensive War to Spread Islam," *Behind the Veil*, http://www.answering-islam.org/BehindVeil/btv2.html.
5. Jacques Jomier, *How to Understand Islam* (New York: Crossroad, 1991), 20. Jomier analogizes the apostle Paul to Umar, as we also do.
6. "The Rightly-Guided Caliphs," University of Southern California Compendium of Muslim Texts, http://www.usc.edu/dept/MSA/politics/firstfourcaliphs.html.
7. John Kelsay, *Islam and War* (Louisville: John Knox, 1993), 33–34.
8. "Discrimination Between a Muslim and a Non-Muslim," *Behind the Veil*, http://www.answering-islam.org/BehindVeil/btv4.html.
9. "The Rightly-Guided Caliphs," http://www.usc.edu/dept/MSA/politics/firstfourcaliphs.html.
10. George Braswell, *Islam* (Nashville: Broadman and Holman, 1996), 26.
11. Paul Halsall, "Medieval Sourcebook: Arabs, Franks, and the Battle of Tours, 732: Three Accounts," http://www.fordham.edu/halsall/source/732tours.html.
12. Braswell, *Islam*, 31.
13. It must be noted that evangelicals such as the Petrobusians, Henricans, and Arnoldists, who were themselves persecuted by the Roman Catholic Church, were personal pacifists who did not partake in the warfare. All of Christianity cannot be blamed for the events that transpired since there was a great contingent of dissenters in the Church.
14. Annalist of Nieder-Altaich, "The Great German Pilgrimage of 1064–65," trans. James Brundage, *Internet Medieval Source Book*, http://www.fordham.edu/halsall/source/1064pilgrim.html.

15. The Mongol Empire: A Historical Web Site, "Genghis Khan," http://www.geocities.com/Athens/Forum/2532/page2.html.

16. Muhammad El-Halaby, "The Liberation of Constantinople," *Nida'ul Islam* (July–September 1996).

17. J. Dominguez, "Islam: The So-Many Totalitarian Regimes," http://biblia.com/islam/islam.htm (accessed December 17, 2001; site no longer available).

18. Lewis, "Roots of Muslim Rage," 50.

19. Paul Marshall, *Their Blood Cries Out* (Dallas: Word, 1997), 44–68.

20. *Anabaptist* literally means "re-baptizer." The name was given to sixteenth-century Christians who believed that only adult believers should be baptized.

21. H. Wayne Pipkin and John H. Yoder, *Balthasar Hubmaier, Theologian of Anabaptism* (Scottdale, Pa.: Herald, 1989), 62.

4

THE QUR'AN:
"MOTHER OF BOOKS"

Tony's Story

As a FRESHMAN in college, Tony was paired with Asklar as his residence hall roommate. Tony had been raised in an evangelical church, accepted Christ as his Savior at age twelve, and had been president of his youth group. It seemed that God had used him to reach others on two mission trips. Yet Tony was frustrated in his attempts to share his faith with Asklar. Nothing he said seemed to faze his roommate.

Every time Tony cited a biblical text from his evangelism training Asklar repudiated his text with an Islamic teaching that contradicted Tony's very premise. Muslims knew the Old Testament stories, Tony learned, but somehow each story came out changed.

Tony was learning an essential element of Islamic theology. Many stories of the Old Testament and the Gospels are found in the Qur'an, but with amendments. The Qur'an, written about six centuries after Christ, "retells" the Bible with a bent toward Muslim beliefs. To reach his friend, Tony must first learn about the book Asklar was always reading.

Authority

According to orthodox Islamic scholarship, the Qurʾan was compiled in the years 646–50 from materials written by Muhammad before his death in 632. The Arabic word *Qurʾan* is derived from the root *qaraʾa*, which means "to read or recite." The angel Gabriel thrice commanded "read" and "recite" when he confronted Muhammad in July 610 in the Hira cave, three miles northeast of Mecca.

According to Islam, the Qurʾan is the final revelation from Allah. In Arabic the Qurʾan is also referred to as *Al-Kitab* (the book), *Al-Furqan* (the distinction), and *Al-dikhr* (the warning).

Christians sometimes assume that the Qurʾan is as large as the Bible, yet the book consists of 114 chapters (suras), 6,616 verses (*ayat*),[1] 77,943 words, and 338,606 Arabic letters. According to Islamic scholars, 86 suras were revealed in Mecca, while 28 were revealed at Medina. In contrast, the Bible has 1,189 chapters, and is about three times as long as the Qurʾan.

Revelation

Islamic doctrine runs into a conundrum at the point of revelation. Allah is remote and does not reveal himself on an intimate level, but he nonetheless wants to communicate his truth with humanity. This seeming chasm is spanned by *arasul* ("the sent ones"), human prophets who were given a special status and able to communicate Allah's will.

The communication, however, was decidedly a monologue from Allah to humanity. While each prophet supposedly fulfilled his mission by producing a book, the final revelation, and therefore—according to Muslims—the most important, was given to the final prophet, Muhammad.

Islam teaches that the Qurʾan is an exact word-for-word copy of God's final revelation, words inscribed on tablets that have always existed in heaven. Muslims point to sura 85:21–22, which says "Nay, this is a glorious Qurʾan, [inscribed] in a tablet preserved."

According to Muslim tradition, these revelations were sent down to the lowest of the seven heavens in the month of Ramadan, during the night of power (*lailat al Qadr*; sura 17:85). From there they were revealed to Muhammad through the angel Gabriel (sura 25:32). Because of Muslim belief that the Qur'an is an exact dictated revelation, Muslims kiss the book, place it to their forehead, and store it on the highest shelf in the house. For this reason, too, Muslims regard any translation of the Qur'an with suspicion, for the true words are impossible to fully understand except in their Arabic original. Only in the Arabic does the Qur'an contain fully the words and testimony of Allah.

Muslims call the Qur'an the "Mother of books" (sura 43:3), and believe no other book or revelation can compare. Suras 2:23 and 10:37–38 challenge anyone to "present some other book of equal beauty."

Inspiration

The Arabic term for explaining the process of revelation is *wahy*, which can mean "divine inspiration." Wahy is explained in sura 42:51:

> It is not fitting for a man that Allah should speak to him except by inspiration, or from behind a veil, or by the sending of a Messenger to reveal, with Allah's permission, what Allah wills, for He is most high, most wise.

The Qur'an tells little concerning how Muhammad actually received his revelations, so we rely upon the accounts of others, such as Ibn Ishaq, Ibn Hisham, Ibn Athir, and 'Ali Halabi for insight. Their writings refer to seven forms of wahy experienced by Muhammad:

1. Muhammad had seizures, during which he sweat vigorously during revelations, according to his wife Aishah. Bells rang in his ears. He became upset, and his face changed. Umar ibnu'l Khattab tells that Muhammad shivered, his mouth foamed, and he roared like a camel.

2. Revelation came in dreams.
3. Sometimes he saw an angel in the form of a young, tall man.
4. At other times he saw actual angels (sura 42:51).
5. During one evening (known as the Mi'raj) he received his revelation as he crossed the "seven heavens" to receive the revelation.
6. Allah spoke to him from behind a veil (sura 42:51).

The accounts of seizures are recorded in Muslim sources. Some authors have compared them to epileptic seizures, but it is best to allow the accounts to speak for themselves without comment. To identify Muhammad with a neurological disease or demon possession does little to advance the gospel witness. Still, it is interesting to note that, according to 'Amr ibn Sharhabil, Muhammed himself told his wife Khadija that he feared he was possessed by demons and wondered whether others might consider him possessed.[2]

Periods and Methods of Revelation

According to tradition, the revelations of suras were received and written down by the illiterate Muhammad, through the angel Jibril (Gabriel) during three periods. Suras of the first Meccan period (611-15) were writings of judgment and revelation concerning the nature of Allah and his rule (suras 1, 51-53, 55-56, 68-70, 73-75, 77-97, 99-104, 111-14).

The second Meccan period (616-22) produced longer suras dealing with doctrines, many taken directly from the Pentateuch. During this time, Islam first declared that it was the exclusively true religion (suras 6-7, 10-21, 23, 25-32, 34-46, 50, 54, 67, 71-72, 76).

The Medina period (623-32) lasted through roughly the last ten years of Muhammad's life. These last writings deal predominately with government and ethics (suras 2-5, 8-9, 22, 24, 33, 47-49, 57-66, 98, 110).

If Muhammad could not read nor write, how did he collect the Qur'anic texts? Some *aulema* (scholars) believe that companions of the prophet memorized the words Muhammad communicated, and it is they who could have been used to corroborate the final collation by Muhammad's secretary, Zaid ibn Thabit. Islam teaches that Muhammad did not foresee his death, and made no preparations for the compilation of his revelations. The work of collecting the revelations fell to Muhammad's compatriots.

Sahih al-Bukhari, a Muslim scholar of the ninth and tenth centuries, wrote that when Muhammad fell into one of his unpredictable trances, his revelations were written on whatever was handy. Leg or thigh bones of dead animals were used, as well as palm leaves, skins, mats, stones, and bark.[3] When nothing was available, his disciples ('Abdullah ibn Mas'ud, Abu Musa, and Ubayy ibn Ka'b) attempted to memorize the revelations. These oral collections were passed on by "reciters," who memorized the suras and recounted them before the people.

According to al-Bukhari, during the years following Muhammad's death large sections were lost when a number of reciters died at the Battle of Yamama. This compelled Hazrat Omar, who had been a companion of Muhammad, to ask the caliph Abu Bakr that the existing revelations/recitations be gathered into one collection. Muhammad's secretary, Zaid ibn Thabit, was designated by Abu Bakr to collect the sayings.

Zaid's text was later given to Hafsah, one of the wives of Muhammad and the daughter of Umar, the second caliph. One of the major controversial issues of transmission begins with the reign of Uthman, the third caliph (644–56).

By the time of Uthman, various versions of the Qur'an had spread across the Islamic community. Setting out to dispose of the variations in the codices and standardize the text, Uthman chose the collection of Zaid ibn Thabit, taken from the manuscript of Hafsah, as the model. According to Islamic tradition, Zaid's collection was chosen because its Qoraishi dialect was the language spoken by Muhammad and was considered to be "standard" Arabic. (This dialect is no longer extant, however, and linguists cannot distinguish between modern Arabic and Qoraishi.) Copies of Zaid's collection were sent throughout the Muslim provinces, while all other manuscripts—some twenty-four variants—were summarily burned.

The final choice for a "canon," then, had little to do with its authenticity. One can deduce that at the time of Uthman, no two Qur'ans were alike, yet in one edict they were all destroyed—except one.

How the Qur'an Views the Bible

The Qur'an, in presenting itself as the final, infallible witness of Allah, portrays the Bible as unfulfilled (so needing the Qur'an to complete the revelation) and flawed (corrupted at its core).

First, the Qur'an describes the Bible as a book from which Muslims can draw teachings. Sura 2:136 notes, "Say ye: 'We believe in Allah, and the revelation given to us, and to Abraham, Ismail (Ishmael), Jacob, and the Tribes, and that given to Moses, and Jesus, and that given to all prophets from their Lord: we make no difference between them.'"

The Scriptures are viewed, in fact, as given by Allah to Moses and Jesus, here viewed as prophets of Allah: "He sent down the Law (of Moses) and the Gospel (of Jesus) . . . as a guide to mankind" (sura 3:2–3). The belief that Allah sent the Old and New Testaments as a precursor to the Qur'an is clearly seen in the fifth sura:

> It was We who revealed the Law (to Moses); therein was guidance and light. . . . If any do fail to judge by the light of what Allah hath revealed, they are (no better than) unbelievers. . . . We sent Jesus, the son of Mary, confirming the Law that had come before him: We sent him the Gospel: Therein was guidance and light . . . a guidance and an admonition to those who fear Allah. Let the people of the Gospel judge by what Allah hath revealed therein. If any do fail to judge by the light of what Allah has revealed, they are (no better) than those who rebel. Judge . . . what Allah hath revealed, and follow not their vain desires. (sura 5:44, 46, 47, 49)

The fifth sura is confirmed by three additional interesting texts:

> People of the Book! . . . Stand fast by the Law, the Gospel, and all the revelation that hath come to you from your Lord.

> It is the revelation that has come to thee from your Lord. (sura
> 5:68)

> The Quran is . . . a confirmation of (revelations) that went be-
> fore it. (sura 10:37)

> If thou were in doubt as to what We have revealed unto thee,
> then ask those who have been reading the Book from before thee.
> The truth had indeed come to thee from thy Lord. (sura 10:94)

The devout Muslim is, in fact, commanded not to argue with the Jew or the Christian over the revelation, but to emphasize that Allah has added the Qur'an to the divine revelation. Sura 29:46 states, "and dispute ye not with the People of the Book . . . but say: 'we believe in the revelation which has come down to us and that which came down to you.'" This point proves most important: Muslims see the Qur'an not as contradicting the Old and New Testaments, but rather as fulfilling them. The Jew and Christian are called to testify to this truth in sura 21:7: "Before thee, also, the apostles We sent were but men, to whom We granted inspiration: If you realize this not, ask of those who possess the message."

So the Old and New Testaments are seen to be divinely given but humanly corrupted. The Jew and the Christian are called by the Qur'an to recognize that the Bible was corrupted by lies and distortions:

> You People of the Book! Why do you clothe truth with false-
> hood and conceal the truth, while you have knowledge? (sura
> 3:71) . . . There is among them a section who distort the Book
> with their tongues: you would think it is part of the Book, but
> it is no part of the Book. (sura 3:71, 78)

The Qur'an, therefore, is the final, complete and exact revelation of Allah. Eerily reminiscent of the warnings in Revelation 22:18–19, one reads the Qur'anic admonitions:

There is none that can alter the words of Allah. (sura 6:34)

No change can there be in the words of Allah. (sura 10:64)

Conflicts with the Bible

Many teachings in the Qur'an directly contradict the Bible. These contradictions draw attention to discrepancies of thought between the Muslim and Christian as we attempt to witness to Muslims. Since Islam teaches that the Bible has been corrupted, they view their versions of the biblical narratives to be correct. A number of suras teach that Allah sent the revisions of the biblical stories to Muhammed to "fix" the corrupted Bible (suras 4:82; 6:34; 10:65). Here are a few samples of these changes.

Pharaoh's Wife Adopted Moses (Sura 28:9)

Exodus 2:10 states that Pharaoh's daughter adopted Moses, but the Qur'an says that it was his wife. Had Pharaoh's wife adopted Moses, he would have been the son of Pharaoh himself and heir to Egypt's throne.

The Trinity Includes Mary (Sura 5:116)

Sura 5:116 states that Christians worship three gods: the Father, the Mother (Mary), and the Son (Jesus). A heretical sect of Christianity, the Choloridians, did teach such a doctrine, and Muhammad could have encountered them in Arabia. For whatever reason, the Qur'an badly misrepresents Christian teaching.

A similar misrepresentation occurs in sura 5:73–75: "They do blaspheme who say: Allah is one of three." Obviously the accusation is against Christians and is an errant assumption that the Trinity makes God one of three. Orthodox Christianity teaches that God is one substance, and three persons.

Pharaoh and the Tower of Babel (Sura 28:38; 40:25)

The Qur'an says that a man named Haman, a servant of Pharaoh, built a high tower to ascend to God. But the Babel tower occurs in Genesis 11, long before there were pharaohs, and the name "Haman" is an even later linguistic name. The only "Haman" in Scripture is in the story of Esther in Babylon, long after the height of Egypt's glory.

Samaritans Built the Israelite Calf (Sura 20:85–97)

The Qur'an says that the calf worshiped by the Israelites at Mount Horeb was molded by a Samaritan. The term *Samaritan* was not coined until 722 B.C., several hundred years after the Exodus, when the idol was crafted.

The Sacrifice of Ishmael (Sura 37:100–11)

Hebrew manuscripts for Genesis 22 do identify the son of Abraham who was laid upon the altar for sacrifice. The context clearly shows that it was Isaac, while sura 37 identifies a son. This can be supported only by tradition and marks one of the two holidays of Islam.

Saul Led Gideon's Army (Sura 2:249)

Judges 7 identifies Gideon as the leader of the three-hundred-man army of soldiers chosen by God. Sura 2 makes Saul the general of this army, although the king was not yet born.

Jesus Was Not Crucified (Sura 4:157)

The Jews boast in sura 4:157, "'We killed Christ Jesus the son of Mary, the Apostle of Allah',—but they killed him not, nor crucified him, but so it was made to appear to them."

Blood Is Unimportant to Allah (Sura 22:34–37)

"And the beasts of sacrifice—We have appointed them for you as among Allah's waymarks; therein is good for you. . . . The flesh of them shall not reach Allah, neither their blood. But godliness from you shall reach Him." Christianity teaches the essential nature of blood, pointing toward the atoning work of Jesus Christ. Leviticus 17:11 notes, "The life of the flesh is in the blood, and I have given it to you upon the altar to make atonement for your souls; for it is the blood that makes atonement for the soul." The New Testament continues the theme in the work of Jesus Christ (see Heb. 9:22–28).

Odd Teachings of the Qur'an

In addition to the obvious misunderstandings of history and theology that reached Uthman's edition of the Qur'an, a number of teachings can be regarded as eccentric, especially when looked at from the twenty-first century. Examples include:

Seven Earths (Sura 65:12)

Sura 65:12 records that God created seven heavens (or levels of heaven) and seven earths as well.

Jinn and Shooting Stars (Suras 37:6–10; 55:33–35; 67:5; 72:6–9)

Meteors and shooting stars are missiles fired at "satans" and jinn who try to listen to the reading of the Qur'an in heaven, and then pass on what they hear to men in suras.

People Become Apes (Suras 2:65–66; 7:163–67)

According to suras 2 and 7, Allah turned certain fishing people into apes for breaking the Jewish Sabbath.

Contradictory Statements in the Qur'an

One can also find a number of facts and statements in the Qur'an that simply do not match well with other statements found therein. These internal inconsistencies and disagreements seldom sway the Muslim, but they do illustrate human fallibility in the central source of Islamic teaching.

Mary and the Angel(s)

Describing the Annunciation, the Qur'an says that one angel came to Mary (sura 19:17-21), but suras 3:42 and 45 mention several angels at the announcement of Jesus' conception.

Allah's Day

How long is a "day" to Allah? Sura 22:47 states that Allah's day is equal to a thousand solar years, but sura 70:4 states that a day is fifty thousand solar years long.

Soul Reaper

Different passages offer conflicting accounts regarding who takes away human souls at death: the Qur'an says it is the Angel of Death (sura 32:11), angels generically (sura 47:27), or Allah (sura 39:42).

Days of Creation

How long did Allah take to create the earth? Suras 7:54, 10:3, 11:7, and 25:59 state that creation required six days, but in 41:9-12 the creation narrative adds up to eight days.

Is heaven or earth older?

Which was created first? Sura 2:29 states clearly that Allah created the earth first and then heaven, but sura 79:27-30 reverses the order.

Humankind's Creation

From what substance were people made? The answers given are a blood clot (sura 96:1-2), water (sura 21:30), burned clay (sura 15:26), dust (sura 3:59), nothing (sura 19:67), earth (sura 11:61), or a drop of thick fluid (suras 16:4, 75:37).

Shirk as the Unforgivable Sin?

Does Allah ever forgive *shirk* (idolatry)? The Qur'an is unclear. The sin is listed as unforgivable in suras 4:48 and 116, but forgivable in suras 4:153 and 25:68-71. Abraham committed this sin of polytheism in worshiping moon, sun, and stars (sura 6:76-78), yet Muslims believe that all prophets are without any sin.

Noah's Son Drowned?

According to sura 21:76, Noah and all of his family survived the flood, but sura 11:42-43 reports that one of Noah's sons drowned.

Punishment for Adultery

The punishment for adultery in sura 24:2 is one hundred lashes for both the man and the woman. In sura 4:15 the punishment is life imprisonment for the woman but no punishment to the man who repents and makes amends.

Christians in Heaven or Hell?

The eternal destination of Christians is in doubt. Suras 2:62 and 5:69 teach that Christians shall enter Paradise, but suras 5:72 and 3:85 say they will go to hell.

Pharaoh Drowned or Saved?

The Qur'an is unclear as to what happened to the Pharaoh who pursued Moses. Sura 10:92 states that he survived the battle, but three other texts say that he drowned (suras 17:103; 28:40; 43:55).

Muslims in Hell?

Would Allah send his own servants to hell? According to sura 19:71 every Muslim will go to hell (for some period), while other numerous texts state that those who die in jihad go immediately to Paradise.

Jesus Alive or Dead?

Sura 3:144 states that all messengers died before Muhammad, but sura 4:158 claims that Jesus was raised to God without death. In his commentary on sura 3:46, Yusaf Ali teaches that Jesus lived until He was about thirty-three, but sura 5:110 says He taught the people as an old man.[4]

Notes

1. Each verse or portion of the sura is known as an *aya*, which means "miracle" in Arabic. Muhammad claimed that the Qur'an was his sole miracle, although the Qur'an did not exist in its written form during his lifetime.
2. Al Waqidi recorded this fear. He also noted the extreme aversion of Muhammad to the cross. Muhammad broke everything brought into the house that had such a form.
3. Sahih al-Bukhari, Hadith, 6.477.
4. For more analysis of the Qur'an, see Robert Morey, *Islamic Invasion* (Eugene, OR: Harvest House, 1992); and Anis Shorrosh, *Islam Revealed* (Nashville: Thomas Nelson, 1988).

5

SUNNAH AND HADITH: THE OTHER BOOKS

The Hendersons' Story

THE HENDERSONS WONDERED why it was so difficult to form a relationship with their Muslim neighbors. The Hendersons only wanted to be friends and along the way earn a hearing for the gospel. After the Askars settled into their new home next door, Shane and Cheryl Henderson soon appeared at their door to say hello and to offer a loaf of freshly baked bread. The couple, obviously Islamic in dress, were polite but reticent and gingerly set aside the bread. Shane and Cheryl went home discouraged.

Strike one.

During the waning summer months, Shane invited their neighbors for a barbecue. Knowing that Muslims do not eat pork, Shane purchased pounds of shrimp, lobster, and clams. The Askars saw the spread and suddenly remembered that they had made a "prior engagement."

Strike two.

After a few other self-conscious and clumsy approaches, Shane gave up. Then one day Mr. Askar noticed that Shane was struggling

to carry armloads of groceries from the car. He came over to
help. Mr. Askar seemed friendlier than normal and eager to help.
Surprised, Shane jumped on the gesture, quickly extending the only
hand he had free—the left—to his neighbor. But instead of shaking
it, Mr. Askar stared at it a moment, then excused himself.

Strike three.

Many well-intentioned Christians stumble into egregious insults
against their Muslim acquaintances. The cause is usually ignorance
of lesser-known prescriptions of Islam. Some of these social prescriptions are found in the Qur'an, but Westerners are more likely
to break rules that are found in a text they likely have never heard
about—the Hadith. The Qur'an contains teachings that Muhammad
believed he had received directly from Allah. But some of the more
idiosyncratic cultural rules are actually in the Hadith and Sunnah
collections of the sayings (ahadith) and examples (sunnahs) of
Muhammad. The Hendersons would have been embarrassed to
learn that the Hadith prohibits the eating of shellfish and lard-
based baked goods. Shaking a left hand is insulting, according to
this compendium of Islamic teaching.

The Hadith as Explanation

The Qur'an is the highest authority in Islam, having been
transmitted to Muhammad from Allah through the angel Gabriel.
Secondary to the Qur'an, the Sunnah and the Hadith serve as
instruction to the Muslim in much the same way as the Midrash
serves the Hebrew. As the Sunnah and Hadith are always placed
together in compilation, it is the purpose of this chapter to examine
them for insight into Islamic teaching.

The Sunnah is the basis of the legal code of Islamic jurisprudence (sharia, "the path"), and is authoritative in rulings among
Islamic states. It depicts the events of the life of Muhammad, and
offers examples for ethics and living.

Hadiths (or ahadith) are similar to the sunnahs, but not iden-
tical. Each hadith is a narration from the life of the prophet and
what he said, as opposed to a biographical sketch. Therefore, as the
entirety of the Sunnah gives the significant story of Muhammad, the

volumes of the Hadith expound Muhammad's crucial, everlasting commandments.

According to the South African Council of Muslim Theologians, the Hadith/Sunnah is the sensible explanation of an otherwise sporadically ambiguous Qur'an. They explain, "The Holy Qur'an without the Hadith or Sunnah of the Prophet remains unintelligible in certain instances and in view of that, the Holy Qur'an has, in several verses, ordered Muslims to follow the Prophet in all his deeds and sayings. Therefore, if one believes in the Holy Qur'an, there is no other alternative but to uphold the Hadith of the Prophet."

In M. M. Azami's *Studies in Hadith Methodology and Literature*, the following definition of a hadith is given:

> According to Muhaddithiin [scholars of Hadith] it stands for "what was transmitted on the authority of the Prophet, his deeds, sayings, tacit approval, or description of his sifaat [features] meaning his physical appearance. However, physical appearance of the Prophet is not included in the definition used by the jurists.[1]

The expansion of Islam in the century following Muhammad's death presented Islamic scholars with a daunting task—preserving knowledge of the teachings of the prophet. Hence the science of hadith evaluation was born. There are four versions of the Hadith, all of which have achieved popularity.

The collection of Sahih al-Bukhari is recognized by the overwhelming majority of the Muslim world to be one of the most authentic collections of the words of Muhammad. According to Islamic scholars, each report in his collection was checked for compatibility with the Qur'an, and the veracity of a chain of reporters had to be painstakingly established. Bukhari (810–870)—full name Abu Abdullah Muhammad bin Ismail bin Ibrahim bin al-Mughira al-Ja'fai—spent sixteen years compiling his research, and ended up with 3,295 ahadith divided into 97 "books" with 3,450 chapters.[2] His criteria for acceptance into the collection were among the most stringent of all the scholars of ahadith, categorizing each memory and oration as follows: sound (*sahih*), good (*hasan*), weak (*da'if*), and fabricated or forged (*maudu'*). All the citations in this chapter come from Bukhari's version of the Hadith.

The translation of Sahih Muslim is a much larger collection. Muslim (817–875)—full name Abul Husain Muslim bin al-Hajjaj al-Nisapuri—was a student of Bukhari. Out of three hundred thousand ahadith he evaluated, about twelve thousand, based upon a less stringent acceptance criteria than that used by Bukhari, were accepted into his collection.[3]

Two partial collections have a smaller following in Islamic academia. The partial collections of Sunan Abu Daawuud and Malik'i Muwatta are about one-half the size of those by Bukhari and Muslim, but they influence such Islamic sects as the Druze.[4]

Evaluating the Hadith and Sunnah

According to Qur'an sura 15:9, Muslims believe that the sunnahs and the ahadith are a fulfillment of prophecy: "We have, without doubt, sent down the message: and we will assuredly guard it (from corruption)." In the fourteen centuries since the Qur'an was formulated, Muslims have protected a living record of Muhammad's example of how Islam is to be lived. Thus, a science of transmission was developed to preserve the prophet's teachings, sayings, and life accounts (see "Criteria for Establishing Ahadith").[5]

Aulema, men trained in memorization, developed an academic study of transmission. These aulema became scholars of the Islamic community, who exposed the forgeries and false attributions to which communities of Muslims had been exposed.

The aulema developed four classifications of ahadith: (1) *qudsi*, supposedly the exact words of Muhammad; (2) *marfu*, reports from a direct witness to Muhammad's words, such as "I heard the Prophet say . . . "; (3) *mauquf*, a statement by a companion who heard Muhammad make a statement; and (4) *maqtu'*, a narration from a successor.

Criteria for Establishing Ahadith

1 Reference to
a particular authority

Qudsi —sacred
Marfu—elevated
Mauquf—stopped
Maqtu'—severed

2 Links of Isnad
(interrupted or
uninterrupted)

Musnad—supported
Mursal—hurried
Muttasil—continuous
Munqati—broken
Mu'dal—perplexing
Mu'allaq—hanging

3 Number of
reporters at each
stage of Isnad

Mutawatir—consecutive
or
Ahad—isolated
which
includes
Mash'hur—famous
Aziz—rare
or
Gharib—scarce/strange

4 Nature of
the text
and Isnad

Ziadatu Thiqah—addition by a
reliable reporter
Munkar—denounced
or
Mudraj—interpolated

5 Reliability
and memory
of the reporters

Sahi—sound
Hasan—good
Da'if—weak
or
Maudu'—
fabricated/forged

Topics Covered

While no topical index of Bukhari's Hadith is authoritative, Muhsin Khan of the University of Southern California has worked out a descriptive set of chapter headings (see "Hadith Chapter Topics" on the next page). These headings illustrate the variety of topics covered.[6]

Camel Urine, Shoes, and Evil Eyes

Some unusual teachings are found in the Hadith. One should not mock ancient health cures, but if Islam holds to the infallibility of its sacred texts, the Hadith presents Muslims with a quandary. Are Muhammad's teachings historical citations within a cultural context, or actually prescriptive?

Muhammad espoused, for instance, the medicinal virtues of camel urine: "The prophet ordered them to follow his camels, and drink their milk and urine, so they followed the camels and drank their milk and urine till their bodies became healthy" (7.590). He believed that "fever is from the heat of hell, so put it out (cool it) with water" (7.619). A housefly in one's cup is a sign of guaranteed health: "Mohammed said, 'If a housefly falls in the drink of anyone of you, he should dip it (in the drink), for one of its wings has a disease and the other has the cure for the disease'" (4.537).

Muhammad believed that a child's appearance is determined by whether the man or the woman has the first orgasm: "Mohammed said, 'As for the child, if the man's discharge precedes the woman's discharge, the child attracts the similarity of the man, and if the woman's discharge precedes the man's, then the child attracts the similarity of the woman" (5.275).

Muhammad was a superstitious man. He taught that "the effect of an evil eye is a fact" (7.636), and "If you want to put on your shoes, put on the right shoe first, and if you want them off, take the left one first" (7.747).

Sunnah and the Life of Muhammad

In ethics, the Muslim is encouraged to follow Muhammad's

Hadith Chapter Topics

1. Revelation
2. Belief
3. Knowledge
4. Ablutions (Wudu')
5. Bathing (Ghusl)
6. Menstrual Periods
7. Rubbing Hands and Feet with Dust (Tayammum)
8. Prayers (Salat)
9. Virtues of Prayer Hall
10. Times of the Prayers
11. Call to Prayers (Adhaan)
12. Characteristics of Prayer
13. Friday Prayer
14. Fear Prayer
15. The Two Festivals (Eids)
16. Witr Prayer
17. Invoking Allah for Rain (Istisqaa)
18. Eclipses
19. Prostration During Recital of Qur'an
20. Shortening the Prayers (At-Taqseer)
21. Prayer at Night (Tahajjud)
22. Actions While Praying
23. Funerals (Al-Janaa'iz)
24. Obligatory Charity Tax (Zakat)
25. Obligatory Charity Tax After Ramadan
26. Pilgrimage (Hajj)
27. Minor Pilgramage (Umra)
28. Pilgrims Prevented from Completing Hajj
29. Penalty of Hunting While on Pilgrimage
30. Virtues of Madina [Medina]
31. Fasting
32. Praying at Night in Ramadan
33. Retiring to a Mosque to Remember Allah
34. Sales and Trade
35. Sales in Which Goods Are Delivered Later
36. Hiring
37. Transference of Debt
38. Representation, Authorization, Business by Proxy
39. Agriculture
40. Distribution of Water
41. Bankruptcy
42. Lost Things Picked Up by Someone
43. Oppressions
44. Partnership
45. Mortgaging
46. Manumission of Slaves
47. Gifts
48. Witnesses
49. Peacemaking
50. Conditions
51. Wills and Testaments (Wasaayaa)
52. Fighting for the Cause of Allah (Jihad)
53. One-fifth of Booty to the Cause of Allah (Khumus)
54. Beginning of Creation
55. Prophets
56. Virtues and Merits of the Prophet
57. Companions of Prophet
58. Merits of the Helpers in Madina [Medina]
59. Military Expeditions Led by the Prophet
60. Prophetic Commentary on the Qur'an
61. Virtues of the Qur'an
62. Marriage (Nikaah)
63. Divorce
64. Supporting the Family
65. Food, Meals
66. Sacrifice for a Birth
67. Hunting, Slaughtering
68. Al-Adha Festival Sacrifice
69. Drinks
70. Patients
71. Medicine
72. Dress
73. Good Manners, Form
74. Asking Permission
75. Invocations
76. To Make Heart Tender
77. Divine Will (Al-Qadar)
78. Oaths and Vows
79. Expiation for Unfulfilled Oaths
80. Laws of Inheritance (Al-Faraa'id)
81. Limits and Punishments set by Allah (Hudood)
82. Punishment of Disbelievers at War with Allah
83. Blood Money
84. Dealing with Apostates
85. Speaking Under Compulsion
86. Tricks
87. Interpretation of Dreams
88. Afflictions and the End of the World
89. Judgments (Ahkaam)
90. Wishes
91. Accepting Information from a Truthful Person
92. Holding Fast to the Qur'an and Sunnah
93. Uniqueness of Allah

hadithic example. Muhammad said, "Adhere to my Sunnah" and elsewhere, "Whoever neglects my Sunnah does not belong to me."

Some aspects of the Sunnah are obligatory (*waajib*) and some are recommendations (*mustahabb*). Prescriptions in the two categories cover virtually every area of life.

Reading ahadith can go a long way toward helping the Christian understand the lifestyle of a Muslim. The Hadith decrees such actions as

- sitting cross-legged in prayer with the right leg on top (muftarishan; Bukhari, 784);
- sacrificing a camel while it is standing up, and its left foreleg is tied (Bukhari, 1598);
- passing a drinking vessel to one's right (Muslim, 3785);
- dividing one's time equally among co-wives (Bukhari, 4813).

Virtually every action taken by Muslims, from how they approach your home to how they brush their teeth, has precedent in the Hadith. Certain acts of protocol must be approached with careful consideration. When in doubt, and to avoid offense, the non-Muslim should allow the Muslim to act first.

Shane and Cheryl learned their lesson. May we do so before we lose our opportunity in witness.[7]

Notes

1. M. M. Azami, *Studies in Hadith Methodology and Literature* (New York: American Trust, 1978), 23.
2. *Survey of Islam* (Institute for the Study of Islam and Christianity, 2000), CD-ROM version, chapter 4.
3. Bill Musk, *The Unseen Face of Islam* (London: Monarch, 1989), 277.
4. Malik'i was a law professor and founder of a judicial school who reportedly taught more than one thousand students. Malik'i revised his *Muwatta* throughout his life.
5. From http://www.usc.edu/dept/MSA/fundamentals/hadithsunnah/ (site no longer available).

6. Muhsin Khan, adapted from a paper presented at the Islamic Society of Greater Kansas City, Kansas, http://www.usc.edu/dept/MSA/fundamentals/hadithsunnah/ (site no longer available).

7. Portions of this chapter were first presented as a paper by the authors in a seminar at the annual meeting of the international Evangelical Theological Society, November 15, 2001, Colorado Springs, Colorado.

6

ALLAH: NAMES OF TERROR,
NAMES OF GLORY

God's "Divine Nicknames"

A FEW DAYS after the World Trade Center and Pentagon bombings, a memorial service was held in a baseball stadium. Thousands gathered to mourn and pray. On a large platform at the center of the infield, leaders of the gathering huddled around the microphone. At center stage stood Oprah Winfrey, the American talk show host and ubiquitous media mogul. In a variety of high-visibility media settings, Ms. Winfrey was becoming the teacher of America. All of her instruction centered in the doctrine that Islam is a peaceful and loving religion.

That day in the stadium a Christian minister stood at the microphone and began the invocation: "We pray in the name of our God—the God of Christianity, Judaism and Islam. . . ."

Were all the people gathered in that stadium—Christian, Jew, Muslim, and others—in fact speaking to the same "God," who just happens to have different "divine nicknames" that are invoked among adherents to the different religions? Are the progeny of the Oprah-style spirituality correct that every person has "inner light," which equalizes every faith system, since each person's journey of discovery is a search for the "inner light of meaning and purpose"?

Oprah's message regarding the benevolence of Islam and its similarity to other faiths is now assumed in media coverage of terrorism and Middle East crises. Yet strangely absent from the discussion at this point have been orthodox, evangelical Christians, or for that matter, orthodox Muslim aulema (scholars).

Is postmodernism correct? Are all religions saying the same spiritual truths using different words?

Near Riot in Texas

After September 11 the debate became heated. That November, Ergun lectured at the University of North Texas on the subject of "Terrorism, Tolerance, and Truth." The lecture, sponsored by the Denton Bible Church and Campus Crusade for Christ, was originally scheduled to take place in Lyceum Hall. Because of intense interest, however, the organizers arranged for a larger facility—the main auditorium.

For weeks, fliers had been distributed. The Muslim population on campus and in the community was enraged that a Muslim turned evangelical Christian was to speak on such a topic. Threats had been made, so security was tight, but as the crowd gathered, it was clear that this was to be an intellectual debate, not a physical confrontation.

The tension was thick in the hall, and discussion was, to say the least, lively. The moderator and speaker had agreed that, if possible, only Muslims and skeptics were to ask questions in the open forum after the lecture.[1] Too often, such lectures have "planted" questioners, who lob easy queries to the speaker, like a bad 1970s Christian movie. Here the skeptics would be allowed to ask questions and also to present their case.

Questions directed toward Ergun followed a predictable pattern, for Ergun has participated frequently in such forums. The statements inevitably would attack the speaker's credibility ("You are not an expert on Islam"), or knowledge ("You have not read the Qur'an enough"), or integrity ("You are lying about us"), without actually dealing with an issue.

Tension heightened as one older Islamic gentleman rose to speak. Instead of yelling (as had been the style of some questioners), he spoke quietly but firmly on the central issue of Allah's divine character and name. The speaker, he noted, had presented only half of the issue. Allah is benevolent and merciful, he continued, and does not send every Muslim into jihad. It is difficult, he conceded, to answer the verses of the Qur'an and the Hadith that Ergun had cited. He believed, however, that the suicide bombers in the World Trade Center tragedy were now in "the hell fire."

Knowing that the media wanted to meld all religions into one "brotherhood," Ergun directed a question to the Islamic gentleman. "Sir, may I ask you—Is Allah the same god as Jehovah?"

The gentleman looked at the speaker, and then the crowd, and said, "No, of course not."

If nothing else was accomplished that night, one point was clear. Muslims and Christians had agreed that Allah and Jehovah are not the same.

Are We Using Divine Nicknames?

If any subject stirs controversy in the Christian academic community, it is the subject of semantics versus theology. Since Christians use *God* in referring to our deity, and since the generic Arabic term for "god" is *Allah*, do Muslims and Christians speak of the same Being?

Some Christian academics see the difference between God and Allah as solely a matter of language. In their excellent book, *Answering Islam*, Norman Geisler and Abdul Saleeb make a point with which we, the authors of this book, respectfully but emphatically disagree:

> Allah is the personal name for God in Islam. We make no distinction . . . between the word "Allah" and the English word "God." As one well-known Muslim author puts it, "Al Lah" means "the Divinity" in Arabic: it is the single God, implying that a correct transcription can only render the exact meaning of the word with the help of the expression "God." For the

Muslim, "al lah" is none other than the God of Moses and Jesus.[2]

Philosophy, logic, and etymology determine the response of Geisler and Saleeb. Muslims throughout history have meant by the term *Allah* an Uncaused Cause and Necessary Being. The concept of Islam's "Necessary Being" is similar to that of the Christian apologists, such as Thomas Aquinas, when they design proofs of God. The concepts of Allah and of God result in a position of "word similarity." As Geisler and Saleeb continue, they cite Kenneth Craig, who notes, "The Arabic 'ilahun' means 'a god,' and it is similar to the Hebrew and Aramaic words for deity."[3]

Yet the questions of origin and intent remain: Did Muhammad see Islam as fulfilling and redacting Judaism and Christianity? Or was he aiming at a complete revision of religion altogether? Did he view Christians and Jews as unintended worshipers of Allah, the one true God, or were they pagans and *kafir* (infidels)? Although he made copious revisions of Old Testament stories and the nature of Jesus, he clearly viewed followers of Moses and of Christ as children of Satan, not separated brethren.

The process of redefining an established set of terms to fit one's own ideas is called "redaction." Therefore, while the Muslim man says that he is a son of Abraham, he pours new meaning into the essential nature of Abraham. In sura 3:66, the Qur'an states emphatically, "Abraham was not a Jew or a Christian, but he was an upright man, a Muslim; and he was not one of the polytheists." The story of Abraham has been redacted to fit an agenda.

Missiology and the Unknown God

Some Christian apologists use these semantic similarities as a bridge to understanding. If we can use the word *Allah*, we can point the Muslim toward an understanding that Allah truly is the triune God of the Bible. Acts 17 records that in Athens Paul used a false god of Mars Hill to proclaim Christ (see Acts 17:16–31).

For those who hold to this missiological principle, the essential argument can be expressed thusly:

Paul shows that these philosophers were ignorantly worshiping the true God of Christianity. (Acts 17:23)

He used their false gods to preach the true God to them.

In their worship, they had established a place in their hearts for the true Creator.

Therefore, we can, on the mission field, speak of Allah as God, because Muslims simply do not know His nature.

But there are flaws in this argument.

First, Paul did not confuse the false gods that Athenians worshiped with the one true God of Christ. He pointed to an idol that the Athenians had built to "cover their tracks." This "unknown God," whom Paul took to be our Lord, was different in nature and name than the other idols. The argument we cited above would only be true if Paul had pointed to Zeus or another god in the Greek pantheon and said, "This god I shall proclaim to you. You do not know this god's true nature." Rather, he differentiated the one true God from the false ones, which he clearly viewed as idols.

Whether or not the Athenians "ignorantly worshiped" the True God, Paul was not saying that they were believers, or else he would have had no need to proclaim Christ to them. Instead of condemning their syncretism in combining all of the gods to worship into one, Paul included a possibility of an unknown god, one that they did not know, and it was this God—Jesus Christ—whom he was now going to preach. He was not simply filling in the blank of the idol with Jesus' name. Christ was not the god they had. Even the philosophers saw that Paul's "strange God" was not one they knew.

Making a close connection between Yahweh and Allah, in fact, only damages the proclamation of Christ in Arabic-speaking countries. When one asks Muslims if they know "Allah," their response is in the affirmative. But the suggestion that Allah is triune and personal then becomes a personal attack on their god and on their religion, rather than the proclamation of Christ. Many Arabic-speaking Christians use the Persian term *khudu* for God, rather than cause confusion by calling God by the name Allah.

The Allah we worshiped as Muslims was a remote judge. When Christians speak of the intimacy and grace of God, it confuses a Muslim who has no concept of the God-man in their religion, except by negation.

Messianic Muslims?

When Ergun spoke in one church on the East Coast of the United States, an Arab who had become a Christian disagreed with his assessment of the term *Allah*. Since this man spoke Arabic and was now a believer, he believed that, since Allah was simply an Arabic word, he could use it to represent Jesus Christ or the entire Godhead. He was unwilling to use the word *Jehovah*, as this was not his native tongue. His second point was even more startling. He regarded himself as a *Messianic Muslim*. Just as Messianic Jews had discovered that Jesus was Yahweh, he had discovered that Jesus was Allah. Could he not continue to use the term *Allah* in that light?

Such an argument goes against the very nature of Messianic Judaism. Israel had always been looking forward to a Redeemer and Savior, the Messiah, and the Messianic Jew has recognized that Jesus is in fact that Messiah, the fulfillment of their hope. A devout Muslim, however, looks back at the life of Christ. Muhammad, who knew the teaching of Jesus Christ as Lord, rejected Him. The rejection of Jesus' claim to lordship is, in fact, a fundamental tenet of Islam.

> As they say the Beneficient has taken to Himself a son. Certainly you make an abominable assumption. . . . It is not worthy of Allah that He should take to Himself a son. (sura 19:88–92)

A Muslim who accepts Jesus Christ as Lord must therefore reject his or her former religion, which explicitly denies Christ as God. Christianity is not the fulfillment of Islam's hope, but it rejects Islam at its core.

No Syncretism

This issue of what is meant by *Allah* is so essential and so seminal that it cannot be overstated. The question of the name of God must be centered in the nature of God. If a Scientologist speaks of "god" in terms of *engrams*, is he or she speaking of the God of the Bible simply because he uses the generic English word for divinity? If a Mormon discusses the nature of God, is he or she philosophizing about Jesus Christ, Immanuel, because he or she invokes the word *God?* It is incumbent on us to be precise. One cannot discuss the "name" of God without first being explicit about the nature of the God attached to the name.

In discussions with well-intentioned but imprecise Christians, we, the authors, often use a series of rhetorical questions to show how ridiculous it is to identify Allah with Yahweh:

- Is Allah triune? If not, then we are not talking about the same God.
- Does Allah have a Son? If not (see sura 19:88–92), then we are not discussing the same God.
- Is Allah the vicarious Redeemer and atoning Lamb of God, taking away the sins of the world? If not, then we are not talking about the same God.

In a politically correct, politically charged, postmodern culture, these principles are neither popular nor welcome. But they are essential to an effective witness (see Phil. 2:5–11).

The Nature of Allah

It is incumbent upon the Christian to examine the nature of Allah in light of the Qur'an. Sura 112 defines *Allah* in this manner: "In the name of Allah, Most Gracious, Most Merciful. Say: He is God, The One and Only; God, the Eternal, Absolute; He begetteth not, Nor is He begotten; And there is none Like unto Him." As

Geisler and Saleeb note, the Hadith states that this sura "is held to be worth a third of the whole Qur'an and the seven heavens and the seven earths are founded upon it. To confess this verse, a tradition affirms, is to shed one's sins as a man might strip a tree in autumn of its leaves."[4]

Allah as Absolutely One (Tawhid)

In more than one hundred passages, the Qur'an emphasizes the absolute monotheistic nature of Allah as being both self-existent and necessary. This simple confession is found at every juncture of Islamic life: *La illaha illa Allah, Muhammad rasul Allah* ("There is no god but Allah, and Muhammad is the messenger of Allah"). This profession, the first pillar of Islam, is made at every rite of passage—birth, marriage, and death. It is uttered countless times a day and is an exclusivistic claim: Allah alone must be worshiped.

Muhammad confessed that Allah alone is God: "Fight those who believe not in Allah nor in the last day" (sura 9:29). Islam alone is central to the salvation of humanity: "If anyone desires a religion other than Islam, it shall never be accepted of him" (sura 3:85).

Allah as Deterministic (En sh'Allah)

En sh'Allah means "Allah wills it." One of the foundational doctrines of Islam is the absolute sovereignty, to the point of determinism, of Allah. Allah knows everything, determines everything, decrees everything, and orders everything. Allah is even the cause of evil:

> We first send a definite order to those among them who are given the good things of this life to transgress, so that the word is proved true against them: then it is We destroy them utterly. (sura 17:16)

Chapter 9 of this book addresses the Islamic concept of salvation, and will look more closely at the fatalism reflected in virtually every act of the Muslim. Our father used to say, "If you fall and

break your leg, say, 'Allah wills it,' because he caused it to happen."
Even during the prayer time (*rakats*), no Muslim truly makes supplication. It is the repetition of the first sura of the Qur'an that
takes up most of the prayer time in each of the five positions of
prayer. This repetition is a type of mantra, invoking the power of
Allah, but does not request anything. For the Muslim, prayer is
an act of obedience (and escaping the punishment due those who
neglect prayer), not petition.

One insight to this fatalism is one of the names of Allah, *Al-
Jabbar*, "the Mighty One," in sura 59:23. The term speaks of an
ability to compel, with a power that cannot be resisted.

The Names of Allah

Islamic tradition teaches that Allah has ninety-nine names. The
Hadith records, "Muhammed said, 'Verily there are ninety-nine
names of Allah and whoever recites them shall enter paradise'"
(8.419). The lists of names for Allah are as varied as the compilers
and aulema themselves. Thus, a comprehensive compilation is difficult
to ascertain. The 1880 *Journal of the Royal Asiatic Society* collected
552 different names of Allah, taking them from the Qur'an and the
Hadith. Still others use eighty-one names found in the Qur'an, and
eighteen in the Hadith.

The following list assimilates two major compilations, one by
Muhammed al-Mandani and the other by Abu Huraira.[5] Neither
this list nor any other version is meant to be exhaustive, but these
names illustrate streams of thought in Islam. The annotations in
extract form are by the compilers. English spellings vary in different
transliterations.

- Allah, The name that cites the essence of being
- Al-Aakhir, the Last, who is the consummation of the
  ages (sura 57:3)

Muhammad has explained this. He said, in Saheeh Muslim,
"Allah, You are the First [al-Awwal], for there was nothing before
You, and You are the Last [al-Aakhir], for there is nothing after

You, and you are the Triumphant [ad-Dhaahir], for there is no one above You, and You are the Perspicacious [al-Batin], for there is nothing beyond You. Remove our debt, and relieve us from poverty." Muhammed meant the Triumphant [al-Ghaalib] with ad-Dhaahir, and the All-Knowing [al-Saalim] with al-Batin. And Allah knows best (Al-Qurtubi for sura 57:3).

- Al-Adl, the Just (6:115)
- Al-Afuw, the Pardoner, who forgives his servants (4:99–100; see also under Al-Ghaffar)
- Al-Ali, the High One in might and power (2:225–56)
- Al-Alim, the All-Knowing (2:29)
- Al-Awwal, the First, who precedes the beginning (57:3; see under Al-Aakhir)
- Al-Azim, the Mighty (2:225–56)
- Al-Aziz, the Sublime in Sovereignty (59:23)
- Al-Badi, the Contriver, who created the entire art of creation (2:117). A related term is Al-Wahid, the Unique Creator, and Al-Khaliq, the Creator (13:16–17)
- Al-Baith, the Raiser, who will raise up a Muslim witness in every region (6:89–91)
- Al-Baqi, the Enduring, who maintains and survives forever (20:73, 75)
- Al-Bari, the Maker, from whose hand we all come (59:24)
- Al-Barr, the Beneficent, whose mercy appears in all creation (52:28)
- Al-Basir, the Observant, who sees and hears all things (57:3)
- Al-Basit, the Extender, who extends his mercy to whom he wills (13:26)

Narrated Anas: "The people said: 'Apostle of Allah, prices have shot up, so fix prices for us.' Thereupon the Apostle of Allah said: 'Allah is the One who fixes prices, the One who takes, the One who gives [al-Basit], and I hope that when I meet Allah, none of you will have any claim on me for an injustice regarding blood or property.'" (Sunan Abu Daawuud hadith 23.3444)

- Al-Batin, the Inner, who is immanent within all things (57:3)
- Ad-Darr, the Afflicter (48:11)
- Al-Fattah, the Opener, who clears the way (34:26)
- Al-Ghaffar, the Pardoner (71:10). As "Pardoner," Allah conceals and overlooks sins. He turns in forgiveness to whomever *repents*, even to someone who has committed deep sin (shirk). But Allah only conceals sin. Islam does not have the concept of cleansing from guilt.
- Al-Ghafur, the Forgiving (2:235)
- Al-Ghani, the Rich, who possesses all (2:267)
- Al-Hadi, the Guide, who leads believers (22:54)
- Al-Hafiz, the Guardian, who watches all (11:57). An intensive form of *al-hafid*, it means "the One ever mindful and constantly on guard."
- Al-Hakem, the Judge among his servants (40:48)

Narrated Hani ibn Yazid: "When Hani went with his people in a deputation to the Apostle of Allah, he heard them calling him by his kunyah [surname], Abul-Hakem [father of al-Hakem]. So the Apostle of Allah called him and said: 'Allah is the judge [al-Hakem], and to Him judgment belongs. Why are you given the kunyah Abul-Hakem?'

"He replied: 'When my people disagree about a matter, they come to me, and I decide between them, and both parties are satisfied with my decision.' He said: 'How good this is!'" (Sunan Abu Daawuud hadith 41.4937)

- Al-Hakim, the Wise (6:18). A more intensive form of the Arabic word *hakim*. Among its meanings are the Ruler or Sovereign, and the Judge. Some have also said that it means the One who prevents or stops corruption.

- Al-Halim, the Kind, who is forgiving of his own (2:225)
- Al-Hamid, the Praiseworthy, to whom all praise is due. Ibn Katheer writes that this name indicates that Allah is the One who deserves praise in "all His deeds, sayings, laws, commands, and prohibitions." (2:225)
- Al-Haqq, the Truth (20:114)
- Al-Hasib, the Accounter, who is the Reckoner (4:6–7); that is, the One who will take account of all people's deeds, and who will reward or punish them accordingly. Al-Qurtubi points out that this is a warning in particular to those who deny Allah: Ultimately they will answer to him for their deeds.
- Al-Hayy, the Living, who is the source of life (20:111)
- Al-Jabbar, the Mighty One, whose might and power are complete (59:23). Al-Jabbar is the omnipotent, All-Powerful One, who is absolutely free of weakness. He can compel others, and his power cannot be resisted. Others have said that another possible meaning is the One who Sets Right or Fixes.
- Al-Jalil, the Majestic (59:23)
- Al-Jami, the Gatherer of men for the final day of judgment (3:9)
- Al-Kabir, the Great One (22:62)
- Al-Karim, the Generous Noble (27:40). *Karim*, the superlative form of *kareem*, means "noble-hearted and magnanimous." It may refer specifically to understanding and patience—all traits of the noble-hearted—that Allah shows in overlooking the ignorance of his servants. The reference to "ignorance of his servants" is based upon the revelation of this particular name. It appears in the Qur'an in 96:1–5, as the first words revealed by Allah to a man who could neither read nor write—Muhammad.
- Al-Khabir, the Well-Informed (6:18)
- Al-Khafid, the Humbler, who humbles some and exalts others (56:3)
- Al-Khaliq, the Creator (13:16–17)

- Al-Latif, the Gracious to his servants (42:19)
- Al-Majid, the Glorious (11:73)
- Al-Malik, the King of all (59:23)

Abu Huraira reported that the Prophet said, "Allah will hold the whole earth and roll all the heavens up in His Right Hand, and then He will say, 'I am the King, where are the kings of the earth?'" (hadith 6.60.336)

Abu Huraira reported from Allah's Messenger so many ahadith and one of them was this: that Allah's Messenger said, "The most wretched person in the sight of Allah on the Day of Resurrection and the worst person and target of His wrath would be the person who is called Malik al-Amlaak (the King of Kings) for there is no king but Allah." (Sahih Muslim hadith 5339)

- Malik Al-Mulk, the Possessor of the kingdom (3:26)
- Al-Matin, the Firm in strength (51:58)
- Al-Mubdi, the Originator (85:13)
- Al-Mudhill, the Humiliator (3:26)
- Al-Mughni, the Enricher, who provides bounty (9:74–75)
- Al-Muhaimin, the Preserver (59:23)
- Al-Muhsi, the Computer, who numbers everything (19:94)
- Al-Muhyi, the Resuscitator, who brings life to the dead (30:50)
- Al-Muid, the Restorer, who rebuilds (85:13)
- Al-Muizz, the Honorer, who chooses to whom he will bestow honor (3:26)
- Al-Mujib, the Answerer, who responds to his servants (11:61) To avoid confusion, the aulema often quote the following ahadith in the context of the name Al-Mujib:

He [the Prophet] then made mention of "a person who travels widely, his hair dishevelled and covered with dust. He lifts his hand toward the sky (and thus makes his supplication): 'O Lord,

O Lord,' whereas his diet is unlawful, his drink is unlawful, his clothes are unlawful, and his nourishment is unlawful. How, then, can his supplication be accepted?" (Sahih Muslim hadith 2214)

Abu Huraira reported Allah's Messenger as saying: The supplication of a servant is granted in case he does not supplicate for sin or for severing the ties of blood, or he does not become impatient. It was said: Allah Messenger, what does: "If he does not grow impatient" imply? He said: That he should say like this: I supplicated and I supplicated but I did not find it being responded, and then he becomes frustrated and abandons supplication. (Sahih Muslim hadith 6595)

- Al-Mumin, the Faithful, who grants security to his servants (59:23)
- Al-Mumit, the Killer at His Will (15:23)
- Al-Muntaqim, the Avenger, whose vengeance is just (30:47)
- Al-Muqaddim, the Forerunner, who sends help ahead (50:28; see also under Al-Mutaakhkhir)
- Al-Muqit, the Well-Furnished with Power (4:85)
- Al-Muqsit, the Judge who sets the scales (21:47–48)
- Al-Muqtadir, the Prevailer over Enemies (4:85)
- Al-Musawwir, the Shaper, who creates as he wills (59:24)
- Al-Mutaakhkhir, the Defender (14:42–43)

Narrated Ibn ʾAbbas: "When the Prophet got up at night to offer the Tahajud prayer, he used to say: 'O Allah! All the praises are for you, You are the Holder of the Heavens and the Earth, and whatever is in them. All the praises are for You; You have the possession of the Heavens and the Earth. . . . Your Word is the truth And Paradise is true And Hell is true And all the Prophets are true; And Muhammed is true, And the Day of Resurrection is true. O Allah! I surrender [my will] to You; I believe in You and depend on You. And repent to You, And with Your help I argue [with my opponents, the non-believers] and I take You as a judge [to judge between us]. Please forgive me my previous and future sins; And whatever I concealed or revealed. You are the One who make some people forward [Al-Muqaddim] and [some] backward [Al-Mutaakhkhir]. There is none to be worshiped but you." (Sahih Al-Bukhari hadith 2.21.221)

- Al-Mutaali, the Self-Exalted, who sets himself high above all creation (13:9–10)
- Al-Mutakabbir, the Proud (59:23)
- Al-Muti, the Giver (20:50)
- Al-Muzil, the Separator (10:28–29)
- An-Nasir, the Helper of His Own (4:45)
- An-Nur, the Light, of both heaven and earth (24:35)
- Al-Qabid, the Seizer (2:245–46)
- Al-Qadir, the Able, who does as he pleases (17:99)
- Al-Qahhar, the Irresistible, Over-Powering One (13:16–17). Al-Qurtubi points out that this irresistibility is especially distinct from Al-Qadir, in that Allah can *prevent* his servants from achieving their desires, or help them.
- Al-Qawi, the Strong in Power (13:19)
- Al-Qayyum, the Self-Sufficient (3:2)
- Al-Quddus, the Most Holy One (62:1)
- Ar-Rafi, the Exalter (6:83)
- Ar-Rahim, the Compassionate, to his own (2:143)
- Ar-Rahman, the Merciful, specifically to those who show mercy (1:3 and 12:64)

Narrated Abu Huraira: "Allah's Apostle said: 'There are one hundred [parts of] mercy of Allah and He has sent down out of these one part of mercy upon the jinn [spirits] and human beings and the insects and it is because of this [one part] that they love one another, show kindness to one another and even the beast treats its young one with affection, and Allah has reserved ninety-nine parts of mercy with which He would treat His servants on the Day of Resurrection." (Sahih Muslim hadith 36.6631)

- Ar-Raqib, the Watcher, who guards his creation (5:117)
- Ar-Rashid, the Guide, who leads believers (11:87)
- Ar-Rauf, the Gentle, who is compassionate to his own (2:143)
- Ar-Razzaq, the Provider, who asks no provision (51:57–58)
- As-Sabur, the Forebearing, who has great patience with his own (51:57–58)
- As-Salam, the Peacemaker, whose name is Peace (59:23)
- As-Samad, the Eternal, who begets not and is not begotten (112:2)
- As-Sami, the Hearer (17:1)
- Ash-Shahid, the Witness (5:117)
- Ash-Shakur, the Grateful, who accepts the service of his own (64:17)
- At-Tawwab, the Relenting, who relents in mercy to Adam and creation (2:37)
- Al-Wadud, the Loving One, who loves his own (11:90)
- Al-Wahab, the Giver (3:8)
- Al-Wahed, the Unique One (13:16–17)
- Al-Wakil, the Administrator, who rules all (6:102)
- Al-Wali, the Safety (13:11–12)
- Al-Waliy, the Patron of His Own (4:45–47)
- Al-Warith, the Inheritor, to whom all will return (19:40)
- Al-Wasi, the All-Emcompassing (2:268–71)
- Az-Zahir, the Outer, who is everywhere (47:3)
- Dhul-Jalal Wal-Ikram, Lord of Majesty and Honor (55:27)

Differences Between Gods

The Distant One

When Allah is discussed within the Islamic community, the absence of intimacy, atonement, and omnibenevolence becomes apparent. In all the terms and titles of Allah, one does not encounter terms of intimacy. In Christianity, we learn that each of us is a "temple of the Holy Spirit" (1 Cor. 6:19), suggesting immanence in the life of the believer. Jesus stresses this dimension in His Garden prayer on the night before the crucifixion. God is the Father, "Abba" (e.g., Mark 14:36), the term of endearment for a loving parent. Even the most faithful and devout Muslim refers to Allah only as servant to master; Allah is a distant sovereign. Some titles for Allah connote mercy, but it is a redefined mercy: Allah is merciful because he did not kill me or leave me in peril. Yahweh is a caring, loving, and intimately involved Father.

The Cold Judge
Islam also looks to a god of the scales, as opposed to the atoning God the Son. Allah forgives only at the repentance of the Muslim, and all consequences for sin and the debt of guilt fall on the Muslim, who comes to Allah in terror, hoping for a commutation of his sentence. Allah is a "Liberal Giver," (Al-Wahab) but with the character of a fierce warrior who decides to be merciful in response to victory. Again, one sees a judge, as opposed to a God of love.

The Hater
Allah's heart is set against the infidel (*kafir*). He has no love for the unbeliever, nor is it the task of the Muslim to "evangelize" the unbelieving world. Allah is to be worshiped, period. Any who will not do so must be defeated, silenced, or expelled. The theme is conquest, not conversion, of the unbelieving world. Allah has called the Muslim to make the name of Allah alone to be worshiped.

Notes
1. The moderator was Jason Martin, the leader of Venue, the philosophical collegiate ministry of the Denton Bible Church, and a student at Criswell College. He led with a spiritual maturity beyond his years, as the situation could have quickly escalated into a riot, but his firm and evenhanded leadership allowed for a free discourse of ideas. Both Venue and Campus Crusade achieved the "almost impossible":

an open debate between Christians and Muslims without physical violence or intellectual warfare.

2. Norman Geisler and Abdul Saleeb, *Answering Islam* (Grand Rapids: Baker, 1993), 13–14. The Muslim author cited is Maurice Bucaille, *The Bible, the Qur'an and Science,* trans. Pannell and Bucaille (Paris: Editions Seghers, 1988), 120–21. *Answering Islam* has become a standard for Christian apologetics to Islam, and, with the exception of their position on Allah, it is in our, the authors', estimation an indispensable work overall.

3. Ibid., 15, citing Kenneth Craig, *The Call of the Minaret* (New York: Oxford University Press, 1964), 36.

4. Geisler and Saleeb, 17, citing Al-Bukhari, *The Translation of the Meanings of Sahih Al-Bukhari,* trans. Muhammad Muhsin Khan (Al-Medina: Islamic University) 6:493–495.

5. Muhammed al-Mandani's list is reproduced in Geisler and Saleeb, *Answering Islam,* 22–24. Abu Huraira's list is found in H. U. Weitbrecht Stanton, *The Teaching of the Qur'an* (New York: Biblio and Tannen, 1969), 33.

7

FUNDAMENTALS:
THE FIVE PILLARS

The John Walker Lindh Story

TO THE AVERAGE American who grew up between the hippie 1960s and the pluralistic new millennium, John Walker Lindh is an enigma. Raised in the comfortable center of liberal and tolerant America, John Walker was given every benefit in life, from education to affirmation. He was taught to search out his own reality and that his parents would be pleased with any decision he made. To his parents, he had no method of rebelling since he himself was allowed to determine his own path.

Freedom gives a person the right to rebel against absolutes, authority, and society. The benefactor of relativism is the modern teenager who is told he can believe whatever he wishes and still be correct, especially as it pertains to religion.

And John Walker was given unbridled freedom. He was raised to "choose his own spiritual path." At the age of sixteen, after reading a biography of Malcolm X, he opted for Islam. Believing that the religion of 1.2 billion people was peaceful, Walker traveled to Yemen to learn Arabic. He later joined a *madrassah* school in Pakistan known for its strict training and close connection with the Taliban. The nineteen-year-old chose simplicity instead of luxury, militancy instead of modernity. He had chosen one of the most intolerant and segregated sects in Islam. *Newsweek* journalist Evan Thomas explains the motivation behind the resolve:

> Most teenagers, when they rebel, say they want more freedom. John Walker Lindh rebelled against freedom. He did not demand to express himself in different ways. Quite the opposite. He wanted to be told precisely how to dress, to eat, to think, to pray. He wanted a value system of absolutes, and he was willing to go to extreme lengths to find it.[1]

Then John Walker Lindh emerged, a fighter for the Taliban against his own countrymen. The next time his parents saw their son, he was on the front page of numerous newspapers. Their son was a traitor.

President George W. Bush called the young man "misled." But who or what misled him? Charles Colson gives the answer:

> Walker was first misled by the way Americans talk about religion. In what is sometimes called "civil religion," all religions are considered to be equal. Not just in legal terms, which is proper in a democracy, but also in validity and truth. Our culture, starting at the top, sends the message that all religions are essentially interchangeable and equally good for individuals and for society.
>
> But that's not true. And it brings us to the second way in which Walker was misled. Since September 11, many of our elites have bent over backwards to obscure, even hide, Islam's true nature. That's why people like Walker and his parents believe that Islam is a peaceful faith. That's why they bought into the utopian vision they had been sold.[2]

John Walker Lindh chose his own destiny. Although his path was flawed in many ways, his journey demonstrated the lure of

Islam: a faith that gives believers strict, concrete rules and practices to which they can adhere.

Community (Umma): A Central Factor in Islamic Rites

The sense of solidarity within the confines of Islam is prized above all else among Muslims. They are a family of believers in Allah who value spiritual kinship more than individual freedom. Islamic Law in many Muslim countries is based on the five pillars of Islam, the five fundamentals that serve as a rallying point in the cause of Allah, unifying believers under the umbrella of essential beliefs.

The pillars are non-negotiable. They are not to be questioned, but believed to the utmost. To criticize the five pillars is, in fact, paramount to treason, perceived as heresy and blasphemy, and punishable in many Muslim countries by imprisonment or worse.

The Five Fundamentals of Faith

1. The Creed (Shahada)

A baby boy is born at the Saddam Hussein hospital in Baghdad, Iraq. After the doctors finish inspecting the child, making sure he is healthy, the father whispers into his son's ear words that will become all too familiar: "*Ilaha illa Allah. Muhammad rasul Allah.*" ("There is no god but Allah. Muhammad is the messenger of Allah.")

These words are repeated to the child throughout his life, and if possible, at his death. He must memorize them himself in their original language of Arabic. Daily he should repeat these words to demonstrate his allegiance to the strict monotheistic faith and its founder.

What seems like a simple statement is actually comprehensive in its scope. The admission of Muhammad as the final messenger of Allah places the believer within the prophet's belief system. Therefore, the Muslim maintains what the prophet believed, including that the Qur'an is the final and perfect revelation of Allah, that prophets are messengers to all people groups, and that angels do the will of Allah. In addition, theological tenets of resurrection, judgment day, heaven, and hell are accepted as factual.

But mere intellectual assent of these details is not sufficient. The devout Muslim must unite belief with practice. The combination of right principles with dedicated performance will guide the Muslim through the course of this life into the hereafter.[3]

2. Prayer (Salat)

Surrounding the Kaaba in Mecca, countless thousands of Muslims prostrate themselves to pray to Allah. Prayer is the most basic tenet of Islam and acts as the lifeline to the Muslim.

Prayer is the ultimate worship of the Muslim. In the call to prayer, notice how prayer is joined to the concept of worship:

> God is Great.
> God is Great.
> God is Great.
> God is Great.
> I testify that there is none worthy of worship except God.
> I testify that there is none worthy of worship except God.
> I testify that Muhammad is the messenger of God.
> I testify that Muhammad is the messenger of God.
> Come to prayer!
> Come to prayer!
> Come to success!
> Come to success!
> God is Great!
> God is Great!
> There is none worthy of worship except God.[4]

This call to prayer also illustrates the importance of repetition in the Muslim's prayer life. In the ablution (*wudu,* "cleansing") preceding the prayer, Muslims are called to purify themselves. They must

- wash their hands up to the wrist three times;
- rinse out the mouth three times;
- clean the nostrils by sniffing water three times;
- wash the face from forehead to chin and from ear to ear;

- wash the forearms up to the elbows three times;
- pass a wet hand over the whole of the head;
- wash the feet up to the ankles three times, the right then the left.[5]

Muslims can expect Allah to hear their prayers only if they are clean physically. Certain acts, in fact, invalidate the cleansing ritual and require the Muslim to repeat it:

- Flatulation

Abu Huraira reported that the Messenger of Allah said, "Allah does not accept the prayer of a person who has released gas until he makes a new ablution." A person from Hazhramaut asked Abu Huraira, "What does releasing gas mean?" He answered, "Wind with or without sound."

- Touching genitals. Ash-Shaf'i related: "Any man who touches his penis must perform ablution. Any woman who touches her vagina must perform ablution."[6]

Muslims must also cleanse when there is no water:

But if you are ill, or on a journey, or one of you comes from the privy [restroom] or you have been in contact with women, and you find no water, then take for yourselves clean sand or earth, and rub therewith your faces and hands. Allah does not wish to place you in a difficulty, but to make you clean, and to complete His favour to you, that you may be grateful. (sura 5:6)

Prayer, then, is not a personal conversation between a human and God; rather, it is an external practice saturated with formal procedures and required customs. The formality is only exacerbated for those Muslims who live outside the Middle East, where Arabic is not the native tongue, but who must still recite their prayers from memory in Arabic.

The importance of humility in Islam is unquestioned. During the prayer rituals, known as rakats, Muslims prostrate themselves before Allah, an act of submission. In fact, "mosque" (*masjid*), the term designating the place of Islamic worship, literally means "a place of prostration."[7]

Finally, prayer in the mosque is elevated above individual prayer. One hadith expounds, "The reward of the prayer offered by a person in congregation is twenty-five times greater than that of the prayer offered in one's house or in the market."[8] The community must be reminded publicly of their duties. If prayers were not repeated five times daily, believers would soon forget about Allah and his greatness.

3. Almsgiving (Zakat): Socialism in Religious Dress

Retaining the theme of purity, almsgiving (literally, "purification") cleanses the Muslim of greed and selfishness while exacting the equitable distribution of goods to the entire community. It is intended to bring unity and betterment to the society as a whole. As the UNN (University of Northumbria at Newcastle) Islamic Society explained, "Zakat represents the unbreakable bond between members of the community, whom prophet Muhammad described to be 'like the organs of the body, if one suffers then all others rally in response.'"

The Muslim must recognize that everything is the property of Allah Almighty. Muslims are obligated to give 2.5 percent of their incomes, after excluding outstanding debts. In an era of modern financial transaction a detailed explanation is required. Each Muslim calculates his or her own *zakat* individually:

> Zakah [sic] is paid on the net balance after paying personal expenses, family expenses, due credits, taxes, etc. Every Muslim male or female who at the end of the year is in possession of the equivalent of 85 grams of gold (approx. $1400 in 1990) or more in cash or articles of trade, must give Zakah at the minimum rate of 2.5%. Taxes paid to government do not substitute for this religious duty. The contributor should not

seek pride or fame but if disclosing his name and his contri-
bution is likely to encourage others, it is acceptable to do so.[9]

Almsgiving also encourages hard work while discouraging
begging, not only benefiting this life, but earning salvation in the
hereafter. Muhammad articulated, "And give Zakat: and whatever
good you send forth for your souls before you, you shall find it with
Allah: for Allah sees well all that you do" (sura 2:110).

Charitable giving also alleviates emotional distress and fear of
judgment. Muhammad confirmed, "Those who believe, and do
deeds of righteousness, and establish regular prayers and give Zakat,
will have their reward with their Lord: on them shall be no fear,
nor shall they grieve" (sura 2:277).

The key word in sura 2:277 is "and." Notice all of the stipula-
tions required of the believer in Allah. Notice how zakat is central
to the theme of salvation, mingled in the midst of other good actions. One recites the creed, offers prayers, and does good, but to
neglect charitable giving nullifies salvation. It is integral to earning
the mercy of Allah. The Hadith illustrates the consequences of
withholding one's required giving:

> Allah's Apostle said, "Whoever is made wealthy by Allah and
> does not pay the Zakat of his wealth, then on the Day of
> Resurrection his wealth will be made like a bald-headed poi-
> sonous male snake with two black spots over the eyes. The snake
> will encircle his neck and bite his cheeks and say, 'I am your
> wealth, I am your treasure.'" (2.486)

> Save yourself from Hell-fire even by giving half a date-fruit in
> charity. (2.498)

> The Prophet said, "Do not with-hold your money by counting
> it (i.e. hoarding it), (for if you did so), Allah would also with-
> hold His blessings from you." (2.514)

Additional voluntary giving is also encouraged. The devout

Muslim can exhibit cheerfulness as a charity or urge others in doing good. If a Muslim abstains from doing evil, it is observed as a part of voluntary almsgiving (*sadaqa*).

In the end, the Muslim hopes that Allah will compensate him or her proportionally and comparably to that which he or she has given.

4. Ramadan: Fast (Sawm) Honoring the Arrival of the Qur'an

At the end of Ramadan in 2001, President George W. Bush invited Muslim leaders for the festival of 'Eid-ul-Fitr, a celebration breaking the month-long fast and bringing back normalcy to Muslim lives. Before the dinner, a Muslim offered a prayer of thanksgiving to Allah. Yet Bush had no right to partake of the holiday since he is a Christian. One Muslim scholar elucidates,

> Fasting is not obligatory on a non-Muslim because he is not commanded to fast and even if he decides to fast and follows all the regulations, it will not be accepted by Allah (SWT). If he or she wants to fast the Islamic fast, he has to declare the *Kalimah* first, and only then will the fast be accepted.[10]

Conversely, however, a devout Muslim would never celebrate Christmas since he or she does not believe Jesus Christ, the Son of God, came to take away the sins of the world, as the biblical Christian story explains. Instead, Ramadan is the antithesis to Christmas. It pits the revelation of the Holy Bible against the revelation of Qur'an. Muslims believe that Muhammad first received his revelation from Allah in the form of the Qur'an during this holy month. Therefore, they lay aside special times to worship and meet.

Fasting is an annual lifelong requirement for every devout Muslim. The Qur'an states, "O you who believe! Fasting is prescribed to you as it was prescribed to those before you, that you may [learn] self-restraint" (2:183). The Muslim, from sunrise to sunset, is required to abstain from sexual intercourse, eating, drinking, and smoking. In its place, he is to read the Qur'an introspectively, performing an act of worship in his or her self-restraint.

Not all Muslims are permitted to fast. Those excluded include women who are menstruating or pregnant, the elderly incapable of holding the fast, pre-pubescent youths, and the sick.

Yet failure to participate without legitimate excuse is deemed an unpardonable sin with potential eternal effects. One scholar notes, "Abu Hurairah reports the Messenger of Allah said: 'Whoever breaks one day's fast of Ramadan without an authorized permission from Allah, he will never be able to redeem it (with another) day's fast, even if he fasts to eternity.'"[11] The sin of abandoning this duty, therefore, is irreversible.

5. Pilgrimage (Hajj): Honoring Abraham

Michael Wolfe, whose mother is Christian and father is Jewish, converted to Islam and made his first hajj to Mecca, the holiest city in Islam, in 1991. He explained the mystical experience:

> Here I join people from all over the earth, all these human be-ings drawn together by the call of an idea, by the oneness of God. We have left daily life behind and come to a place hardly belonging to this world, a place filled by the almost tangible presence of God.[12]

Muslims call attention to the fact that millions of believers from all over the globe come together to celebrate the oneness of Allah, contributing substantial credibility in affirming their faith.

The Kaaba, the focal point of Mecca, is an ancient stone building some thirty-three feet wide, forty feet long, and fifty feet high. A black stone (thought to be a meteorite) is set in a corner of the building.[13] Surrounded by hundreds of thousands of Muslims every year as they fulfill their duty to Allah and make their pilgrimage, its heritage allegedly goes back to the time of Abraham.

As Islamic tradition records, Abraham was commanded to sacrifice Ishmael, but Allah offered a ram in his stead. Abraham, in gratitude to Allah, built a place of worship, called it "Kaaba," and requested that people make an annual pilgrimage to it. In years to come, local Arabs corrupted the ritual, set up idols in the structure, and began a tradition of polytheism. Muhammad finally restored monotheism and the pilgrimage.

The pilgrimage is the climax of the Muslims' spiritual journey. They prepare themselves mentally and spiritually for the trip. Only Muslims are allowed inside the city of Mecca, and all are required to dress in a simple white robe to demonstrate unity. Yet the diversity among the people is obvious. People of all races speak in countless languages.

The pilgrims first cleanse themselves before they begin their rituals. The first stage begins as thousands circle (*tawaff*) the Kaaba seven times, reciting verses from the Qur'an and offering prayers along the way. Wolfe gives details of his journey: "When you first see the Ka'bah [sic], if you're a Muslim, you've been praying toward it for years. It's very sweet. And it's very exciting. And people are routinely crying at the first sight of this—this nothing, this simple square building."[14]

The circling of the Kaaba, however, is just the beginning of the journey. Muslims also must run seven times between the two hills of Mecca, reenacting Hagar's frantic search for water for her son Ishmael. Finally, pilgrims find water at the well of Zamzam and take a drink, displaying the fulfillment of Hagar's quest for her son's needs.[15]

Now immersed in the journey, the pilgrims must yet travel a long way in order to accomplish their duty.

- They must travel thirteen miles to the Plain of Arafat, where Muhammad preached his last sermon. Here, they stand from noon to sunset in honor of Muhammad's standing in the community.
- Pilgrims must go to Mina, the site of the sacrifice of Ishmael by his father Abraham. Here pilgrims throw seven stones, memorializing how Ishmael threw stones at the Devil to resist his temptations.
- Next, pilgrims sacrifice an animal in remembrance of the ram offered in place of Ishmael.

- Muslims return to Mecca and repeat their encircling of the Kaaba and running of the hills.[16]

The arduous journey is now complete. The Muslim has worked intensely for one main purpose—the ultimate forgiveness of sin. As one Muslim expert writes, "The Hajj is designed to develop God consciousness and a sense of spiritual upliftment. It is also believed to be an opportunity to seek forgiveness of sins accumulated throughout life. Prophet Muhammad had said that a person who performs Hajj properly 'will return as a newly born baby [free of all sins].'"[17] The hajj, then, is the perfect illustration of what it takes to get to heaven: hard work, meditation, and the mercy of Allah.

Such is the ultimate goal for all five pillars of Islam, which are eternally interwoven together. The five pillars act as a tapestry that gives Muslims a portrait of their task in life, a journey that they hope ends as it began—as a newborn baby free from all sins.

Notes

1. Evan Thomas, "American Taliban," *Newsweek*, December 17, 2001, 30.
2. Charles Colson, "The Strange Odyssey of John Walker," *Breakpoint*, December 17, 2001, 2.
3. George Braswell, *Islam* (Nashville: Broadman and Holman, 1996), 59–60.
4. Ishaq Zahid, "The Five Pillars of Islam," http://islam101.com/dawah/pillars.html#Salah.
5. Braswell, *Islam*, 62.
6. "Figh-us-Sunnah, Volume 1: Ablution (Wudu')," http://www.usc.edu/dept/MSA/law/fiqhussunnah/fus1_02.html.
7. George Braswell, *What You Need to Know About Islam and Muslims* (Nashville: Broadman and Holman, 2000), 33.
8. Quoted in Braswell, *Islam*, 63.
9. http://www.unn.ac.uk/societies/islamic/islam/charity.htm (accessed December 17, 2001; site no longer available).
10. Sheikh Tajuddin B. Shu'aib, "Essentials of Ramadan, The Fasting Month," http://www.usc.edu/dept/MSA/fundamentals/pillars/fasting/tajuddin/fast_1.html.

11. Ibid.
12. Michael Wolfe, "An American in Mecca" *Nightline*, ABC News (April 18, 1997).
13. Braswell, *What You Need to Know*, 36.
14. Wolfe, "An American in Mecca."
15. Braswell, *What You Need to Know*, 36.
16. Ibid., 36–37.
17. Council on Islamic Education, "Hajj Intro for People of Other Faith," http://www.islamicity.com/mosque/hajj/hajjintro.htm.

8

WOMEN: LOVE, MARRIAGE, AND PROPERTY

Cynthia's Story

CYNTHIA LOVED ASHAM.[1] They met at college and dated steadily through her junior and senior years. With Asham, she felt like a princess. He showered her with gifts and treated her with a gracious chivalry she had not known with any American man. He was thoughtful, considerate, ruggedly handsome, intelligent, and oddly spiritual. She did not give much thought to his devout Muslim faith. A casual Baptist, Cynthia assumed that everyone who attended church, synagogue, or mosque was basically on the same track. His morality certainly seemed higher than that of the heathen white boys she'd dated.

They married in the summer and vacationed in his home country, a beautiful, majestic place, with tall spires and rolling hills. At the mosque, she was bemused by the practices. Back in the United States, they settled into a routine of work, play, and eventually children.

The changes in Asham appeared slowly. Occasionally he became abrupt with her and their five-year-old son. He constantly sent money overseas, supposedly for his family, and was secretive, especially when his friends came around. Every Friday, Asham took their son to the mosque, although Cynthia no longer went with them. Then one Friday she discovered that Asham had left the country with their son. In the subsequent weeks, she discovered to her horror that she and her child were considered Muslims, converted at least on paper. Thus, her son had to be raised in Islam. Because her rights to her child were minimal in his country, her child was gone, and her life forever marred.

Cynthia did not know that she had joined a growing subculture, a subculture of white American women who marry foreign Muslim men.

A Woman's Genetic Inferiority

In Islam, one finds a disturbing yet fascinating dichotomy. Most Muslims will declare that their men hold women in an elevated regard and believe that they must be protected. In comparison with the cultural context from which Islam emerged, there truly was an elevation of women. Yet Islam has deserved its reputation around the world for stifling and even enslaving women. Many Islamic women are both educated and successful, but most remain illiterate, hidden, and treated as property.

Muslim apologists have a difficult task in defending Islamic doctrines regarding gender and sexuality, for Muhammad was painfully specific about his beliefs concerning women. Some Qur'an texts are a public relations nightmare in societies conditioned by the feminist movement to assume gender equality. That a Muslim man practices gender equality can be a dangerous assumption for non-Muslim women such as Cynthia. Since Muslim men usually are thoughtful and superficially attentive, it is important to examine the Qur'an's and the Hadith's teachings concerning women and the ramifications of these doctrines on Muslim society.

Islam teaches that women are inherently inferior to men. While some imams disagree with this assessment, it is difficult to change what the Qur'an says. Sura 2:228 states in part, "Women shall have rights similar to the rights against them, according to what is equitable; but men have a degree over them."

How is this subordinate status defined? According to hadith 3.826, Muhammad said that women are genetically and legally inferior: "Muhammad asked some women, 'Isn't the witness of a woman equal to half of that of a man?' The women said, 'Yes.' He said, 'This is because of the deficiency of the woman's mind.'" Muhammad reiterated this same point in hadith 2.541, speaking again to a group of women: "I have not seen anyone more deficient in intelligence and religion than you."

Consigned to Hell

Three times in the Hadith, Muhammad's vision of hellfire is recorded, each time including the same feature: "Muhammad said, 'I was shown the Hell-fire and that the majority of its dwellers are women.'" As a result of this teaching, women are regarded as both harmful to men and a bad omen. "Muhammad said, 'Bad omen is in the women, the house and the horse . . . after me I have not left any affliction more harmful to men than women.'"[2]

A woman, thus being a lesser creature, has fewer rights and privileges in Muslim society. In apportioning inheritance, a woman should receive half of what a man receives: "To the male a portion equal to that of two females" (sura 4:11). In judicial proceedings, a woman's testimony is given one-half the value and credibility as that of a man: "Get two witnesses out of your own men, and if there are not two men, then a man and two women such as you choose, for witnesses" (sura 2:282).

Marriage, Sexuality, and Desire

Muslim men are allowed to marry two, three, or four wives, according to sura 4:3.[3] Western women who marry Muslim men often discover that their husbands have other wives overseas. Such is a common practice of Muslim men living in Western countries with laws regarding polygamy. Western women are usually naive about Islamic teachings and practices concerning wives, women, and marriage, or they are certain that such teachings would not be followed by the man they have come to know and love.

Even though the Qur'an gives men a limit of four wives,

Muhammad received special dispensation directly from Allah to marry as many as he wished. As was discussed in chapter 2, that amounted to thirteen wives and concubines, one of whom he married at age six and had sexual relations with at age nine.[4] Aishah was the daughter of Abu Bakr as Siddiq, who was a close friend of the prophet and in charge of his books. When he offered her as a legitimate wife to Muhammad she was eight years old. He added in jest, "She is eight but dependable!"[5] Throughout history, even in cultures oppressive to women, sexual relations with someone as young as nine years old have seldom been acceptable. No woman that young has the psychological or biological maturity to willfully consent to a mutual act of love. Another wife, Zaynab bint Jahsh, had been Muhammad's daughter-in-law. When his adopted son Zaid saw that Muhammad wanted his wife, he divorced her so that his father could have her (see pp. 57–58).

Discrepancies occur in counting Muhammad's wives, because Muhammad's own "classification" system of wives and concubines creates confusion. Muhammad married at least nine women after the death of his first wife, Khadija.[6] Muhammad divided these wives into classifications of "intimate" (*Muqarribat*) and "remote" (*Ghair Muqarribat*). At the head of the list of intimates was Aishah, then Hafsah, Um Salma, and Zaynab. Among his remote wives he counted Um Habeeba, Maimoona, and Sawda. Then come Juweiriyeh and Sufia.

Muhammad gave his own twelve-year-old daughter, Fatima, in marriage to his cousin Ali bin Abu Taleb. She is reputed to have been quite mature mentally for her age, reading the Qur'an with one hand while grinding barley with the other. Arranged marriages of girls as young as twelve is not unknown, though it is not a common cultural practice. Fatima's prepubescent age would still demand her protection in almost all modern cultures.

In the Hadith, Muhammad's sexual prowess is raised to legendary proportions. In hadith 1.268, Anas writes, "The prophet used to visit all his wives in an hour round, during the day and night and they were eleven in number . . . the prophet was given the strength of thirty men."

"Special" Marriages

Of special interest are Muhammad's "super-normal" marriages, about which he spoke on occasion. After his virtual "flight into the seven heavens" (*Al Isra'a wal Mi'raj*), he told his first wife, Khadija, as she lay dying, "Oh Khadija, know that God has wedded me to Mary, Christ's mother in paradise." He repeated this to Aishah after the Hijra, saying, "Oh Aiysha [sic], didn't you know that God Almighty in heaven wedded me to Mary the daughter of Imran, to Kulthum, Moses' sister and to Assiya, wife of the Pharaoh."[7]

According to Muhammad, Allah had married him to three women who were already in Paradise—none other than Mary the mother of Jesus Christ, Moses' sister Miriam, and Pharaoh's wife. It was Allah's special divine blessing that Muhammad was husband to three of history's most noted women. Clearly he was not bound to the very Qur'an he said he had received. Some Muslims have speculated that a special dispensation superseded the Qur'an, a dangerous position at best.

The Role of the Wife

One of the most controversial areas of public discourse is the role of women in Islamic society today. Examples of Islamic sharia (law) that seem to suppress and oppress are those that prohibit a woman from even looking directly into a man's eyes, that forbid women from wearing shoes that make noise, that forbid them to become educated. A host of laws regarding women are enforced whenever sharia is strictly followed. True, some women willingly hide their bodies in burkas as an act of modesty and faithfulness to Islam.[8] But when Taliban rule ended in Afghanistan, few women retained the burka.

On November 17, 2001, the wife of the former president of the United States, Laura Bush, took the unprecedented action of producing a radio broadcast in place of the weekly presidential radio address. Her remarks were an indictment of the oppression against women in Afghanistan and other religiously conservative Islamic countries. But the United States and other Western nations show that they remain confused and politically pragmatic about such issues. President George W. Bush took pains to communicate that it is the culture of these countries, rather than the religion, that dictates oppressive regulations. Such traditions are, however, more than a narrow cultural anomaly.

Wives as "Play Things"

In truth, women are considered possessions in any orthodox Islamic regime. Sura 3:14 notes, "Fair in the eyes of men is the love of things they covet: women and sons; heaped-up hoards of gold and silver." A man can threaten divorce if his wife is not meeting his sexual needs, according to sura 66:5: "It may be, if he divorced you, that Allah will give him in exchange consorts better than you." In both public appearance and private sexual encounter, the onus is on the woman to satisfy her husband's desires.

The wife is considered the husband's sex object. The Qur'an states in sura 2:223, "Your wives are as a tilth [field to be plowed] unto you, so approach your tilth when and how you will." Again, the Hadith says, "Wives are playthings, so take your pick."[9]

As has often been noted, according to the Qur'an women are not permitted to divorce their husbands under any circumstance. A man may divorce his wife, however, by simply verbally declaring his intent. If he changes his mind, he must wait until his wife has remarried and divorced again before he can marry her.[10]

In the case of adultery, one again sees a discrepancy in the treatment of men and women. Originally in the sharia a male adulterer's punishment was limited to a flogging, while the woman was to be imprisoned until death. This law was later mitigated to eighty strokes for the man and one hundred strokes for the woman.[11]

In Public Appearance

The protocols for a woman in public are too numerous to mention here. Many Qur'anic admonitions stress the woman's responsibility to submit in public in both gaze and dress:

> And say to the believing women that they should lower their gaze and guard their modesty; that they should not display their

beauty and ornaments except what appear thereof; that they should draw their veils over their bosoms and not display their beauty. (sura 24:31)

Clearly, a woman protected is a woman hidden from the lustful gaze of men. In sura 33:59, Allah instructs Muhammad, "O prophet! Tell thy wives and daughters, and the believing women, that they should cast their outer garments over their persons [when abroad]."

According to Islam, a woman is by nature unclean. In the protocols before prayer, a man is considered unclean if he touches a woman (even his wife) before prayer:

> O ye who believe! Approach not prayers with a mind befogged until ye can understand all that you say; nor in a state of ceremonial impurity . . . until after washing your whole body if you are ill, or on a journey . . . or you have been in contact with women. And if you find no water, then take for yourself clean sand or earth and rub . . . your faces and hands: for Allah doth blot out sins and forgive them again and again. (sura 4:43)[12]

Beating the Wife

One of the most troubling admonitions in the Qur'an allows marital punishment. Because the husband is to train his wife, the Qur'an gives men much latitude in the area of punishment. The man can be physically abusive or withhold sexual favors from a wife whose conduct is sanctioned: "As to those women on whose part you fear disloyalty and ill-conduct, admonish them, refuse to share their beds, beat them" (sura 4:34). In the arena of withholding sexual conduct, the Qur'an notes, "For those who take an oath of abstention from their wives, a waiting period for four months is ordained; if they return, Allah is oft-forgiving, most-merciful" (sura 2:226).

Once the Prophet was asked about this subject: "What rights does the woman have with the man?" He replied, "He should feed her if he eats, clothe her when he dresses, avoid disfiguring her or beating her excessively or abandoning her except at home" (hadith 7.62.77).

In recent years, the world has viewed horrifying videos of women being shot summarily in the city square for exposing one-fourth of their iris in public. Others have been bullwhipped into silence, and become slaves of terrifying violence.

Evaluation

How does one process this disturbing history? Abuse and subjection of women certainly are hardly restricted to the Muslim world. Millions of women have suffered at the hands of adherents to every world religion. Men claiming to be Christian have enslaved women and beaten them into submission—sometimes citing distorted interpretations of biblical teaching.

The difference that must be observed, though, is that any such abusive acts by a Christian are clearly and unmistakably at variance with what the Bible instructs and what Jesus explicitly taught. Jesus elevated women. He did not consider their touch to be unclean. Women are, in fact, given special note in the New Testament record. They were the last to leave the site of Jesus' crucifixion and the first to testify to His resurrection. As male disciples cowered in hiding, the women boldly walked to minister to the body in the tomb. Women surrounded Jesus, not for sexual purposes, but for spiritual ones. Breaking with midrashic tradition, Jesus spoke to the Samaritan woman at the well (John 4) and shared His words with Lazarus's sisters in Bethany (Luke 10:38–42; John 11).

Scriptural admonitions regarding a distinction of purpose between men and women in Ephesians 5:22–33 speak out of a context of declared fundamental and essential equality. Christ, the second Person of the Godhead, is as fully God as the Father, yet they have different functions. Women are equal to men before God, yet men and women have complementary roles. Thus, submission to a husband's servant leadership reflects Christ's desire to do the will of the Father (Phil. 2:1–16).

In addition, Ephesians 5:21–33 stresses that the husband is to love and serve the wife with the same devotion Christ showed in loving the Church. If a woman reflects the passage, entrusting her life to her husband's care, then the husband must also reflect Christ in going further. Jesus did not simply dedicate His life to the church—He died for it. The responsibility for care that is the husband's is a far greater burden than the Christian wife's duties within submission. If the wife sees her husband truly show servant leadership, she is more likely to be willing to submit to his godly care.

Christianity asserts that a husband can never, ever subject his wife to any sort of abuse. An abusive husband violates the very foundation upon which a wife's role of complementary submission is based.

In Islam, the picture is darker. One can, for the sake of Islamic apologetics, state that the Qur'an's passages on women and marriage are culturally outdated, but one cannot say that the passages are not constrained by the context. The Qur'an is so clear that those who regularly abuse their wives are more faithful to their sacred text than those who would rationalize away its teachings. If a woman is honored and respected in an Islamic home, it is in spite of the teachings of Muhammad, rather than because of them. Such is directly opposite to the admonitions of the Lord Jesus Christ and the Bible.

We wish we could have spoken to Cynthia before marriage to Asham. She should have been told of the systematic abuse suffered by women in Islam for over fifteen hundred years. We would have told her of the freedom and liberation of Christ. We would have read the texts to her concerning the treatment of women and begged her not to marry Asham and suffer a lifetime of consequences.

Notes

1. The names of the people in this true story have been changed.
2. Hadith 7.30, 33. Hadith chapter seven also includes an admonition against wearing wigs: "Muhammad said, 'Don't wear false hairs, for Allah sends His curse upon such ladies who lengthen their hair artificially'" (7.133).
3. Sura 4:3 reads: "If you fear that you will not act justly towards the orphans, marry such women as seem good to you, two, three, four;

but if you fear you will not be equitable, then only one, or what your right hands own; so it is likelier you will not be partial." Some Muslim aulema (scholars) note that this is an admonition to graciousness. Christian scholars would hasten to observe that this system makes the decision the man's alone as to whether he can take care of multiple wives. The wives do not have a say if a husband adds another woman to his family.

4. Hadith 7.64. Muhammad was fifty-five years old at the time.
5. Arabic: *Hia thaman, wa alaihad dhaman.*
6. Some have speculated that Khadija was from a Coptic Christian family, and her interpretation of the nature of Jesus may have influenced Muhammad's view of Christ.
7. Related by Abu Umama in later ahadith.
8. By now the burka (variant spellings include "burqa") is the ubiquitous and complete covering of a woman from head to toe, including a screen to cover the eyes.
9. Attributed to Muhammad, according to Al Hakim.
10. Sura 2:229-30.
11. M. Rafiqulhaq and P. Newton, *Al Nisa'a Fil Islam* (The place of women in pure Islam) (New York: Berean, 1996), 26-34.
12. Some scholars have speculated that this is a reference to sexual contact with a woman, but sura 5:6 seems to indicate even casual or accidental contact with a woman makes a man unclean.

9

SALVATION: MATHEMATICAL RIGHTEOUSNESS

Converts' Stories

HERE ARE THREE honest people explaining why their journey in the Christian faith ended in Islam. The born-again Christian must be prepared to answer people who have found Christians and/or the tenets of Christianity to be genuinely unconvincing.

Cultural Significance

I was Cassius Clay then. I was a Negro. I ate pork. I had no confidence. I thought white people were superior. I was a Christian Baptist named Cassius Clay.

—Muhammad Ali

Intellectual Significance

I began to study [the] Qur'an more, and in several months I said [the] *Shahada [i.e. stated and accepted the creed of Islam—ed.]*. That was less than a year ago. I am still learning, striving to find

God's truth. I am so grateful that God has guided me so. *Here is a religion of truth, which can stand up to any test of logic and reason!* Just as I always thought religion should be. It should make sense, it should be logical.

—Diana

Devotional Significance

It's hard for me to express the difference I felt between these two religions. . . . I also feel that with Islam I'm sort of more guided, either by the Qur'an or the hadiths. Whereas, when I was Catholic, it was kind of like I had to figure out what to do in certain situation[s]. People might think that Islam is strict, but I think that's the way it's meant to be. I mean, I feel in this way God tells us very clearly what he expects. And you don't have to just wonder [*sic*] in the world looking for the truth, or the real happiness, or things like that.

—Monica[1]

Such testimonies help us understand the motivation and mind-set of the novice Muslim. The former Cassius Clay found in Islam a truly individual identity for himself. That new identity gave him confidence for this life and its hardships.

Diana's full testimony is disheartening because she inquired of Christians as she compared the Christian and Islamic faiths. But those she asked either were so ignorant of the Bible that they could not give an adequate answer or they simply condemned the Qur'an and the prophet Muhammad out of hand, without any explanation. This left Diana to assume that Christianity is a boorish and foolish religion, while the Muslim faith is logical and sensible.

By birth a Catholic, Monica had never attended church, so she assumed that Christianity was merely a cultural religion. She liked the honesty and strict expectations of Islam, a demanding lifestyle to which she could give all of her heart and mind. Monica shows us the danger of making Christianity so user friendly that nothing is expected by Christ as Lord. She might have been more intrigued if she had heard a biblical gospel that faith is always free but never cheap.

Christians who take their faith lightly and impart to their children a relationship with God that has no boundaries or demands of discipleship should not be surprised if those children drift into skepticism or another faith.

Security: Knowing What to Do

This is the Book; in it is guidance sure, without doubt, to those who fear Allah; who believe in the Unseen, are steadfast in prayer, and spend out of what we have provided for them; and who believe in the Revelation sent to you, and sent before your time, and [in their hearts] have the assurance of the Hereafter. (sura 1:2–4)

Allah's Apostle said, "Whoever can guarantee [the chastity of] what is between his two jaw-bones and what is between his two legs [i.e. his tongue and his private parts], I guarantee Paradise for him." (hadith 8.76.481)

The ultimate question in any religion addresses an eternal life after death: "What must I do to go to heaven?" In Islam, the answer to this question remains as mysterious and complex as was the founder of its religion, Muhammad.

As will be seen in this chapter, the Qur'an hints that the believer in Allah can be confident of his or her eternal destiny, but there is no guarantee, even for the most righteous. So Muslims strive mightily to get to Paradise, but they continually fear that Allah will judge their arrogance and send them to hell. Islamic tradition argues that the guarantee of heaven is as impossible to find as a chaste virgin and pure speech. Consequently, the devout Muslim makes every effort to please Allah and thereby obtain heaven. But fate (*kismet*) in the hands of the all-powerful Allah will decide the outcome.

The Creed (Shahada)

Salvation in Islam is ultimately based upon the creed, "*Ilaha illa Allah. Muhammad rasul Allah,*" which is translated, "There is no god but Allah. Muhammad is the messenger of Allah."

This, then, is the only necessary step in becoming a Muslim. Personal, heart-felt conversions are replaced with an intellectual assent of the facts. But one need also adhere to the six major doctrines of Islam:

1. *Monotheism.* Belief in one god alone.
2. *Angels.* Belief that supernatural beings do the will of Allah.
3. *Revelation.* Belief in the Torah, the gospel (*injil*), and the Qur'an.
4. *Prophets.* Belief that Allah has sent prophets to reveal his will—Adam, Noah, Abraham, Moses, Jesus, and Muhammad.
5. *Judgment.* Belief that Allah will judge all men and women.
6. *Heaven and Hell.* Belief that all men and women will spend eternity in either the splendor of Paradise or the eternal torture of hell.

Prayer (Salat)

Most Americans have heard the melodic call to prayer for Muslims. The prayer leader (muezzin) chants in Arabic, "God is great. There is no god but God. Muhammad is the messenger of God. Come to prayer. Come to prayer. Come to success in this life and the hereafter." In the end, prayer not only gives devout Muslims a greater hope of heaven, it also gives them a greater chance at success in this life.

Devout Muslims pray five times a day, hoping that Allah will see their faithfulness and give them mercy. They pray daily during the following times:

- *Salat al Fajr.* Dawn prayer
- *Salat al Zuhr.* Midday prayer
- *Salat al Asr.* Afternoon prayer
- *Salat al Maghrib.* Evening prayer (after sunset)
- *Salat al Isha.* Late evening prayer

The Qur'an is clear on the absolute necessity of prayer for the Muslim who desires Paradise and its rewards. The unyielding commitment to prayer has many ramifications in the Qur'an:

- Prayer reassures faith: "[The Qur'an] is sure, without doubt to those who . . . are steadfast in prayer. . . . And (in their hearts) have the *assurance* of the Hereafter" (sura 2:3-4, emphasis added).
- Prayer removes evil: "And establish regular prayers at the two ends of the day. . . . For those things that are good *remove* those that are evil" (sura 11:114, emphasis added).
- Prayer receives rewards: "And establish regular prayer for My remembrance. . . . Verily the Hour is coming—I have almost kept it Hidden—for every soul to receive its *reward* by the measure of its endeavor" (sura 20:14-15, emphasis added).

But Muslims must come not only with humble hearts, they must perform the prayers with clean hands. The cleansing ritual (covered in more detail in chapter 7) before prayer begins includes the following: washing the hands, rinsing the mouth, cleaning the nose, washing the face, washing the forearms, and washing the feet.

This ablution is so important that if not done properly, any prayer uttered may not earn the hearing or mercy of Allah. The Hadith expounds, "Once the Prophet remained behind us in a journey. He joined us while we were performing ablution for the prayer which was over-due. We were just passing wet hands over our feet (and not washing them properly) so the Prophet addressed us in a loud voice and said twice or thrice: 'Save your heels from the fire'" (3.57).

Revelation: Knowing What to Trust

No changes can there be in the Words of Allah. This is indeed the supreme Triumph. (sura 10:64)

"I believe in the Torah, Psalms of David (Zabur), and the

Gospels (Injil). I also believe that you are People of the Book." This statement may cause some Christians to go into cardiac arrest, but it is exactly what modern Muslims want Christians to hear.

But Muslims also believe that Christians and Jews have altered the sacred books of God, thereby negating their significance. The Qur'an, on the other hand, cannot be corrupted. As it clearly elucidates, "We have, without doubt, sent down the Message; and we will assuredly guard it from corruption" (sura 15:9).

Therefore, when Muslims look to the source they can trust for their salvation, they will always be drawn to the Qur'an over and above the Bible. In effect, Islamic scriptures have abrogated the Gospel much as Muhammad has overshadowed Jesus. The Qur'an (and its messenger) is the final revelation. Nothing else is needed.

The irony that Muslims seem to ignore is that if the Torah, the Psalms of David, and the Gospels are the "Words of Allah," how can they be allowed to be corrupted?

The Prophets: Guidance on the Path to Salvation

What part do the prophets play in humankind's salvation? Prophets are the very mouthpieces of Allah to *all* people. Each people group has been given a prophet to hear the message of Allah, that prophet removing all doubts and lies about the truth. The Qur'an affirms, "To every people (was sent) a Messenger: when their Messenger comes (before them), the matter will be judged between them with justice, and they will not be wronged" (10:47).

Therefore, Allah's voice has never been silent to any generation, and each generation will be judged according to the *extent* of revelation given to them by various prophets.

Judgment: Accounting for Your Works

We shall bring out from him a scroll, which he will see spread open. [It will be said to him,] "Read thine [own] record: Sufficient is thy soul this day to make out an account against thee." (sura 17:13-14)

Judgment Day is coming for everyone who has ever lived. The Qur'an states, "He raised the heavens and He placed in all things a balance and means of accounting" (sura 55:7). This day will be so terrible and stressful that it will make children "hoary-headed" or white-headed (sura 73:17).

Judgment Day is intended to either humiliate and shame, or purify and reward. The Day of Judgment, too, is evidence of Allah's characteristics of omniscience, omnipotence, mercy, wisdom, providence, and justice. Ultimately, he will show himself to be true in all ways. That is the purpose of the Day of Judgment.

Eternity: The Garden or the Fire

There is no such thing as a non-Muslim since every person has been given the truth of Allah through his prophets. Therefore, infidels (*Kafirs*), those who reject the truth of Islam, are going to hell. The following crimes are mentioned in the Qur'an as especially worthy of eternal punishment: arrogance, false worship, taking innocent life, adultery, and a complete life of sin. The Qur'an illuminates, "But the Chastisement on the Day of Judgment will be doubled to him, and he will dwell therein in ignominy" (sura 25:68).

Hell: Torture and Roastings

> Those who reject our Signs, We shall soon cast into the Fire: As often as their skins are roasted through, we shall change them for fresh skins, that they may taste the Chastisement: for Allah is Exalted in Power, Wise. (sura 4:56)

The reason for eternal torture of infidels in hell is to exalt Allah and demonstrate his omnipotence. As can be seen above, hell is a place of torture where people's pain is renewed. Other details of punishment include drinking boiling fetid water (sura 14:16), wearing garments made of fire-conducive pitch (sura 14:50), and "other Penalties of a similar kind, to match them!" (sura 38:58).

Infidels will desire to die, but it will not be afforded to them as their pleas for destruction will go unheeded by Allah. Every time the wicked attempt to flee from the furious fire, they are forced back into its grasp. This does not in any way illustrate the injustice of Allah, but only the injustice of the sinner (sura 43:76).

Hell, then, is a bottomless pit (sura 2:9-11) in which the infidels will remember their sin (sura 89:23-26) and express humiliation in their faces (sura 88:2-7).

Heaven: Paradise of Luxury

> But those who believe and do deeds of righteousness, we shall soon admit to Gardens, with rivers flowing beneath,—their eternal home: Therein shall they have spouses purified we shall admit them to shades, cool and ever deepening. (sura 4:57)

Heaven, then, is the antithesis of hell as gardens replace fire and shade replaces roasting. Since Allah is satisfied with the righteous, he gives them eternal security, fruit and drink, and chaste women! Men will sit on raised couches drinking new wine and looking at beautiful virgins (sura 37:41-49).

In material rewards, believers enjoy lofty mansions (sura 39:20), thrones (sura 18:31), rivers (sura 16:30-31), and fantastic food (sura 52:17-24). For spiritual rewards they are given joy (sura 36:55-58), peace (sura 19:61-63), satisfaction (sura 43:68-73), and bliss (sura 69:21-24). The soul will be complete and rested, well-pleased with Allah as Allah is well-pleased with the soul (sura 89:27-30).

Heaven in the Balance

> Then those whose balance (of good deeds) is heavy,—they will be successful. But those whose balance is light, will be those who have lost their souls; in Hell will they abide. (sura 23:102-3)

Misery versus magnificence ultimately will be resolved statistically. Muslims believe that each person must be 51 percent good to reach heaven. Therefore, those who know they have lived a life of misery and shame have *no* hope of heaven if they are nearing death. Accordingly, they live in despair and destruction, for they can expect only hell.

The divine balance scale is the ultimate demonstration of precise mathematical judgment. Each person is literally accountable for each act performed. Consequently, the scales become more important as one approaches the end of life, especially for those who are on the edge. They have to work harder, live better, and give more. Then they can hope the scales will tip in their favor.

God's Mercy: Bring out the Damned!

Since eternal life is ultimately given at the subjective whim of Allah and depends upon his mercy and will, Muslims pray that mercy will abide with them. Even Muhammad commented that he could not obtain heaven without the mercy of Allah.

Some will be in heaven although they do not deserve it. As Norman Geisler and Abdul Saleeb point out, "God's mercy is also shown in the belief that after a certain period of time God himself will bring out a large number of the damned from hell, not because of their own merit but to demonstrate his compassion on his creatures."[2]

The Ultimate Issue—Offending a Holy God

Four days before Acar Mehmet Caner, the authors' father, died of prostate cancer, he gave each of his sons a copy of the Qur'an. Knowing that he was on the threshold of death, he said, "Remember, I was a good man." With all of his faults, which were no greater than those of his sons, he was the epitome of a family man. He loved his wife and children, providing for them financially and emotionally.

But Acar Caner possessed a different outlook from that of his sons. He believed that all people are born without sin. We believe that all people are born sinful and in need of a Savior. This is a crucial difference. In Islam, you place your hope in good works, trying to please Allah more than you offend him. Christians believe that *any* sin stands as an infinite offense against God and must be judged with an infinite penalty. Good works no more cover bad works than an act of kindness can take away the guilt of a murderer. If you are a criminal, justice demands that punishment must be meted out. And it was. Jesus Christ *paid* the infinite penalty for sin.

In Islam sin is not paid for, it is weighed on a balance scale. Islam has no understanding that a truly holy and just God cannot simply measure the sin and throw it aside without any punishment. My father wrote his last request on the first page of each copy of the Qur'an that he gave to his sons. Emir's copy reads, "To my son Emir. This is yours. Please take the time and read each word for you and for me. Your father."

Although now a Christian, Emir obeyed that intimate request. The Qur'an contains many words of wisdom and pieces of good advice. What is lacking is the promise of life everlasting. We only pray that our father placed his faith at the end of his life in someone greater than himself. Only God knows what goes through someone's mind when they are at the precipice of death. Perhaps there he met a true Savior.

Notes

1. http://www.arabianebazaar.com/ac/convv.htm (accessed December 1, 2001; site no longer available).
2. Norman Geisler and Abdul Saleeb, *Answering Islam* (Grand Rapids: Baker, 1993), 126.

10

HOLY DAYS: A CALENDAR OF
ISLAMIC COMMUNITY

Mustafa's Story

LIVING AS A MUSLIM in America can be daunting. Certainly no season is so disconcerting as the holiday weeks around Christmas, Hanukkah, and New Year's Day. Mustafa dreaded this time all year long, his discomfort beginning around Halloween, when he noticed the appearance of evergreen trees and gaily decorated wreaths. He heard his fourth-grade classmates plan trips and talk of gifts, lights, ornaments, and carols.

If he visited a non-Muslim friend's home, the walkway to the front door was surrounded with greenery, poinsettias, and multicolored lights. In the home, the smell of gingerbread and cookies was always enticing, and the parents with their red sweaters would greet him with "Merry Christmas." Wistfully, he noticed gifts under the evergreen and listened to songs about bells that jingle, and three wise men.

Around his door was no wreath or lights, his yard held no nativity scenes or glowing reindeer. His home looked the same throughout the year. In his Sunni Muslim home, Mustafa often felt safely removed from the commercialized and ubiquitous seasonal regalia. But television saturated him with Christmas advertising, showings of the movie *It's a Wonderful Life*, and programs with vaguely religious Christian symbolism. Even in the sanctity of his parents' home, Mustafa felt overwhelmed.

If a Christian desires to reach into the life of a Muslim to extend the grace of Christ, it is imperative to understand Islamic culture. Integral to this understanding is the Islamic holidays.

Moon Months and Sun Years

Months of the Islamic year are based on the lunar cycle, consisting of twelve months of twenty-nine or thirty days each, totaling 353 or 354 days for the year. Each new month begins at the new moon, and actual dates differ by a day or two in different hemispheres. Although a lunar calendar confuses Westerners—who are accustomed to more precise dating—imagine what it is like to a Muslim confronted with the Western system.

Although Muslims begin their calendars with the year of the pilgrimage (A.D. 622), that their year is about ten days shorter than the Julian calendar introduces a sense of approximation. The European New Year's Day is always on January 1, but the Muslim New Year, *Mihama*, shifts, as shown in the chart below.

Islamic New Year's Day on the Western Calendar	
In the year of Hijra (A.H., "After Hijra")	Date of Mihama on Gregorian/Western calendar
A.H. 1421	April 6, 2000
A.H. 1422	March 26, 2001
A.H. 1423	March 15, 2002
A.H. 1424	March 5, 2003

While finding worldwide Islamic consensus is difficult, it is possible to list the Islamic months, beginning with Muharram, which is the first month of the year: (1) Muharram; (2) Safar;

(3) Raby' al-Awal; (4) Raby' al-Thaany; (5) Jumaada al-Awal; (6) Jumaada al-Thaany; (7) Rajab; (8) Sha'ban; (9) Ramadan; (10) Shawwal; (11) Dhul-Qi'dah; (12) Dhul-Hijjah.

In months organized around new moons, holidays move. It is mystifying to Muslims that a holiday called Christmas can occur every year on December 25. Consider, too, that Islam operates on two distinct calendars—the lunar calendar and the solar calendar. Most Muslims think in terms of the Islamic solar calendar, on which A.D. 2001 was the year 1380, coinciding with the foundation of Islam following the initial visions of Muhammad. But when the Taliban took over Afghanistan in 1996, they imposed the Islamic lunar calendar, on which 2001/1380 was the year 1422. Small wonder many Muslims do not know their exact age or birth date, although this circumstance is slowly changing.

The perplexity of figuring holidays is compounded further because lunar cycles vary in different regions and hemispheres, so in the same year, holidays can begin and end on different days, depending upon where one lives. Western Christians might be forgiven for some bewilderment at Muslim holidays. This chapter clarifies matters in regard to the Islamic calendar, making some connections to the Gregorian calendar for a sample year— 2002.[1]

Hajj

The fifth pillar of Islam, and the holiest of Muslim journeys, is called hajj, the pilgrimage to Mecca. Each year, about 2 million Muslims converge on Mecca, Saudi Arabia. The world's largest international gathering, hajj is obligatory at least once in a Muslim's lifetime.

The protocols surrounding the hajj (discussed in chapter 7) are exacting. The hajj experience is profound for the Muslim, and is considered one of the highest rites of passage in life. The purpose is the same for every Muslim who makes the journey—the worship of Allah at the Kaaba, the Sacred House in Mecca.

According to the Qur'an, the Kaaba was built by two prophets, Abraham and his son, Ishmael. The Qur'an declares that

Abraham was not a Jew or a Christian,
but he was an upright man, a Muslim;
and he was not one of the polytheists. (sura 3:66)

Islam teaches that it was not Isaac but Ishmael who was to be offered and who was spared by the ram in the thicket (compare with Genesis 22). After that miracle, the two continued to Mecca, where they built the Kaaba. The Hadith teaches, "And when Abraham and Ishmael raised the foundation of the House, [they said] 'Allah accept from us . . . and show us our way of devotion.'"

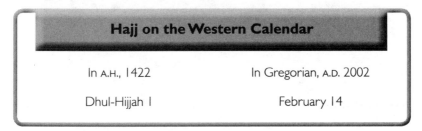

Hajj on the Western Calendar	
In A.H., 1422	In Gregorian, A.D. 2002
Dhul-Hijjah 1	February 14

The Muslim believes that Abraham instituted the pilgrimage and established the rites around the Kaaba. Muhammad resuscitated the pilgrimage after many years of dormancy.

The most important day of the pilgrimage is the ninth day of Dhul-Hijjah, the Day of Arafat. On this day, a huge throng of pilgrims gathers at the Plain of Arafat, which Muslims believe is the prototype of the site of Allah's last judgment. Here, they pray for forgiveness and mercy, in preparation for the next day, 'Eid-ul-Adha, another Islamic holy day.

'Eid-ul-Adha

On the day following the Day of Arafat, Muslims celebrate 'Eid-ul-Adha, the Festival of Sacrifice. This holiday celebrates Abraham's willingness to sacrifice everything, including his son Ishmael. Since the Muslim believes that Allah spared Ishmael by substituting a sheep in a thicket, Muslims honor the day by slaughtering an animal and distributing the meat among family, friends, and the needy.

'Eid-ul-Adha is designed to encourage special acts of mercy

toward poor Muslim families in the community. The day carries many traditions, including the wearing of new or special clothing and the giving of gifts to children after the telling of the story of the sacrifice of Ishmael. While these first two holidays occur early on the Western calendar, they are in fact at the end of the Islamic year. The New Year begins roughly three weeks later, at the inception of the month Muharram (see New Year's dating on p. 153).

'Eid-ul-Adha on the Western Calendar

In A.H., 1422	In Gregorian, A.D. 2002
Dhul-Hijjah 10	February 23

Ramadan

The most universally recognized Islamic holiday period is Ramadan, which is both the name of the month and the name of the fasting period. Observing a fast (sawm) each day of this most special month of the year is one of the five pillars of Islam. The most widely practiced of all the Muslim forms of worship, it calls the world's 1.2 billion Muslims to devotion, inner reflection, and self-control.

The stated purpose for Ramadan is to give a universal and concrete time for the observance of the third pillar of Islam, fasting. While many Muslims practice fasting throughout the year, the obligation to fast comes once a year, and most Muslims, even nominal ones, follow the practice. Abstaining from food during the daylight hours and from marital relations, and beginning new commitments to prayer and Qur'anic study are emphasized as acts of obedience. Every act during the month of Ramadan is dedicated for this purpose.

Ramadan begins with the new moon on the ninth month. As noted earlier, because the new moon is not the same throughout the world, there is some disparity in regard to the beginning of Ramadan, but astronomical calculations are used to bring world continuity. The end of the month, marked by the celebration of 'Eid-ul-Fitr, is similarly determined.

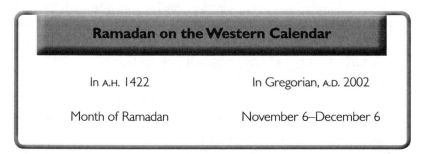

Ramadan on the Western Calendar

In A.H. 1422	In Gregorian, A.D. 2002
Month of Ramadan	November 6–December 6

With the exception of the sick, women in certain conditions, and those traveling, all Muslims are commanded to fast during Ramadan. The daily period of fasting begins at the breaking of dawn and ends with the setting of the sun. During this period, Muslims abstain from food, drink, smoking, marital sex, and all forms of indulgence.

For the Muslim, this does not reflect a period of depression or sadness. The celebrations surrounding the month are, in fact, times of feasting. In the morning, a Muslim rises early to have a meal, called the *suhoor*. The meal is large and foods are prepared with much fellowship. After the meal, the morning prayers are recited, and the fast begins. In the evening, the prayer is said to mark the end of daylight, and the evening fellowship meal, often with family and friends, is celebrated. This meal is called the *iftar* and, following the tradition of Muhammad, begins with the eating of sweet dates. Although Muslims are commanded to read the Qur'an daily, it is often part of the Ramadan celebration to read one-thirtieth of the Qur'an each day, reading the entire text during Ramadan.

The last ten days of Ramadan have special power, as Muslims seek to serve Allah in acts of charity and devotion. The Night of Power (Lailat ul-Qadr) comes on the twenty-seventh night of the month, and is the most holy night of the holy month. According to the Qur'an, this night commemorates the night Muhammad received the first verses of the Qur'an, and the night is "better than a thousand months."

The impact of the celebration within the Islamic community must be experienced to be understood. Anticipation builds for months, during which menus and guest lists are planned. With a feeling of expectancy similar to that which Christians feel as they approach Christmas or Jews feel nearing Passover, Muslims look forward to Ramadan with glee. Small gifts are received each night, and ethnic and spiritual pride escalates as Muslims recognize a single event that encompasses the entire Islamic world. Friends and family greet each other with special phrases during the month, many of which are common throughout Islam:

Kulu am wa antum bi-khair, "May you be well through the year."

Elveda, ey Ramazan, "Farewell, O Ramadan."

'Eid mubarak, "A blessed 'Eid."

This last phrase is the universal Arabic greeting that augurs Allah's blessing in the final Islamic holiday of universal observance, the Festival of Fast Breaking.[2]

'Eid-ul-Fitr

The first day of the tenth month of Islam is the celebration of the breaking of the fast of Ramadan. It is a joyous celebration, marking the completion of special acts of devotion. Muslims around the world dress in festive colors, attend a special prayer in the morning, and visit friends. In many places, larger gifts or money are given to children by parents and relatives.

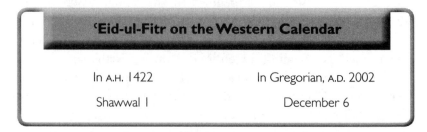

'Eid-ul-Fitr on the Western Calendar	
In A.H. 1422	In Gregorian, A.D. 2002
Shawwal 1	December 6

The celebration of 'Eid-ul-Fitr lasts three days, and in most countries, non-essential work is suspended during this time. Most of the formal observations, however, take place on the first day.

A special offering for the poor is obligatory, funding much of the corporate benevolence for the year. Currently, Muslims in America are attempting to get 'Eid-ul-Fitr recognized as an official holiday.

An Eschatological Holy Day

In Shiite Islam, one holiday has messianic overtones—the celebration of the twelfth imam, Muhammed al-Mahdi, the son of the eleventh imam, al-Hasan al-Askari. According to tradition, Imam al-Mahdi has never died. He is now alive and in hiding, awaiting the day of judgment when he will appear to establish justice on earth. The celebration of his birth date, on the fifteenth of Sha'ban, has many traditions that strangely hearken to a reigning and ruling King.

Celebrations of Human Endeavor

Christians must understand that Islamic holidays differ in both essence and meaning from the holy days that Christians observe.

First, and of most importance, Christian holidays remember divine interventions, while Islamic celebrations are based upon human accomplishment. In Christianity, we celebrate Easter as the resurrection of our Lord Jesus and His completion of the sacrifice for our sins. In Islam, 'Eid-ul-Adha celebrates Abraham's willingness to sacrifice Ishmael, not Allah's substitution of the ram in the thicket. In Christianity we celebrate on Christmas the birth of the Savior, Jesus Christ, for our redemption. Islam celebrates Mawlid al-Nabi, the birth date of Muhammad, their warrior. Christianity and Judaism recognize Passover as the work of God sparing the firstborn children of the Israelites. Muslims mark the end of their own personal sacrifice in Ramadan with 'Eid-ul-Fitr. The complete inversion of the purpose of holy days cannot be overstated.

Second, the communal activities and meals celebrated in Islam are exclusively for Muslims. In Christian terminology, Muslims believe emphatically in "closed communion." While Jews often make a point of inviting their Christian neighbors to celebrate Shabbat or the Passover Seder with them, non-Muslims (even if they are friends or family) are unwelcome at Muslim celebrations.

The import of this principle is disturbing. In November 2002, former President George W. Bush unwittingly committed a religious faux pas, even as he sought to reach out to Muslims. President Bush hosted an iftar, the evening meal of Ramadan. At the beginning of the meal, the perfunctory prayer is recited, pledging the clear devotion of every person at the table to Allah. The president's advisors surely did not tell him that by joining in this prayer he was pledging himself to the Muslim god. As a strong Christian who has been candid in confessing his faith, President Bush made an error common for those who try to find bridges to Islam without understanding the Muslim worldview.

Christians take note: While we should understand Islamic customs, we can easily fall into syncretistic idolatry. Respecting other religious traditions enables us to witness more effectively. Validating their traditions waters down the gospel witness. We center our celebrations on the provision of the Lord, not on our personal endeavors.

Young Mustafa is like many other Muslims. He would appreciate knowing a Christian who understands his traditions and is sensitive to his position, but who does not minimize the differences.

Notes

1. Westerners are not without their own calendar controversies. The Gregorian calendar of 365¼ days has been in use only since A.D. 1582. In the United States that calendar only became the standard in the mid-eighteenth century. Until then we used the Julian calendar, which Russia continued to use into the twentieth century. In 1908, the Imperial Russian Olympic team arrived in London twelve days late for the games.

2. Muslims also celebrate Mawlid al-Nabi, the birth date of Muhammad, which in 2002, for example, fell on May 24.

11

ISLAMIC SECTS AND SPLINTERS

A Blurring of the Lines

SINCE THE ATTACKS on the World Trade Center and Pentagon in September 2001, many lines of distinction have become blurred. Less distinction exists between civilian and soldier, at least here in the United States. The media seems less certain of the boundary between secular and religious. Even in the Islamic world, an important line between two of the major sects has become less distinct.

The blurring of lines is no small matter, since boundaries are important to a culture. Consider, first, the distinction in the United States between citizen and soldier. Assuming that the American Civil War was a domestic conflict, the last time the eastern shores of America were attacked by a foreign aggressor was in the War of 1812. Throughout the history of the United States, American soldiers at war knew that their families at home lived in relative calm. In the face of the bombings and anthrax-contaminated letters, civilians feel exposed.

Second, the line between secular and sacred society is indistinguishable. After the bombing and the release of the fatwa (declared jihad), world media rushed to learn the meaning of jihad. For a brief moment, theologians outnumbered politicians on the airwaves. Prayer services and religious debates were front-page news.

Perhaps the most alarming line that has been crossed is the third. For fifty years, Western politicians have depended upon the supposedly moderate Muslims, Sunnis, to help stabilize Islam's radical fringe, the Shiites. Now a most remarkable shift has taken place. Osama bin Laden was a *Sunni* Muslim, but he drew followers from across sectarian lines, and the demarcation between the various groups within Islam is no longer pronounced. Christians should understand these groups that compose the Islamic population and that help Muslims define themselves in Islamic terms.

A Historical Break: The Caliphate

Following the death of Muhammad, caliphs (or kaliphs) led the quickly growing Islamic community (see pp. 67–70). Muhammed had not established a line of succession, so Muslims had to quickly develop an organization plan for administration, military command, courts, and spiritual teaching. They developed the office of caliph to head the community, although this position was not to be a prophet, on an equal with Muhammad.

Abu Bakr officially became the first caliph, but his claim was not undisputed. Ali, Muhammad's cousin and the husband of his daughter Fatima, was fourth caliph until he was assassinated and replaced by the Umayyad dynasty in 661. A faction had believed Ali was the true first caliph.

Most Muslims supported the "mainstream" line of caliphs and came to be known as Sunnis. They followed the sunnah (custom) of Muhammad as it is practiced and interpreted by the Islamic community, the umma.

The dissenters became known as the Shia (faction) of Ali. In 680, Ali's younger son Husayn revolted against the majority rule of the Sunnis and was killed in a massacre at Karbala, Iraq. Shiites still commemorate his death annually on the tenth of Muharram. This split and subsequent political struggle eventually defined the first division in Islam—that between the Sunnis and the Shiites—and in many countries in the Islamic world the division remains to this day.

Sunni Muslims: Sharia and Fiqh

By far the largest segment of Muslims belong to the Sunni sect. Following the death of Muhammad, the Sunni faction purposed that the successor to Muhammad should be elected from among the people. The Shiites (party of Ali) believed a direct descendancy from Muhammad should be followed, a blood line of succession. Consequently, the Shiites reject as fraudulent the first three caliphs elected. They accept only the election of Ali, Muhammad's cousin and son-in-law.

In the Islamic community, the Sunni Muslims systematized and organized Islamic life and ethics under a structure of theocratic law. The most important concept instituted by the Sunni community was that of sharia (literally "the way to the watering hole") Islamic law. Traditionally, sharia is divided into three arenas: religious duty (*ibadat*), ethics (*m'Amalat*), and jurisprudence (*fiqh*).

The organization of these laws (*Usul al-fiqh*) was formulated by Muhammad ibn Idris al-Shafi before his death in 819. The highest authority in all matters of life was the Qur'an, followed by the Sunnah in the Hadith, and finally the consensus of the community, known as *ijma*. This ijma began as the consensus of the entire community, but later came to indicate the consensus of the scholars, known as the aulema.

Among the Sunnis, community became the final resource for law and ethics. In early Islam, *qiyas* (analogy) and *ijtihad* (independent decision-making) were also taken into consideration, but the Sunnis no longer accept these as authoritative. In the Shiite community, however, ijtihad still exists as a valid process, but is practiced only by the local imam in each mosque. In virtually every arena of life, even the detailing of the prayer times and dietary restrictions in various countries, the Sunni community has kept Islam speaking with one voice. They are committed to furthering Islam in established countries and spreading the religion through the world.

Shiite Muslims: Sharia and Imam

In opposition to the Sunni Muslims, early Shiites believed that the leader must be a descendant of Muhammad, and that

Muhammad had, at the pool of Ghadir al-Khumm, explicitly designated Ali as his successor. Shiites developed a theology that negated
the caliph and enlisted their own leaders, known as the imams.

The imam was believed to be a fully *spiritual* guide, inheriting
some of Muhammad's inspiration, and not merely a contractually
elected administrator like the Sunni caliph. In Shiite Islam, the imam
was believed to be an inerrant interpreter of law and tradition.

Divinely chosen at birth, true imams are direct descendants of
Ali, and Shiites teach that the twelfth generation (twelfth imam)
of that line did not die, but that he was taken by Allah to heaven,
or is in hiding on the earth. He shall return, the Shiites believe, to
the earth to be the Mahdi, a messianic figure.[1]

The draw of early Shiite Islam was compelling, with its theme
of martyrdom and suffering, focusing on the deaths of Husayn and
other important figures in Shiite succession. Shiites attracted other
dissenting groups, especially representatives of non-Arab (*Mawali*)
civilizations (in such societies as Persia and India). These groups
felt they had not been treated fairly by Arab Muslims, who were
predominately Sunni.

Around the world, and particularly in Iraq, Iran, India, Pakistan, and
in parts of Afganistan, millions gather every year to mourn the death
of Husayn and recite the narrative of his "martyrdom." The event is
compared to a vicarious sacrifice, somewhat similar to how Christians
view the death of Christ. Husayn gave everything on the day of Ashura.

The subsequent inclusion of other civilizations accounts for Shiite
Islam's inclusion of some religious tendencies such as mysticism and
meditation. This distinction can often be seen in the emphasis on
dreams as an act of Allah's revelation, especially helpful in decision
making. The interest in retelling and analyzing dreams is evident on
the widely published videotape in which Osama bin Laden discusses
the New York and Washington, D.C., attacks of September 11, 2001

The Shiite community insists on the sharia as a governmental
absolute. In countries where Shiite Islam holds sway, theocracy
(rule of god) is seen as the best option to rule and live. Laws are
determined by the Qur'an and the Hadith, the teachings from which
stem ethics and criminal law.

Sufism: Islamic Mysticism

Sufism developed in response to a perceived legalism within Islam. Because the more mystical Sufis regarded the observance of religious law as *outer* conformity, they encouraged a desire for personal experience with Allah, through *dhikr* (remembrance) and *tariqa*, the *inner* way of meditation.

Sufis based their teachings on the simplicity of lifestyle of Muhammad and the first caliphs, as well as their rejection of wealth. This rejection would lead to the loss of self-desire and a passing away (*fana*) of self into Allah. Sufism appealed to the countries where Buddhism and Hinduism were strong.

Denial of self is accomplished by extreme fasting, long periods of meditation, the whirling dervish (spinning dance), and other meditation aids, which often transcend Islamic law and Qur'anic teachings so far as Sufis are concerned.

In regard to doctrine, Sufis preach the centrality of the love of Allah (*mahabbah*), introduced by the leader Rabi'a in the eighth century. They teach an allegorical and symbolic interpretation of the Qur'an, and they chant the divine names of Allah to commune with him. Each Sufi brotherhood includes a spiritual master (sheikh), who teaches his distinctive path (tariqa) to his disciples (fakirs). The disciples live with the sheikh and practice the path communally.

The Sufi movement now is growing rapidly in Middle Eastern and Eastern countries. The mysticism they practice is welcome and universal to cultures that emphasize self-denial. Even in America, with the trend toward the Cabalic Judaism and Eastern mysticism, Sufi communities continue to spread.[2]

While Sufi Islam does not have a cohesive and systematic theology, certainly pantheism is central to the sect. The journey into Allah communion is directed in each Sufi sect by a leader, called a *pir*, who enlists followers known as *murid*.[3]

Minor Sects

Roughly 98 percent of all Muslims follow one of the three major Islamic groups, but small sects draw followers around the world. Some of these groups are considered to be so far from mainstream

Islam that they are not part of the religion; some are nonetheless
worth investigating.

Nation of Islam

One of the most controversial groups in Islam is the World
Community of Al-Islam in the West, otherwise known as the Nation
of Islam (NOI). Strictly a movement within the United States, the
NOI has drawn attention in the political arena.

Around 1930, the NOI was founded by Wallace Dodd Fard
(Wali Farad Muhammad) in Detroit, Michigan. Fard tended to draw
on the teachings of Timothy (Noble Drew) Ali who founded his
Moorish Holy Temple of Science Organization in 1928.[4]

Drew taught that African-Americans were actually of Arabic heritage and therefore should be referred to as *Moors*. He further taught
that Islam, not Christianity, was the original and therefore correct
faith of Africans in the United States. After Drew's mysterious death
in 1929, Fard spread the teaching that the black man was originally
Muslim (Moors), the white man was the devil, and the empower-
ment that African-Americans sought would be found only within a
separated nation. By 1934, Fard had eight thousand converts.

In June 1934, Fard disappeared, and his main minister, Elijah
Pool Muhammad, succeeded him. Muhammad's strong leadership
expanded the membership and influence of the NOI. At his death
in 1975, his son, Wallace Muhammad, took over and began moving
NOI into the fold of orthodox Islam, with six reforms:

1. Elijah Muhammad's doctrine of black racial superiority
   was abolished.
2. Wallace Fard was said to be a wise man but not God
   himself, as Elijah Muhammad had believed.
3. Business organizations were separated from religious
   organizations.
4. The demand for a separate state for African-Americans
   was dropped.
5. For the first time the authority of the U.S. Constitution
   was accepted.

6. NOI doctrines were aligned with Orthodox Islam, including the Hajj.

Under these changes, the Sunni community accepted the NOI into its fold, but not everyone in the NOI agreed with the changes. Louis Farrakhan, an outspoken proponent of African nationalism, founded a separate Islamic movement.

Wahhabi: Radical Sunnism

Wahhabism is an external designation for the religious movement within Islam that was founded by Muhammad ibn Abd al-Wahhab (1703–1792). Seeing himself as a reformer of Islam, Wahhab declared jihad on all other forms of Islam—a unique occurrence in Islamic history. Members describe themselves as *muwahhidun* (unitarians), and they oppose anything that diminishes the glorification of the one God, Allah. Wahhabism condemns as illegal and heretical the practice of using the name of any prophet or angel in a prayer, and of visitations to graves of saints. Adherents insist on a literal interpretation of the Qur'an and a strict doctrine of predestination.

In their strict purity, the Wahhabi are considered to be among the most radical Muslims in the world. Their teaching on kismet (fate) determines their purpose in jihad, being warfare between Islam and all kafir (infidels) who do not worship Allah. Wahhabis are found in Saudi Arabia and in other regions of the Middle East.

Druze: The Secret Muslims

One of the more unusual sects of Islam, the Druze is a fiercely independent and secretive group in Lebanon and northern Israel. The Druze began as a split from Islam under the leadership of Darazi and Hamza ibn Ali ibn Ahmad. These men taught that Allah had manifested himself in the person of al-Hakim Bi-amr Allah (996–1021), but mainline Islam eventually repudiated this leader.

Strongly mystical, the Druze sect is completely exclusive. They do not accept converts, do not intermarry, and do not discuss their religion. They often assume the local religion of their country as a cover, and only discuss their beliefs with other members (called *mowahhidoon*).

The Alawites

Founded by Ibn Nucair Namin Abdi, the Alawites broke from the Shiites in the ninth century over the teaching of the twelve Shias. Alawites live in Syria, mainly in the mountains near the city of Latakia, but many also live in the cities of Hama and Homs, and in recent decades in Damascus. With a membership of 1.5 million, the Alawites comprise about 10 percent of Syria's population, and two recent Syrian presidents, Bashar and Hafez al-Assad were Alawites.

The Alawite name is a recent one—earlier they were known as Nusairi, Namiriya, or Ansariyya. The names *Nusairi* and *Namiriya* are derived from their first teacher, Muhammad ibn Nusairi n-Namiri. The name *Ansariyya* is derived from the mountain region in Syria where this sect lived.

In their view, Ali was the bearer of divine essence and second only to Muhammad as an elevated prophet. The Alawites have seven pillars in their religion, five being similar to those of other Muslims, but Alawites consider the pillars as symbols only, not requirements. The other two pillars are *jihad* (struggle against Ali's enemies) and *waliya* (devotion to Ali).

Considering themselves to be moderate Shiites, the Alawites have often been in conflict with Islamic rulers as well as with other Muslims, who often have claimed that Alawites are not Muslims.

Nusairiyyah: Secret Paternal Islam

The Nusairis trace their beginnings to the eleventh Shia Imam al-Hasan al-Askari and his pupil Ibn Nusair. The Nusairis lived mostly in Syria, supported by the Shiite Hamdanid dynasty. In the twentieth century, Nusairis enjoyed a degree of political dominance disproportionate to their size. After World War I, the French, who were ruling Syria, made an unsuccessful attempt to establish a separate Nusairi state. Since 1970, following the coup of the Nusairi air force chief, Hafez al-Asad, the Nusairis have been dominant in

Syrian political and military life. An estimated six hundred thousand Nusairis now live in Syria.

Nusairi doctrine is a mixture of Islamic, Gnostic, and Christian beliefs. Sunni Muslims treat them as heretics because of three of their doctrines:

1. Ali was Allah in the flesh. Ali created Muhammad from his spirit, and Muhammad created Salman, an early Shiite saint. These three form a trinity in which Ali is described as the "meaning," Muhammad as the "name," and Salman as the "door."
2. The authority of the Qur'an and all forms of prayer are rejected. All Islamic teaching can be interpreted allegorically and therefore does not have to be taken literally.
3. Men are reincarnated. Women do not have souls, so they do not need to learn the secrets of Nusairi doctrine.

Nusairis have their own distinct religious leaders, called sheikhs, believed to be empowered with a kind of divine authority. Nusairis have special feasts in which they celebrate the anniversaries of their sacred figures. At the age of nineteen, Nusairi men undergo an initiation rite in which they learn secrets of the sect.

The Ahmadiyya Movement: An Islamic Cult

One of the fastest-growing movements within the Islamic countries, Ahmadiyyas, is actually considered a cult by orthodox Muslims. The movement was established in 1889 by Mirza Ghulam Qadiani (1835-1908) in a small Punjabi village of India. Qadiani's life was laden with controversial claims. In 1880, he declared himself to be only a Muslim writer, but in 1885 he announced that he was a revivalist and scholar (*Mujaddid*). In 1891, he claimed to be the promised Messiah, and in 1901 he pronounced that he was himself an authoritative prophet of Allah.

Facing strong opposition by Muslim scholars (aulema) for this declaration and other teachings that contradicted the Qur'anic revelations, Qadiani also announced that he was Muhammad, who had returned with authority to reinterpret the Qur'an. In 1904, Qadiani further infuriated Muslim leaders when he declared himself to be the Hindu Lord Krishna. Appealing to uneducated Indians, he succeeded to an extent that alarmed the Islamic leadership.

After his death in 1908, the movement continued, both in mission activity and opposition. In 1974, after an examination of all the evidence presented for and against the Qadianis, the Muslim World League (Rabita Alame Islami) passed a unanimous resolution declaring that the Qadiani movement and its leaders were apostate and outside the fold of Islam.

Sikhism: A Melding of Islam and Hinduism

One of the most misunderstood religious movements is Sikhism. Often Sikhs are mistaken for Muslims, because they arose from Islamic background. Their founder, Guru Nanak, was born in Talwandi, a village in Punjab, India, in 1469. He challenged the perceived fanaticism and intolerance of the Muslims of his time, also criticizing Hindus for their seemingly meaningless rituals and caste prejudice. During his visit to Mecca, he publicly proclaimed that Allah's house is everywhere, not just at the Kaaba.

Guru Nanak believed deeply in the equality of all men and sought to syncretize Hinduism and Islam. He opposed distinctions of caste, and identified himself with the lowest caste. His teachings drew both Muslims and Hindus, and the number of disciples grew exponentially as word spread of his pacifism and equitable treatment of lower castes of society.

Sikhism is, if it is logically possible to be so, a monotheistic atheism. It recognizes Allah as the only one, not confined to time, space, or mind. Yet Sikhism does not believe in Avtarvada, that Allah takes a human form. Instead, Allah is a divine "principle," with which the Sikh can unite in elevation.

The Sikh religion rejects all rituals and routine practices including fasting and pilgrimage. The goal of human life, to merge with Allah, is accomplished by following the teachings of the guru, by meditating on the "holy Name," and by doing acts of service and charity.

Sikhism emphasizes Bhakti Marg or the "path of devotion." It does, however, say that there is a limited value in Gian Marg ("the path of knowledge") and Karam Marg ("the path of action"). Sikhs also stress the need to earn grace in order to reach the eternal mind.

In summary, like Protestantism, Islam consists of differing factions and branches, birthing variant strands of religion. To think of Muslims as a homogenous group is erroneous and fails to do justice to the diversity of beliefs embraced within the religion. Differences of opinions have existed since immediately after Muhammad's death and they show no signs of abating.

Notes

1. Ignaz Goldziher, *Introduction to Islamic Theology and Law* (Princeton, NJ: Princeton University Press, 1981), 167.
2. Charles Waddy, *The Muslim Mind* (London: Longman, 1976), 151ff.
3. Phil Parshall, *Bridges to Islam* (Grand Rapids: Baker, 1983), 31-37.
4. For further study on the Nation of Islam, see Vibert L. White, *Inside the Nation of Islam: A Historical and Personal Testimony by a Black Muslim* (Orlando: University of Florida Press, 2001).

12

THE ILLUSION OF RELIGIOUS
LIBERTY: TERRORISM FROM WITHIN

Neema's Story

HER BROWN EYES look older than her nineteen years. Neema seems remarkably composed as she recalls the day in 1988 when Muslim invaders swept from the north through her Christian village and carried her into slavery. She speaks quietly, almost in a whisper, pausing while the interpreter repeats in English. "When the Arab militia came, they kidnapped many people, killing anyone who resisted. They concentrated on women and children."

Neema gently calms the small boy who leans against her side, tugging at her garments, trying to catch her attention.

"Did you try to escape?"

Neema nods, "Oh yes. But I was badly beaten. Finally I surrendered, and I was thrown across the back of a horse and taken away."

"Where did they take you?"

"To the north. I was sold to a man who put me to work as a servant, helping his wife pound dura and collect firewood. They gave me a Muslim name and forced me to take part in their Muslim rituals, even though I am a Christian. When I refused, I was harshly beaten. And when my master's wife went to market, or left the home for any reason, he . . ." she lowers her eyes.

Neema motions toward the child.

"When my master's wife found that I was pregnant with his child, she became enraged, chased me out of the house, and I was able to escape."

"How did you get back here?"

"Slave traders helped me. They brought me back and sold me to my family for five cows. My people were glad to have me back, but now I cannot marry. I have been with a man, and I have a child. I am no longer free to marry a husband."[1]

Equal Opportunity Persecutors

The Crusades. The Inquisition. The Reformation Wars. The Pogroms against the Jews. Abundant examples can be cited—atrocities committed by people identifying themselves as Christians against entire communities and nations. In defending jihad, Islamic scholars point to episodes of Christian slaughter. And as have Muslims, Christians have practiced holy war, the Crusades of 1095 to 1291 offering a prime example. But these examples are not analogous to Islam's jihad as historically practiced.

First, Muhammad, both by his life and his writings, affirmed jihad as a strategy for expanding the faith. Jesus did not. Rather, He taught, "Blessed are the peacemakers, for they shall be called the sons of God" (Matt. 5:9). When crusading against the Muslims, Christians were acting contrary to their Savior and His Word. Muslims fighting against pagans are obeying their warrior-prophet and his message.

Second, New Testament Scripture never advocates jihad on any other group, and, in fact, anticipates that persecutions will be practiced only against Christians. Jesus explained to His disciples, "If they have persecuted Me, they will also persecute you" (John 15:20; cf. Matt. 5:11–12, 44–45; 10:22–23; Luke 21:12–13; John 15:20–27; Rom. 12:14). The book of Acts shows how the apostles rejoiced when they were persecuted. Christians in the Bible never retaliated, giving their lives for the faith.

Third, the Qur'an and Hadith traditions lend credence to the Muslim militancy that, through the words of Muhammad, sheds innocent blood for the cause of Allah. Jesus fulfilled Old Testament laws in His own sacrifice on the cross, thereby placing punishment for sin upon Himself.

Fourth, except for isolated heretical groups, Christians have learned (although far too slowly) from their bloody history. Muslims continue their onslaught in numerous nations, including (at this writing) Sudan, Saudi Arabia, Iran, Indonesia, Bangladesh, Nigeria, and Pakistan. In fact, Islamic militancy continues to gain momentum.

Fifth, with rare exceptions of revenge killings in Palestinian refugee camps, modern examples of warring in Christian areas pit Christian groups against each other, not against outsiders. Irish Protestants fight Irish Catholics. Christians do not use war to expand political boundaries, believing that they will thus expand the kingdom of God. Further, examples of violence are aberrations in an otherwise peaceful Christian world. On the other hand, militancy remains the norm in conservative Islam.

The significant difference between Christians and Muslims, then, is not history but theology. Orthodox Christians are taught to live at peace by the living and written Word of God. Muslims are taught by the Qur'an and Allah's messenger to "fight and slay the Pagans wherever you find them" (sura 9:5).

The Political Difference

In recent decades in the United States, many non-Christians who are motivated by a personal agenda have abused the term "separation of church and state." But the original and still appropriate constitutional amendment reads, "Congress shall make no law respecting an establishment of religion, or prohibiting the free exercise thereof." Simply defined, the amendment allows a Christian desiring to pray voluntarily in school to do so. Nor can a Muslim be forbidden to share his or her faith in public.

When religious liberty is congested with unconstitutional interference, other liberties suffer. A central tenet of the freedoms enacted at the founding of the United States was that government would not simply tolerate those who are religious. Rather, we would be a nation that encourages the free expression of worship and witness. This is the principle that the United States has endeavored to uphold. Islam has followed the principle that other faiths must be given no encouragement or opportunity to share.

This principle can be traced to the seventh-century when the Pact of Umar was developed after rapid Muslim expansion. The Pact states that Christians

- "shall not build, in our cities or in their neighborhood, new monasteries, Churches, convents, or monks' cells, nor shall [they] repair, by day or by night, such of them as fall in ruins or are situated in the quarters of the Muslims";
- "shall not manifest religion publicly nor convert anyone to it. . . . [Christians] shall not prevent any of [their] kin from entering Islam if they wish it";
- "shall show respect toward the Muslims, and shall rise from seats when [Muslims] wish to sit";
- "shall not display crosses or books in the roads or markets of the Muslims. . . . [They] shall use only clappers in churches very softly."[2]

Dhimmis, or protected people (especially Christians and Jews), were accorded the rights of second-class citizens, paying extra taxes but nevertheless protected by the Islamic regime. The pact above, however, demonstrates a level of persecution.

Twenty-first-century Turkey practices a similar arrangement. An overwhelmingly Muslim nation, Turkey is the home of the leading figure of the Eastern Orthodox Church, Ecumenical Patriarch Bartholomew I. Religious liberty expert Paul Marshall explains, "The patriarch has been rigidly controlled, consistently denied permission to develop theological education or buildings for the Orthodox minority."[3]

Indeed, Turkey's secular government has not always been kind to its minorities. Between 1905 and 1918, 2 million Armenian Christians were slaughtered by the Ottomans, and as recently as 1994 and 1996, explosives were used in attacks against the Christian church.[4]

Similarly, Morocco allows freedom of worship, but proselytizing is forbidden. Zmamda Mustapha, a convert to Christianity, was given a three-year sentence for passing out Christian literature. Others are imprisoned for not participating in Ramadan. Only in the face of aggressive international pressure have governments in that region ceded even a minimal level of liberty.

In contrast, Western countries in recent centuries have offered increasing freedom and acceptance to Muslims. The authors' father, Acar Caner, helped design and build an incredibly beautiful mosque in Columbus, Ohio. He had every right to do all he wished to expand Islam in a peaceful way. As converts from Islam to Christianity, his sons fight for the Muslim's right to worship freely and spread his or her faith openly in the United States or any other nation. Every Bible-believing Christian knows that saving faith in Jesus Christ should not and, in fact, cannot be coerced.

We would not, however, enjoy that same right in Turkey, the homeland of our father. For all their rhetoric about tolerance, not one Muslim-controlled government offers comprehensive religious freedom. Even the most open-minded of Muslim countries do not recognize the arguments for such liberty. They never have—and we can only pray that one day they will.

Violence in Persecution

To equate all of Islam with religious persecution, however, would be an incredible overstatement.[5] Yet, along with Marxist and Maoist communists and Hindu extremists, Muslims have accumulated a record in modern times as leaders in committing mayhem against humanity. This violence is most often committed by individuals or small groups, but sometimes governments enforce it.

The most horrendous example of brutality in recent years has been in Sudan, a country having more Christians than any other Islamic country. When Muslims came to power in 1983, they immediately declared jihad on the millions of Christians (infidels). As a result of that jihad:

- Between 1.5 and 3 million had been killed as this book fiirst went to press. More Sudanese have become victims than in Rwanda, Bosnia, Somalia, and Kosovo combined.
- Fifty thousand children of the Dinka tribe alone are held as slaves. Their families can buy back their children with cattle, or for as little as fifteen dollars.
- Forced conversion to Islam is governmental policy. The militant Mujahidin (holy warriors) fight alongside government forces.
- Open preaching and evangelizing is illegal and punishable by imprisonment or beating.[6]

Witnesses and investigators have given plentiful evidence and descriptions of these events. Rabbi David Saperstein, Chairman of the United States Commission on International Religious Freedom, remarks that

> In World War II, so many people in Germany, even in the Allied countries, were able to say, "But we didn't know." We know. We know what is happening in Sudan. We cannot stand idly by the blood of our neighbors. And this nation's beginning to stir. But we are compelled to act far more forcefully than we have done.[7]

In the book *Their Blood Cries Out*, Paul Marshall describes devastation in the Nuba Mountains region of south central Sudan. Mass graves hold the remains of entire villages. In internment camps where women and children are kept, Nuba women are systematically raped by Arab soldiers to produce non-Nuba offspring. Some report that Christians have been crucified by soldiers.[8]

Sudan is not an isolated case. Other notable violators of religious freedom include Iran, Saudi Arabia, Turkmenistan, Pakistan, and Uzbekistan. In all of these nations, Christians who openly worship Jesus Christ may be killed, imprisoned, forced out of work, or forced to convert to Islam; and Christian centers of worship are destroyed. It is not a small fringe group of Taliban radicals who are carrying out these actions. Rather, more than a dozen governments

encompassing hundreds of millions of Muslims justify these acts
from followers of the Qur'an and the prophet Muhammad.

If the Muslim world is at all embarrassed by these horrific
events, there has not been an outcry from leaders in the Islamic
community. Muslims were quick to condemn the attacks by terrorists in the United States on September 11, 2001, calling the actions
demonic or satanic. Yet they are silent about less politically offensive
persecutions that they allow and sometimes support in their own
communities. If the attacks on innocent people in New York City
were "demonic," surely the offenses against Christians across Africa,
the Middle East, and Indonesia are equally demonic. In truth, the
carnage on September 11 pales in comparison with what is now
occurring in some nations in the name of Allah.

The Sanctity of Religious Liberty

The Christian ideal is that the inerrant, infallible Word of God
is the basis upon which ethical decisions are made. Christians are
never to be reactionary, that is, simply acting out of an emotional
response to another person's actions. Action based upon Scripture
is an important precept of the Christian theory of religious liberty.
Muslims (and any others) have a God-given right to believe whatever
they wish and to practice that belief so long as their actions do no
violence to others. At the point of violence, Christians can in some
circumstances step in to act, but not out of a desire for revenge. The
motivation must be love and honor for the fundamental laws God
has given to govern humanity. The Bible teaches that Christians "do
not wrestle against flesh and blood, but against principalities, against
powers" (Eph. 6:12). They are to fight the battle spiritually with the
only offensive weapon they need—the Bible.

Further, God the Father gives all people the opportunity to
love Him by accepting the sacrifice of His Son on the cross as forgiveness for sin. Since love must be a choice and cannot be forced
upon anyone, God, in His power, allows people to reject Him, even
allowing people to hate Him.

Therefore, people must be given ample possibility to act in
accordance with their decision for or against the Creator of the

universe. To do otherwise is to indirectly or directly force a person into a legalistic relationship with the Church and its doctrines.

Toppling Walls and Buildings

Millions of people around the world have seen the September 11, 2001, actions of terrorists played out before their eyes on television. Lives were destroyed, and as a nation, the United States was changed. A new era had dawned. Commentators spoke in many languages of the gloom in this new reality. The authors of this book, however, suggest that the events of September 11 have created more hope than we have felt for many years.

First, citizens of free countries have been brought back to a realization of what they have. In the United States, we can feel justifiable pride in the way citizens of our nation pulled together in the midst of unimagined tragedy. We can take pride in the forceful, balanced leadership of our nation and the professionalism shown by armed forces in a time of fast action and tough decisions. What we did in the first weeks and months after September 11 was morally defensible and biblically supportable.

Second, the United States and other Western nations have an opportunity to return religious liberty to the core of liberties. Seeing the results of religion being established and coerced by government, societies can seek the balanced ideal set before the world in the U.S. Constitution. Citizens in Canada, the United States, and other free societies can engage in processes that link political and religious freedoms in any society where our influence extends. Countries that allow a democracy politically but not religiously are doomed to fail.

Third, Muslim-Christian dialogues are taking place across the free world, but Muslims also must accept dialogue in their own lands, where religious liberty is devalued. To do otherwise is hypocritical. Given what has been shown in this volume, perhaps it is overly idealistic to call upon Islamic governments to encourage religious liberty in their laws and society. This much is true: Both Muslims and Christians believe the afterlife is far more important than this temporal journey. Therefore, if heaven is attained by a choice that holds infinite ramifications, then religious liberty must be allowed so that people can have an opportunity to encounter truth.

Notes

1. Paul Marshall, *Their Blood Cries Out: The Worldwide Tragedy of Modern Christians Who Are Dying for Their Faith* (Dallas: Word, 1997), 18. This book is a must read for anyone desiring a balanced view of persecution in the world today. Much of the material for this chapter comes from Marshall's diligent research.

2. This is only a partial list highlighting the most egregious statements found in the document.

3. Marshall, *Their Blood Cries Out*, 49-50.

4. Ibid.

5. Many European countries are considering enacting laws (or have recently done so) curbing religious freedom. Groups targeted include Jehovah's Witnesses, Assemblies of God, Baptists, and evangelicals. Due to the stigma of these groups, mainline Christians have been surprisingly quiet in their opposition. These laws need to be repealed immediately.

6. See persecution.org and projectpersecution.org. These sites also give ways people can help in this tragic situation.

7. "Prayer for the Persecuted Church in Sudan," CBN News, December 12, 1999.

8. Marshall, *Their Blood Cries Out*, 21-22.

13

THE BLOODSHED OF JIHAD

ON FEBRUARY 23, 1998, five Islamic caliphates signed a fatwa declaring war against the United States. Representing five radical factions, these men united to call the Muslim world to common cause against the perceived enemy of Islam. The full text reads:

Statement signed by Sheikh Osama bin-Muhammad bin-Ladin; Ayman al-Zawahiri, leader of the Jihad Group in Egypt; Abu-Yasir Rifa'i Ahmad Taha, a leader of the Islamic Group; Sheikh Mir Hamzah, secretary of the Jamiat-ul-Ulema-e-Pakistan; and Fazlul Rahman, leader of the Jihad Movement in Bangladesh

Praise be to Allah, who revealed the Book, controls the clouds, defeats factionalism, and says in His Book "But when the forbidden months are past, then fight and slay the pagans wherever you find them, seize them, beleaguer them, and lie in wait for them in every stratagem (of war)"; and peace be upon our Prophet, Muhammad bin-'Abdallah, who said "I have been sent with the sword between my hands to ensure that no one but Allah is worshipped, Allah who put my livelihood under the shadow of my spear and who inflicts humiliation and scorn on those who disobey my orders." The Arabian Peninsula has never—since Allah made it flat, created its desert, and encircled it with seas—been stormed by any forces like the crusader armies

now spreading in it like locusts, consuming its riches and destroying its plantations. All this is happening at a time when
nations are attacking Muslims like people fighting over a plate of
food. In the light of the grave situation and the lack of support,
we and you are obliged to discuss current events, and we should
all agree on how to settle the matter.

No one argues today about three facts that are known to
everyone; we will list them, in order to remind everyone:

First, for over seven years the United States has been oc-
cupying the lands of Islam in the holiest of places, the Arabian
Peninsula, plundering its riches, dictating to its rulers, humiliating its people, terrorizing its neighbors, and turning its bases
in the Peninsula into a spearhead through which to fight the
neighboring Muslim peoples.

If some people have formerly debated the fact of the occupation, all the people of the Peninsula have now acknowledged it.

The best proof of this is the Americans' continuing aggres-
sion against the Iraqi people using the Peninsula as a staging
post, even though all its rulers are against their territories being
used to that end, still they are helpless. Second, despite the
great devastation inflicted on the Iraqi people by the crusader-
Zionist alliance, and despite the huge number of those killed,
in excess of one million . . . despite all this, the Americans are
once again trying to repeat the horrific massacres, as though
they are not content with the protracted blockade imposed
after the ferocious war or the fragmentation and devastation.

So now they come to annihilate what is left of this people
and to humiliate their Muslim neighbors.

Third, if the Americans' aims behind these wars are religious and economic, the aim is also to serve the Jews' petty
state and divert attention from its occupation of Jerusalem and
murder of Muslims there.

The best proof of this is their eagerness to destroy Iraq, the
strongest neighboring Arab state, and their endeavor to frag-
ment all the states of the region such as Iraq, Saudi Arabia,
Egypt, and Sudan into paper *statelets* and through their disunion

and weakness to guarantee Israel's survival and the continuation of the brutal crusade occupation of the Peninsula.

All these crimes and sins committed by the Americans are a clear declaration of war on Allah, his messenger, and Muslims. And aulema have throughout Islamic history unanimously agreed that the Jihad is an individual duty if the enemy destroys the Muslim countries. This was revealed by Imam bin-Qadamah in "Al-Mughni," Imam al-Kisa'i in "Al-Bada'i," al-Qurtubi in his interpretation, and the shaykh of al-Islam in his books, where he said "As for the militant struggle, it is aimed at defending sanctity and religion, and it is a duty as agreed. Nothing is more sacred than belief except repulsing an enemy who is attacking religion and life."

On that basis, and in compliance with Allah's order, we issue the following fatwa to all Muslims

The ruling to kill the Americans and their allies—civilians and military—is an individual duty for every Muslim who can do it in any country in which it is possible to do it, in order to liberate the al-Aqsa Mosque and the holy mosque from their grip, and in order for their armies to move out of all the lands of Islam, defeated and unable to threaten any Muslim. This is in accordance with the words of Almighty Allah, "and fight the pagans all together as they fight you all together," and "fight them until there is no more tumult or oppression, and there prevail justice and faith in Allah."

This is in addition to the words of Almighty Allah "And why should you not fight in the cause of Allah and of those who, being weak, are ill-treated and oppressed—women and children, whose cry is 'Allah rescue us from this town, whose people are oppressors; and raise for us from thee one who believes in Allah and wishes to be rewarded to comply with Allah's order to kill the Americans and plunder their money wherever and whenever they find it. We also call on Muslim aulema, leaders, youths, and soldiers to launch the raid on Satan's U.S. troops and the devil's supporters allying with them, and to displace those who are behind them so that they may learn a lesson.

Almighty Allah said "O you who believe, give your response to Allah and His Apostle, when He calls you to that which will give you life. And know that Allah comes between a man and his heart, and that it is He to whom you shall all be gathered."

Almighty Allah also says "O you who believe, what is the matter with you, that when you are asked to go forth in the cause of Allah, you cling so heavily to the earth? Do you prefer the life of this world to the hereafter? But little is the comfort of this life, as compared with the hereafter. Unless you go forth, He will punish you with a grievous penalty, and put others in your place; but Him you would not harm in the least. For Allah hath power over all things."

Almighty Allah also says "So lose no heart, nor fall into despair. For you must gain mastery if you are true in faith."[1]

Thousands of persons lost their lives on September 11, 2001, as the United States saw the first manifestation of this declared fatwa—the World Trade Center towers were reduced to burning rubble. Were the men who flew planes into the towers and into the Pentagon acting out the wild ranting of a cultic leader who has bastardized the peaceful religion of Islam? Or did they offer their lives because they believed orthodox Islamic doctrine? The authors of this book assert that Islam does in fact have an essential and indispensable tenet of militaristic conquest. The terrorists were not some fringe group that changed the Qurʾan to suit political ends. They understood the Qurʾan quite well and followed the teachings of jihad to the letter.

In both the Qurʾan and the Hadith, the infidel (kafir) must be converted or conquered. Muslims who die in the struggle against infidels (jihad) will immediately be translated to the highest level of Paradise. Much of this doctrine draws on admonitions and injunctions in the Hadith, but strong Qurʾanic foundations also exist for holy war.

High Jihad Is Warfare

The Qurʾan, supposedly from the very mouth of Allah, takes a dim view of the nonbeliever. Strictly speaking, jihad means a continuing *warfare* against them. Despite the explanations of Islamic apologists after the terrorist attacks, jihad does not primarily refer to a "struggle of personal piety." Jihad is combat on the fronts of politics, warfare, and culture. Muhammad exemplified this principle when he authorized the slaughter of thousands of men throughout the Arabian Peninsula in the name of Allah. If jihad is only a personal internal struggle, the Prophet misled the people through his actions and words as recorded in the Hadith. In the end, he was the personification of a militaristic theologian, which the Hadith accurately illustrates. In sura 2:190, Allah says, "Fight [jihad] in the cause of Allah those who fight [ajihad] you." The definition of this struggle includes the possibility of violence: "And slay them wherever you catch them, and turn them out from where they have turned you out, for tumult and oppression are worse than slaughter" (sura 2:191).

The apparent contradiction of conquering the oppressors so all through oppression have faith in Allah can be understood with a proper interpretation of jihad. Military warfare is an absolute necessity if Allah is to be honored and worshiped.

The very presence of the infidel stirs turmoil and requires Islam to win victory: "And fight them on until there is no more tumult or oppression, and let there prevail justice and faith in Allah; but if they cease, let there be no hostility except to those who practice oppression" (sura 2:193).

The current Muslim apologists who stress the concept of intellectual debate in this warfare must hasten to sura 2:216: "Fighting is prescribed for you, and you dislike it. But it is possible that you dislike a thing which is good for you, and that you love a thing which is bad for you. But Allah knows, and you know not." It is impossible to translate the word *fighting* in this text to mean anything but the traditional combat sense.

The Hadith also interprets jihad as a "fight, struggle, or battle." Bukhari's very first volume notes, "Allah's Apostle was asked, 'What is the best deed?' He replied, 'To believe in Allah and His Apostle (Muhammad).' The questioner then asked, 'What is the next (in goodness)?' He replied, 'To participate in Jihad in Allah's cause'" (sura 2:25). In hadith 3.46.724, which is narrated by Abu Huraira, Muhammad said, "A pious slave gets a double reward," and Abu Huraira added, "By Him in Whose Hands my soul is but for Jihad [holy battles], Hajj, and my duty to serve my mother, I would have loved to die as a slave." Thus, death is seemingly a possible end of such jihad.

Of special interest to the student of the Hadith is the title of Book 52 of Bukhari's Hadith, *Fighting for the Cause of Allah* (jihad). The volume presents with explicit clarity some of the mandates for the Muslim in combat. In the volume, Ibn 'Abbas relates,

> Allah's Apostle said, "There is no Hijra (i.e. migration) (from Mecca to Medina) after the Conquest (of Mecca), but Jihad and good intention remain; and if you are called (by the Muslim ruler) for fighting, go forth immediately." (4.52.42)

In complete agreement with Ibn 'Abbas, Sahl bin Sad as-Sa'idi continues:

> I saw Marwan bin al-Hakam sitting in the Mosque. So I came forward and sat by his side. He told us that Zaid bin Thabit had told him that Allah's Apostle had dictated to him the Divine Verse: "Not equal are those believers who sit [at home] and those who strive hard and fight in the Cause of Allah with their wealth and lives." (sura 4:95)

In so doing, as-Sa'idi cites the Qur'an to substantiate the teaching of combat as holy fighting.

The Kafir Cannot Be Tolerated

Certainly the Qur'an declares the expulsion or destruction of the infidel (kafir). Even a cursory reading of the Qur'an or the Hadith gives evidence of a missiological endeavor that calls for the complete eradication of the nonbeliever:

> If anyone desires a religion other than Islam, it will never be accepted of him. (sura 3:85)

Seize them and slay them wherever you find them: and in any case take no friends or helpers from their ranks. (sura 4:89)

For the Unbelievers are open enemies to you. (sura 4:101)

For the Unbelievers, Allah has prepared a humiliating punishment. (sura 4:102)

I will instill terror into the hearts of the unbelievers, smite ye above their necks and smite all their fingertips of them. It is not you who slew them; it was Allah. (sura 8:13–17)

Fight those who believe not in Allah nor the last day. (sura 9:29)

Of special interest to the hypothetical or potential Muslim who converts to Judaism or Christianity is hadith 9.57: "Mohammed said: Whoever changes his Islamic religion, kill him."

Christianity is a specific enemy of Islam, and is held out for specific scorn in the Qur'an. Our belief in a triune God, with Christ as the begotten Son of God in hypostatic nature, caused Muhammad to record a scathing critique of the core doctrines of orthodox Christianity:

O People of the Book! Commit no excesses in your religion: nor say of Allah anything but the truth. Christ Jesus the son of Mary was no more than a Messenger of Allah. . . . Do not say "Trinity": desist: it will be better for you: for Allah is One God: Glory be to Him: far exalted is He above having a son. (sura 4:171)

From those too, who call themselves Christians, We did take a covenant, but they forgot a good part of the Message that was sent to them: so We estranged them, with enmity and hatred between one and the other, to the Day of Judgment. And soon will Allah show them what they have done. (sura 5:14)

In blasphemy indeed are those that say that God is Christ the son of Mary. (sura 5:17)

They do blaspheme who say: "God is Christ the son of Mary."
They do blaspheme who say: God is one of three in a trinity:
for there is no God except one God Allah. If they do not desist
from their word of blasphemy, verily a grievous penalty will befall the blasphemers among them. . . . Christ the son of Mary
was no more than a Messenger; many were the Messengers that
passed away before him. (sura 5:72–73, 75)

Jews, too, are held in contempt as corrupters of the truth of
Allah:

O you who believe! Take not the Jews and the Christians for
your friends and protectors: they are but friends and protectors
to each other. And he among you that turns to them for friendship is of them. (sura 5:51)

It is He Who got out the Unbelievers among the People of the
Book from their homes at the first gathering of the forces. Little
did you think that they would get out: and they thought that
their fortresses would defend them from Allah! But the wrath of
Allah came to them from quarters from which they had little expected it, and cast terror into their hearts, so that they destroyed
their own dwellings by their own hands and the hands of the
Believers." (sura 59:2)[2]

The Hadith Against the Infidel

The Hadith enlarges upon the necessity for the expulsion of the
kafir from the land of the Muslim, recording Muhammad's final earthly
words: "Turn the pagans out of the Arabian Peninsula" (hadith 5.716).

Central to Islamic doctrine is also the sociopolitical emphasis
on the land. Ibn 'Abbas quotes Muhammad:

On the day of the Conquest [of Mecca] the Prophet said,
"There is no emigration after the Conquest but Jihad and intentions. When you are called [by the Muslim ruler] for fighting,
go forth immediately." (hadith 4.52.79)

Thus, the conquest of the land—here specifically Mecca—is seen as the victorious fulfillment of the cause of Islam, although jihad continues. The promise of their "holy land" in Mecca as the "sanctuary" given by Allah, is seen as the proper fulfillment of their faith system:

> Allah's Apostle also said, on the day of the conquest of Mecca, "Allah has made this town a sanctuary since the day He created the Heavens and the Earth. So, it is a sanctuary by Allah's Decree till the Day of Resurrection. (hadith 4.53.412)

As volume 4 continues in Bukhari's ahadith collection, the reader is confronted with Allah's clear intention to expel the infidels:

> When the Prophet returned [from jihad], he would say Takbir thrice and add, "We are returning, if Allah wishes, with repentance and worshipping and praising [our Lord] and prostrating ourselves before our Lord. Allah fulfilled His Promise and helped His Slave, and He Alone defeated the [infidel] clans." (hadith 4.52.317)

The alliance of Muhammed, Allah, war and victory eternally intermingles the idea of struggle with the shedding of blood. The parallel between military victory and the will of Allah is key in understanding that Islam at its core desires both physical and metaphysical victory, and the use of force is not only acceptable, but it is commendable.

The final promise of the expulsion and destruction of the infidel is seen in the final triumphant song of the Hadith:

> Narrated 'Ata bin Abi Rabah: "'Ubaid bin Umar Al-Laithi and I visited Aisha and asked her about the Hijra (i.e. migration), and she said, 'Today there is no [Hijra] emigration. A believer used to run away with his religion to Allah and His Apostle lest he should be put to trial because of his religion. Today Allah has made Islam

triumphant, and today a believer can worship his Lord wherever
he likes.'" (hadith 5.58.240; repeated in 5.59.602)

Forgiveness and Power in Jihad

The reward for jihadic endeavor has been a topic of debate.
Were the suicide pilots and hijackers indeed expecting forgiveness
of sin and a certain degree of honor in Paradise for their horrific
deeds? Both the Qur'an and the Hadith illustrate exacting and
precise protocols that were clearly enunciated by Sheikh Osama
bin-Muhammad bin-Ladin, and explicitly followed by the terrorists.
The Qur'an is clear in the policy of atoning martyrdom:

> Let those fight in the cause of Allah who sell the life of this
> world for the Hereafter. To him who fights in the cause of
> Allah,—whether he is slain or gets victory—soon shall We give
> him a reward of great value. (sura 4:74)

The Hadith is more explicit regarding both the protocols followed and the promises made to the one who dies in jihad. The
standards by which Muhammad measured jihad resonate eerily in
light of suicide attacks in the United States and elsewhere.

1. The scales are balanced:

> Narrated Abu Burda bin Abi Musa al-Ashari: Your father [i.e. Abu
> Musa] said, "No, by Allah, we took part in Jihad after Allah's
> Apostle, prayed and did plenty of good deeds, and many people
> have embraced Islam at our hands, and no doubt, we expect re-
> wards from Allah for these good deeds." On that my father [i.e.
> Umar] said, "As for myself, By Him in Whose Hand Umar's soul
> is, I wish that the deeds done by us at the time of the Prophet
> remain rewardable while whatsoever we did after the death of the
> Prophet be enough to save us from Punishment in that the good
> deeds compensate for the bad ones." (hadith 5.58.254)

2. Jihad requires a pledge of life:

Narrated Mujashi bin Masud: "I took Abu Mabad to the Prophet in order that he might give him the pledge of allegiance for migration. The Prophet said, "Migration has gone to its people, but I take the pledge from him [i.e. Abu Mabad] for Islam and Jihad." (hadith 5.59.599)

3. Jihad is required for all those within the fatwa:

Narrated Ibn 'Abbas: "The Prophet said, on the day of the Conquest of Mecca, 'There is no migration (after the Conquest), but Jihad and good intentions, and when you are called for Jihad, you should immediately respond to the call.'" (hadith 4.52.311)

4. Jihad encourages fighting to the death:

Narrated Nafi': "During the affliction of Ibn Az-Zubair, two men came to Ibn Umar and said, 'The people are lost, and you are the son of Umar, and the companion of the Prophet, so what forbids you from coming out?' He said, 'What forbids me is that Allah has prohibited the shedding of my brother's blood.' They both said, 'Didn't Allah say, "And fight then until there is no more affliction?"' He said 'We fought until there was no more affliction and the worship is for Allah (Alone while you want to fight until there is affliction and until the worship become for other than Allah.'" (hadith 6.60.40)

5. Jihad is one of the highest calls of life:

Narrated Al-Walid bin 'Aizar: "I heard Abi Amr 'Ash-Shaibani saying, 'The owner of this house,' he pointed to 'Abdullah's house, 'said, "I asked the Prophet 'Which deed is loved most by Allah?' He replied, 'To offer prayers at their early [very first] stated times.'" 'Abdullah asked, "What is the next [in goodness]?" The Prophet said, "To be good and dutiful to one's parents." 'Abdullah asked, "What is the next [in goodness]?" The Prophet said, "To participate in Jihad for Allah's Cause."

'Abdullah added, "The Prophet narrated to me these three
things, and if I had asked more, he would have told me more.""""
(hadith 8.73.1)

In contradiction to the Muslim who engages in jihad is the
slothful Muslim who does not endeavor in the "holy cause." Those
who choose not to fight in holy battle are seen as less pious, and
they will lack reward. Hadith 4.52.85, narrated by Sahl bin Sad
as-Sa'idi, warns:

> I saw Marwan bin al-Hakam sitting in the Mosque. So I came
> forward and sat by his side. He told us that Zaid bin Thabit had
> told him that Allah's Apostle had dictated to him the Divine
> Verse: "Not equal are those believers who sit [at home] and
> those who strive hard and fight in the Cause of Allah with their
> wealth and lives." (sura 4:95)

No person enlisted in holy war can be found guilty of murder:
"Muhammed said: No Muslim should be killed for killing a Kafir"
(hadith 9.50). Therefore, the notion that terrorists might be turned
over to a non-Islamic authority to be indicted on a capital offense
is beyond reason to the Muslim caliphate.

Virgins and Feasting in the Martyr's Heaven

One perk of jihad that always astounds non-Muslims is the
promise of special dispensations for the jihad martyr. It is not
enough that the martyr's sins are forgiven and the balance of his
scales weigh entirely in his favor. He also is given a special dwelling,
where he will be treated to a feast of unprecedented proportions.

Muhammad himself testified to the nature of this "added
blessing" of the martyr's Paradise. In the book *Kitab ul Isra'a wal
Mu'raj* the author, Ibn Serene, quotes Muhammad as describing
the trip he took one night from Jerusalem to the "Seven Heavens":

> Among other things he reports about the paradises prepared
> for Muslims that each of them contained a variety of fruits,

unpicked and not forbidden. Also there were rivers flowing underneath rivers of honey, milk and wine in which the believers were swimming as well as drinking. As he looked, he saw palaces made of crystal, sapphire and diamonds, the likes of which he had never seen. When he entered these palaces he saw that in each there were seventy couches made of gold and emerald on which lay virgins, untouched by man prepared for their bridegrooms. . . . When this reached the ears of his disciples and followers there were many questions asked. Among them, whether sexual intercourse was permitted in heaven. Were there female angels whom God had prepared for that purpose? When one of his followers posed the question: "Oh Messenger of God, do we have sexual intercourse in paradise?" He replied in extravagant words, indicating the intensity and total preoccupation with sexual expression. . . . Then he added: "There is no bachelor in paradise." When another asked him how one man could have the strength to (be intimate with) seventy girls in one day he responded: "He would be given the strength of one hundred men!"

The Three Prohibitions of Jihad

According to the Hadith, certain classes of people should not be involved once a holy jihad is declared: women, the disabled, and men caring for elderly parents. For women, the pilgrimage of Hajj (the fifth pillar of Islam) is considered their jihad, and thus seen as a holy struggle as well.

> Narrated 'Aisha, the mother of the faithful believers: I requested the Prophet permit me to participate in Jihad, but he said, "Your Jihad is the performance of Hajj." (hadith 4.52.127)

Also, the disabled are prohibited by Allah to fight in holy war, although their desire to do so is seen as blessed in the Hadith. Zaid said,

> Ibn-Maktum came to the Prophet while he was dictating to me that very Verse. On that Ibn Um Maktum said, "O Allah's

Apostle! If I had power, I would surely take part in Jihad." He
was a blind man. So Allah sent down revelation to His Apostle
while his thigh was on mine and it became so heavy for me
that I feared that my thigh would be broken. Then that state
of the Prophet was over after Allah revealed ". . . except those
who are disabled [by injury or are blind or lame etc.]." (hadith
4.52.85)[3]

Thus, that the physically disabled cannot involve themselves in
holy war further demonstrates the definition of jihad as a physical
struggle and not an internally spiritual one. Muhammed found
spiritual victory in physical success and so too are modern Muslims
commanded to do so whenever called upon.

Finally, the last group exempted from jihad in any form includes
those caring for parents. In hadith 4.52.248, 'Abdullah bin 'Amr
narrates, "A man came to the Prophet asking his permission to take
part in jihad. The Prophet asked him, 'Are your parents alive?' He
replied in the affirmative. The Prophet said to him, 'Then exert
yourself in their service.'"

The Promised Victory

The Hadith explicitly states that the Muslim is promised eternal
victory in the act of holy war. Victory includes both the success
of battle, the promise of eternal forgiveness, and translation to the
highest level of Paradise. Here, the authors of this book note the
most stark contrast of Islam to Western culture and life: The terrorists who died in the bombing sincerely believed that they would
be forgiven of all sin by Allah. They followed a route completely
antithetical to the Christian mind, since Muslim beliefs are antipa-
thetic to the Christian faith. Since Allah is completely removed from
his people and is in no way incarnational or personal, the terrorists
followed the route imposed upon them by the only sources they
trusted and that guaranteed them Paradise: the literal rendering of
the Hadith and Qur'an.

First, Allah promises victory in the conquest of land. In reference to the capture of Mecca, it is recorded,

'Ubaid bin Umar Al-Laithi and I visited Aisha and asked her about the Hijra (i.e. migration), and she said, "Today there is no [Hijra] emigration. A believer used to run away with his religion to Allah and His Apostle lest he should be put to trial because of his religion. Today Allah has made Islam triumphant, and today a believer can worship his Lord wherever he likes." (hadith 5.58.240; see also 4.42. This verse is repeated in 5.59.602)

Second, and most important to the Muslim, Allah promises to jihad martyrs eternal forgiveness and blessing in Paradise. For the Muslim who fears that the scales may be weighted toward his eternal damnation, jihad provides the only true eternal security. For the Muslim in fear or without hope, death in jihad is not only a viable option—it may be the only option. Twice Allah guarantees entrance into Paradise for the Muslim who dies in jihad:

Narrated Abu Huraira: Allah's Apostle said, "Allah guarantees to the person who carries out Jihad for His Cause and nothing compelled him to go out but the Jihad in His Cause, and belief in His Words, that He will either admit him into Paradise or return him with his reward or the booty he has earned to his residence from where he went out." (hadith 9.93.549)

Narrated Abu Huraira: Allah's Apostle said, "Allah guarantees [to the person who carries out Jihad in His Cause and nothing compelled him to go out but Jihad in His Cause and the belief in His Word] that He will either admit him into Paradise [martyrdom] or return him with reward or booty he has earned to his residence from where he went out." (hadith 9.93.555)

The nature of the heavenly abode is detailed explicitly in Hadith volume 9, book 93. A literal exposition demonstrates that militaristic jihad gives the greatest of rewards to the Muslim striving to serve Allah with all his heart. The devout Muslim is, therefore, compelled into militaristic service. The term "Muslim fundamentalist" is correct insofar as it refers to someone who desires to follow Allah wholeheartedly and with an honest, simple devotion to the Islamic scriptures. Muhammed is cited as saying in the chapter,

> Narrated Abu Huraira: The Prophet said, ". . . There are one-hundred degrees in Paradise which Allah has prepared for those who carry on Jihad in His Cause. The distance between every two degrees is like the distance between the sky and the Earth, so if you ask Allah for anything, ask Him for the Firdaus, for it is the last part of Paradise and the highest part of Paradise, and at its top there is the Throne of Beneficent, and from it gush forth the rivers of Paradise." (hadith 9.93.519)

It is therefore clear to even the most casual reader that jihad is more than just an intellectual exercise of struggle, but rather a struggle and warfare, with death as the hoped-for conclusion. Muhammed echoed this conclusion in hadith 4.73: "Mohammed said: Know that paradise is under the shades of the sword."

A Horrific Application of Jihad

Few illustrations of Islamic holy war are more disturbing than the letters left by the leaders of the World Trade Center/Pentagon attacks. On September 28, 2001, the *Washington Post* published excerpts of a letter found in the luggage of Muhamed Atta, who was alleged to be the leader of the suicide bombers. The excerpts as published did not include some significant doctrinal points made by the letter writer, but the complete text shows the doctrinal dimension of the mind-set. Copies of the five-page handwritten letter, released by U.S. Attorney General John Ashcroft, also were found in luggage of other members of the team.

Even if Islamic scholars and media consultants do not agree with the doctrine of jihad or would change its definition, they cannot argue that the attackers and their leaders were unequivocal about what jihad involves. Their actions were jihad, based on the fatwa reproduced at the beginning of this chapter. Although the letter's invectives are difficult to comprehend or even read, we must examine them, if only to process this dark day in American life. Following are some significant excerpts from the letter:

> Read the Chapter of Tobah from the Qur'an.
>
> Think about what God has promised the good believers and the martyrs.
>
> Remember the battle of the prophet . . . against the infidels, as he went on building the Islamic state.
>
> You should engage in such things, you should pray, you should fast. You should ask God for guidance, you should ask God for help. . . . Continue to pray throughout this night. Continue to recite the Qur'an.
>
> Purify your heart and clean it from all earthly matters. The time of fun and waste has gone. The time of judgment has arrived. Hence we need to utilize those few hours to ask God for forgiveness. You have to be convinced that those few hours that are left you in your life are very few. From there you will begin to live the happy life, the infinite paradise. Be optimistic. The prophet was always optimistic.
>
> Say your rakats and blow your breath on yourself and on your belongings.
>
> Always remember the verses that you would wish for death before you meet it if you only know what the reward after death will be.
>
> Everybody hates death, fears death. But only those, the believers who know the life after death and the reward after death, would be the ones who will be seeking death.
>
> Keep a very open mind, keep a very open heart of what you are to face. You will be entering paradise. You will be entering the happiest life, everlasting life. Keep in your mind that if you are plagued with a problem and how [you are] to get out of it. A believer is always plagued with problems. . . . You will never enter paradise if you have not had a major problem. But only those who stood fast through it are the ones who will overcome it.[4]

The letter clearly links the intentions of the attackers to jihad doctrine, illustrating the intricate set of protocols by which they operated. Their motivations, actions, and even preparation followed the prescriptions of the martyrs' edicts.[5]

Notes

1. Published in *Al-Quds al-'Arabi*, February 23, 1998. Translation and emphasis by the authors of this book.
2. "People of the Book" is a common Islamic term for Jews, especially current in Shiite circles and among aulema (scholars).
3. It is interesting that Muhammad blessed his desire to fight, even though he was excluded from the necessity to fight.
4. "Letter to the Attack Leaders," released by the United States Federal Bureau of Investigation and printed in the *Washington Post*, September 28, 2001, A18.
5. Portions of this chapter were first presented as a paper by the authors in a seminar at the annual meeting of the international Evangelical Theological Society, November 15, 2001, Colorado Springs, Colorado.

14

CLASH OF CULTURES: CHRISTIANITY THROUGH THE EYES OF THE TYPICAL MUSLIM

A Seeking Muslim's Story

"EVERYTHING CHANGED." These were familiar words after September 11, 2001. The terrorist attacks caused some people to reassess long-held worldview assumptions. Their entire perceptions of life were shaken.

In *Christianity Today* magazine, author Philip Yancey shared a letter he received from a Pakistani Muslim living in the U.S., who questioned his faith after September 11:

Considering the terrible tragedy that happened yesterday in this nation, I don't know whether this is the appropriate time to write about something personal. But perhaps because of what happened, I think I should write this letter, because I am convinced now that evil does exist in this world.

Growing up in Pakistan, I was a moderately religious Muslim. During the past few months, some of the events in

my life caused me to think about God. A friend of mine had a
brain tumor, and that caused me an immense amount of pain
and sent me searching for the answer for "Why?" I read some
books about the prophet Muhammad and the Islamic faith by
Western scholars. I was shocked to learn a lot of things about
my religion that I never knew. I felt—and still feel—betrayed and
hurt. In a closed society like Pakistan, any sort of criticism of
Islam is punishable by death, so one cannot have an unbiased
view of the faith.[1]

The words gripped Yancey in a life-altering way. He explained,
"For me, everything going on in the world took on a different slant
because of this letter." Most compelling is the final paragraph of
the letter, in which the seeking Muslim raises candid questions:

Do you think I would find loving and open-minded friends in
the church? Would it be fair to say some people would put their
guards up and won't want anything to do with someone who
belongs to some different Asian Indian race? Someone who has
a different color of skin and speaks with an accent?[2]

The modern Muslim is increasingly knowledgeable of Christianity. But the contrast between Christianity and Islam in theology
and thought pattern creates great difficulty for the inquisitive Muslim.

As cultures clash, perceptions will be sharpened on both sides.
But how do Muslims view Christianity now? We won't achieve an
accurate answer by perusing old Muslim-Christian dialogues to find
commonalties between the two faiths. Ecumenism has offered little
solace; it has ignored substantive disagreements and refused honest
engagement. Such an approach might bring a stagnant calm, but
never healing of the bitterness. True understanding can come only
as honest perceptions are confronted truthfully and answered frankly.

Approaching the Problem from History

The clash of cultures between Christianity and Islam dates back
to Muhammad. The violent disagreement that began in the Arabian

Peninsula between Christians and the prophet has never ceased. The two sides have paused only occasionally for a brief respite in their contest.

Since the Crusades, both Christians and Muslims are ever reminded of the bloody past. The Reformation Wars of the sixteenth century continued the bloodshed, as Turks from the East laid siege to much of Europe. These cultures today stand at another impasse, still largely segregated and uninformed about each other.

The clash is not just a matter of dissimilar cultures. Many Muslims and Christians do not know what they themselves believe. Consequently, their reactions are improper since their information is inaccurate. Confusion through politically correct ecumenism and relativism has prolonged ignorance.

A postmodern "seeker," one who does not believe in ultimate truth, is not truly seeking, but rather merely observing. A true seeker will find truth and hold on to it passionately, whatever the consequences.

Underlying Belief: Allah Is Your God!

Muslims interpret all religions according to the central tenet of their faith, their confession (Shahada): "There is no god but Allah, and Muhammad is his messenger." Therefore, Allah is everyone's god. No one has a choice of the god they serve. No one has the right to call anyone or anything else god, and to do so is an unforgivable sin if not repented.

Muslim scholar Ishaq Zahid unashamedly declares, "It may surprise many in the West, but it is the plain truth. Allah is the One God of everyone."[3] Although he defends his opinion by pointing out that an Arabic Bible contains the word *Allah* for Jehovah, his belief is based primarily on the Qur'an.

The following perceptions of Islam in regard to Christianity are founded upon this underlying principle: Allah and his message is unalterable; hence, it cannot be Islam that changed the doctrines of Christianity, but Christianity changed the doctrines of Islam.

Perception 1: The True Christian Gospel Has Been Changed

Muslims believe Christians are not following the historical Jesus. Jesus was a good servant of Allah whose task it was to call the Israelites back to worship the God of Abraham and Moses. Jesus, as a result, never intended anyone to worship Him or to identify Him as God.

Muslim scholars charge that Paul and his companions altered the message of Christ almost immediately following Jesus' ascension. In an attempt to win over non-Jews, Paul denounced the Hebrew Torah, revised the life of Christ, and cheapened salvation. Modern Christians are following Paul, not Christ.

The "real" life of Jesus is narrated by the Qur'an. Jesus was born without a father as Mary was a single, chaste young woman. Although the Qur'an is scant in its detail of Christ's life, it does have details not mentioned in the Bible. For example, Jesus spoke as a baby:

> Verily, God is my Lord and your Lord: Him therefore you serve: this is a Way that is straight. But the sects differ among themselves: and woe to the Unbelievers because of the [coming] Judgment of a momentous Day! (sura 19:36–37)

Muslims believe, however, that Jesus was a messenger and not a sacrifice for sin. Muslim scholars attempt to prove that the disciples were not present at the cross (a patently false claim), that Jesus never died, and that the Bible is inaccurate, corrupted by counterfeit followers of God.

Perception 2: Christians Are Divided and Weak

Muslims point out all of the divisions of Christian denominationalism, in which it does not seem that any two groups agree. On the other hand, Muslims, Islamic apologists claim, are unified under one confession (Shahada) and five pillars. All believers in Allah are required to pray similarly, give equally, and fast annually.

Christians cannot even agree upon what Bible to use. Catholics have more books in their version than have Protestants, and Protestant translations are numerous. Denominations disagree on the issues of ritual. There are broad theological differences between modernists, conservatives, neo-orthodox, and fundamentalists. Such divisions show weakness and corruption.

Perception 3: Christians Have Maligned True Islam

With Islam at the center of spiritual curiosity, many Muslims are skeptical about novice seekers or Christian inquisitors. They fear misrepresentation or undue criticism. The greatest threat, they believe, is misuse of the Qur'an to defame the Islamic religion. The prime distortion comes in the doctrine of jihad, which means not "holy war," but rather refers to an internal struggle to better oneself and the community.

Muslims believe that spreading deceit about Islam is organized and has two goals. First, in terms of argumentation, it will place upon the Muslim a violent trademark. Second, in terms of missionary activity, Christians distort the truth in order to obtain conversions, especially among those Muslims who are ignorant about Islam. The Muslim must therefore protect Islam's reputation and community, for to convert to Christianity is to commit the unforgivable sin of shirk, the equating of the divine and human natures in Jesus Christ.

Perception 4: Christians Are Blind and Unreasonable

When Muhammad was leading caravans through the Arabian Peninsula, he encountered many Christians, most of them confused and contentious people who were unable to explain their faith logically. Many Christians today are just as ignorant. Muslims believe that a Christian cannot defend the Bible, Jesus as the Son of God, or the Trinity.

Muslims say, for example, that Christians seem unaware that the twenty-seven-book New Testament is not representative of Christ's words or works. Paul, who wrote one-third of it, was a fraud who changed the course of history through his ambition and lies. Christians who hold to the four Gospels as authentic are deceived or lying.

Nor can Christians explain the hundreds of contradictions in the Bible, while the Qur'an has been preserved in its original language since its inception in the seventh century. Muslims, then, can accept only those parts of the Bible that do not conflict with the Qur'an. The injil (gospel) is to be treated with respect but also caution, since it has been contaminated by such false prophets as Peter, Paul, and John.

Christians are to be commended for believing in the virgin birth of Christ and the miracles He performed. But they commit a great sin in believing in the deity of Christ and His sacrificial death for the sins of humankind.

Muslims cringe at the thought of worshiping a mortal human being. Further, because execution on a cross is not a sign of strength but a demonstration of failure, Jesus could not have been so incompetent as to let Himself be crucified. See how Muhammad demonstrated his success as a warrior, affirming himself as a prophet.

To believe that God can partner and have a son is the ultimate irrationality; to believe that God's Son acted as a slave and servant is only somewhat less irrational. The Muslim is even less prone to believe that God will place Himself within humanity. He is utterly removed and distinct from humankind and would never sink to the level of creation.

Thus, Jesus was not the atonement for the world, but only a messenger of the straight path to Allah. Salvation, consequently, is not based on faith alone (as in Eph. 2:8–9), but on Allah's mercy melded with man's good works. How can there be a secure faith that has nothing to do with works? As one imam remarked, "That is too good to be true!"[4] To do nothing is to receive nothing, eternally or temporally. To believe otherwise is egotistical.

The Trinity is the definitive example of the unreasonableness of Christian faith. How can 1 + 1 + 1 = 1? It doesn't make sense. Belief in the Trinity—that is, the Father, Son, and Holy Spirit being three persons within one Godhead—is the supreme profanity against Allah. Jesus, Muslims avow, never believed in the doctrine, but only advocated belief in the oneness of God. They argue that the Bible itself never holds to a trinitarian formula.

Islamic debaters say that the Trinity did not become an official doctrine until the Council of Nicea in 325. For that reason, it is a man-made concept that many in the Christian faith do not even believe, for example, Unitarians and Jehovah's Witnesses.

Perception 5: The Christian Faith Overlooks Immorality

At the grassroots level, a great disgust exists among Muslims for the loose morality of "Christian" Europe and America. The rampant sexual immorality, drunkenness, drug abuse, greed, and crime illustrate the vanity of the Christian religion. Secularization and modernization, too, are looked upon with disdain.

Further, the Christian church ignores immorality and hypocrisy. What is the difference between the lives of a Christian and a non-Christian? The strictness of Islam gives the believer in Allah a high standard to hold and demands that people live up to their faith commitments. If not, punishment can be severe, since sin must be dealt with swiftly. Otherwise, the Muslim world will become like the "Christian" world.

A Christian Response

The Christian response to these five perceptions must be clear and intelligent. Faith must be both steadfast and based upon reason. The objective is not to answer every argument a Muslim may have but to demonstrate the reasonableness of Christianity while assisting Christians to defend their faith (1 Peter 3:15). This book is not, after all, a call to go to seminary; it is a call to get into the Bible.

Response to the Underlying Assumption: We Believe in a Very Different God from That of Islam

Christians and Muslims do not worship the same God, unless Muslims wish to agree that Jesus is God and Lord. The popular notion that Jews, Christians, and Muslims all worship the same God is blasphemous to all three religions and founded only in modern pluralism. Jews do not worship Jesus, nor do the Muslims. For the Christian, to not adhere to the Trinity is to not be Christian at all.

Yes, there is one God and He is in control of everything and everyone. Yes, everyone (according to the teachings of all three faiths) will stand before Him for judgment. But to say that all worship the same God because we use the same generic word is like saying that all references to the name "Mike" must refer to the same person.

Response to Perception 1: Historical Evidence Affirms Christianity

To claim a change of the gospel message perpetrated by the apostle Paul is to attack the Bible itself, a book that the Qur'an calls "the Book of God," "the Word of God," "a light and guidance to man," "a decision for all matters," "a guidance and mercy," and "the lucid Book."[5] How can such commendation be heaped upon a corrupt book? How can "the Book of *God*" be corrupt at all? And how can Almighty Allah allow this book to become corrupt? This itself would go against the very nature of Allah.

Second, this premise assumes that the New Testament is inconsistent between the Pauline letters and epistles and the four gospels. The Christian must be able to match what Paul said about Christ in Colossians 2:9 ("In Him [Jesus] dwells all the fullness of the Godhead bodily") with what the apostle John said in the fourth Gospel ("In the beginning was the Word, and the Word was with God, and the Word was God. . . . And the Word became flesh and dwelt among us" [John 1:1, 14]).

No evidence can be presented that Paul altered anything that Jesus said. On the contrary, history from extrabiblical, and many times pagan sources, affirm every detail of the Bible as authentic. Further, why would the eyewitnesses who walked with Jesus and eventually gave their lives for Him allow a Jew to change what they had seen with their own eyes and believed with their whole hearts?

Finally, biblical evidence through manuscript copies illustrates the preservation of the Bible, not the corruption.

Response to Perception 2: Christians and Muslims Are Both Divided

There is no doubt that Christianity is separated into too many denominations. Many Christians advocate removing denominational barriers, but to say that Muslims are unified is ridiculous.

Shiites, Sunnis, and Sufis separate the Muslim world into different authority structures that are every bit as divergent as the Christian divisions of Roman Catholics, Eastern Orthodox, and Protestants. The word *Shia* means "partisan" and is quite similar in meaning to the word *protestant*. Shia Muslims hold to a direct succession within the family of Ali, and they adhere to this doctrine so intensely that they have altered the supposedly non-changing confession, adding that Ali is the commander of true believers and is the friend of God.[6]

Muslims point out differences among fringe groups that are not accepted as Christian by the vast majority of believers in Jesus Christ. Comparing quasi-Christian cults with traditional Christianity is akin to associating all of Islam with the theology of the Nation of Islam. True Muslims deny any connection with Elijah Pool's syncretistic faith, yet they claim Christianity has heretical diversity. The fundamental beliefs of the Trinity, the deity of Christ, and the bodily resurrection of the Lord are nonnegotiable among orthodox Catholics, Orthodox, and Protestants alike. In this sense, Christianity retains a high degree of unity.

Response to Perception 3: Muslims Malign Christianity Far More Than Christians Malign Islam

Muslims blame Christians for maligning Muhammad and Islam, but the Muslim world has not helped its own cause. Muslim-led countries remain locked in intolerance. It is rare to hear any Muslim advocate democracy, much less religious liberty. The Christian is in far greater danger when speaking of his beliefs in a Muslim country than is a Muslim who advocates Islam in a democratic nation. Where the mosque is intertwined with the state, religious laws are as much a part of society as are civil laws.

Jihad plays out violently in many nations around the world. If the vast majority of Muslims are peaceful, why is there such an outpouring on a popular level of militant violence across the globe?

Muslims do not desire Christian missionaries in their countries, yet they are determined to spread Islam across the world. That too is jihad. They will not allow open Christian witness in Saudi

Arabia, Pakistan, and other countries, but they assume a right to
enjoy these freedoms in the West. Christians should not fight to
close any society to anyone—but they should call upon Muslims
to open their cultures to the world.

Response to Perception 4: Christian Faith Is Reasonable and Can Be Understood

One problem of Muhammad's day has not changed—Christians
frequently cannot express or defend their faith. Few Christians
can honestly and intelligently discuss the Trinity, revelation, and
the Person of Jesus Christ. Muslims also have a point that many
Christians take their faith lightly and without much regard to trans-
formation of the mind. Christianity is much like Islam in regard to
these difficulties.

Few Muslims (especially outside the Middle East) know Arabic,
the only language in which the true Qur'an can be read. Translations
are not the very words of the Qur'an and so are no more than
interpretations. Relatively few Muslims can recite the call to prayer
or understand what is being said. The situation is reminiscent of
that in the medieval Roman Church—when the Roman Church
made Latin the language of Scripture, few Christians knew it or
could read the Bible for themselves.

Christians must be able to trust their Bible, defend their faith,
and openly discuss controversial issues. True, the Trinity is a difficult
mystery to explain. Yet it is fully taught in the Bible and can be
defended by anyone with a functional understanding of what the
Bible teaches. A God in any religion who transcends our being
can be explained only within the limits of analogy. To be able to
explain God exhaustively in human conception is to have a small
conception of God.

In any debate between Christianity and another religion, the
ultimate issue revolves around the Person of Jesus Christ. If Jesus
Christ is the Son of God who came in the flesh to die for the sins of
the world, then all other arguments must fit around that fact. Aware
Muslims know that if Jesus died on the cross and conquered death
in the bodily resurrection, their faith is vain. Thinking Christians

likewise recognize that unless Jesus did those things, their own faith is empty.

It is not within the scope of this book to defend the fact of Jesus' life, death, and resurrection, but the start of that defense revolves around such certainties as these:

1. Eyewitness testimony in the four Gospels is much more credible than the legends about Jesus that Muhammad and other Muslims assembled centuries later.
2. Pagan testimony such as Tacitus's *Annals*, written in the first century, express no doubt that Christ was executed under Pontius Pilate. Thallus, a Palestinian historian writing twenty years after Jesus' death, verifies the unnatural darkness of that day.[7]
3. Jesus was seen as raised from the dead by more than five hundred people. If His death had been staged or His resurrection a fraud, plenty of witnesses were available to correct the record.

There are abundant reasons to believe, of which these are only a sample. Christians must become familiar with how to use these evidences to respond to any unbeliever.

Response to Perception 5: Western Nations Are Not Christian Nations

Muslims assume, given the mosque-state ties in Islamic nations, that contemporary Western societies represent Christian values. Every Western secular government is, however, thoroughly pagan. Many nations of Europe are among those with the highest percentages of atheists. As governments have strayed from Christian principles, immorality has increased. Europe is not Christian, and there is no society more diverse in religion than that in North America.

Muslims have a more valid criticism, too, in pointing out the hypocrisy that infects churches. This indictment carries more weight, in fact, than any other argument Muslims advance. Many churches fail to heed the admonitions of the Bible, and many so-called Christians feel no sense of shame or fear for their sin patterns.

A Christian intellectual response to Islam must reflect a personal Christian commitment, because a person who knows right and habitually does wrong persuades no one. Christians are called upon to transform their minds and their entire selves (e.g., Rom. 12:1–2). Only then will they find more opportunities for a hearing with someone who may not have knowledge of Christianity but honestly seeks the truth.

When a seeking Muslim walks into your church, will you be ready to answer difficult questions that are obstacles to faith in Jesus Christ?

Notes

1. Philip Yancey, "Letter from a Muslim Seeker," in *Christianity Today* 45, no. 15 (December 3, 2001): 80.

2. Ibid., 81.

3. Ishaq Zahid, "Allah in the Bible?" http://www.islam101.com/ religions/christianity/aibible.htm.

4. Quoted in Wendy Murray Zoba, "How Muslims See Christianity," in *Christianity Today* 44, no. 4 (April 3, 2000): 40.

5. Norman Geisler and Abdul Saleeb, *Answering Islam* (Grand Rapids: Baker, 1993), 207.

6. George Braswell, *What You Need to Know About Islam and Muslims* (Nashville: Broadman and Holman, 2000), 64.

7. For greater analysis of such poignant facts, see Geisler and Saleeb, *Answering Islam*, 271–86.

15

Jesus According to the Qur'an

"We Believe in Jesus"

"No Muslim is a true Muslim unless he believes in Jesus!" Muslims place this statement at the forefront of any discussions with Christians about the person of Jesus Christ. Muslims are quick to demonstrate charity for Jesus and His mother Mary. Jesus' name occurs twenty-five times in the Qur'an, including these texts:

> We gave Jesus the son of Mary clear (signs) and strengthened him with the holy spirit. (sura 2:87)

> And in their footsteps we sent Jesus the son of Mary, confirming the Torah that had come before him: We sent him the Gospel: therein was guidance and light. (sura 5:46)

> And Jesus and Elias [Elijah]: all in the ranks of the Righteous. (sura 6:85)

Such quotations lend credence to the Muslims' position that they honor the son of Mary. Yet if one looks past the superficial, politically correct desire for unity, the differences between Islam's and Christianity's views of Jesus are vast and fundamental. A high view of the person Jesus Christ does not necessarily mean a correct view of Jesus. Muslims take great pains to assure the public of their beliefs that He was virgin born and that He preached the truth. Christians believe that Jesus was virgin born and *was* the truth (John 14:6).

Jesus was not merely an example of righteousness, He was the sacrifice that allows mankind to obtain righteousness. He is the Savior. In the end, the differences between Muslims and Christians are proportional to the importance of the cross in salvation.

The Qur'an's Jesus vs. the Bible's Jesus

The seeker for the true historical Jesus cannot turn to the Qur'an for answers. As one author points out, "The Qur'an records no sermons, no parables, none of his gentle words to the poor and dispossessed, none of his cutting challenges to the religious establishment of the day."[1] Indeed, it seems that the Qur'an only revises what the Bible portrays of Christ.

Ask the average Muslim about his or her view of the historical Jesus and they will tell you that everyone should honor the life of the great prophet. Yet what better evidence is there of the historical Jesus than the Bible? The Muslim apologist will answer, "The Gospels are now corrupt!" How do they logically know this? For the Qur'an—in their minds the superior revelation of Allah—says so. Furthermore, how then do they know that Jesus was a righteous man in history if not through the primary source used by historians for the past two thousand years?[2]

Jesus Through the Eyes of Unbelievers

Many secular scholars discount both the Bible and the Qur'an as corrupt and errant. Giving these skeptics the benefit of the doubt, a very brief survey from outside sources can be helpful in determining the historical Jesus.

Flavius Josephus, a Jewish priest in the first century, retells the story of Jesus' trial and death:

Now there was about this time Jesus, a wise man; for he was a doer of wonderful works, a teacher of such men as receive the truth with pleasure. He drew over to him both many of the Jews and many of the Gentiles. And when Pilate, at the suggestion of the principal men amongst us, had condemned him to the cross, those that loved him at the first did not forsake him; And the tribe of Christians, so named from him, are not extinct at this day.[3]

Fellow Jews considered Josephus a traitor of the worst sort. He had sympathized with Jesus and given credibility to Christ's actions on the cross. The Sanhedrin, the highest Jewish council, which protected the religious laws of Israel, supported Josephus' facts when it explained, "As nothing was brought forward in [Jesus'] defense, he was hanged on Passover Eve."[4]

Pliny the Younger, governor of Pontus and Bithynia, provides more relevant information from the view of Christ's disciples, some of whom had direct contact with the historical Jesus. In a letter to the Roman emperor Trajan in A.D. 96, he explains his first encounter with the Christian sect and their view of the risen Savior:

They asserted, however, that the sum and substance of their fault or error had been that they were accustomed to meet on a fixed day before dawn and sing responsively a hymn to Christ as God, and to bind themselves by oath, not to some crime, but not to commit fraud, theft, or adultery, not falsify their trust, nor to refuse to return a trust when called upon to do so. When this was over, it was their custom to depart and to assemble again to partake of food—but ordinary and innocent food.[5]

Note that these Christians, only two generations removed from the historical Jesus Christ, worshiped Him as God in songs of praise. Nonetheless, Muslims assert that Jesus was not worthy of worship and praise, but only of admiration as a messenger of Allah.

Making Jesus a Seventh-Century Muslim

> When Jesus found unbelief on their part He said: "Who will be
> My helpers to [the work of] Allah?" Said the Disciples: "We are
> Allah's helpers we believe in Allah, and do you bear witness that
> we are Muslims." (sura 3:52)

According to the above sura, Jesus was ultimately only a good
Muslim. His life was spent spreading the gospel of Islam to all that
would listen. It was not His purpose to "seek *and to save*" those
who are lost (Luke 19:10, emphasis added). Instead, His mission
was limited due to His nature and Allah's will. "And it was never
the part of a messenger to bring a Sign except as Allah permitted
(or commanded)" (sura 13:38).

A Man . . . Like Adam

The problem of who Jesus is can be traced to the origin of
mankind itself. Muslims believe that Jesus had the same beginning
as Adam. The Qur'an states, "The similitude of Jesus before Allah
is as that of Adam; He created him from dust, then said to him:
'Be': And he was" (sura 3:59). Therefore, Jesus was a mere man,
and not the eternal Son of God.[6]

The comparison with Adam is important to the Muslim. The
birth of Jesus parallels that of Adam—creation without need of a
father. The greatness of Jesus was not from His character, however,
but from Allah's word "Be." He was paltry dust before Allah created Him, clay to the potter's hands.

Christmas in the Qur'an

Surprising to some, Muslims believe in the virgin birth of Christ.
The Qur'an states, "[Mary] said: 'O my Lord! How shall I have
a son when no man hath touched me?' He said: 'Even so; Allah
creates what He wills'" (sura 3:47). The virgin birth was not,
however, to be a sign of Christ's nature and power, but a sign
(*aya*) of Allah's omnipotence and sovereignty. He can and will
do as he pleases.

Similarities exist in the two accounts of the birth of Jesus Christ.

The Bible says:

And the angel said to her, "Do not be afraid, Mary, for you have found favor with God. And behold, you will conceive in your womb and bring forth a Son, and shall call His name Jesus. Rejoice, highly favored *one*, the Lord is with you; blessed are you among women!"

Then Mary said to the angel, "How can this be, since I do not know a man?" (Luke 1:28–34, authors' translation)

The Qur'an says:

Behold! The angels said: "O Mary! Allah gives thee glad tidings of a Word from Him."

His name will be Christ Jesus, the son of Mary.

Behold! The angel said: "O Mary! Allah has chosen you and purified you—chosen you above the women of all nations."

She said: "O my Lord! How shall I have a son when no man has touched me?"

But, many variances can be found between the two.
The Bible says:

And she will bring forth a Son, and you call His name Jesus, for He will save His people from their sins. (Matt. 1:21, authors' translation)

Then Joseph her husband, being a just man, and not wanting to make her a public example, was minded to put her away secretly. (Matt. 1:19, authors' translation)

An angel of the Lord appeared to him in a dream, saying, "Joseph, son of David, do not be afraid to take to you Mary your wife, for that which is conceived in her is of the Holy Spirit." (Matt. 1:20, authors' translation)

He will be great, and will be called the Son of the Highest; and the Lord God will give Him the throne of His father David . . . and of His kingdom there will be no end. (Luke 1:32–33, authors' translation)

The Qur'an says:

And Allah will teach him the Book and Wisdom, the Torah and the Gospel, and [appoint him] a messenger to the Children of Israel.

There is no mention of Joseph in the Qur'an:

We gave Jesus the son of Mary Clear (Signs) and strengthened him with the holy spirit. The Christians call Christ the Son of Allah. This is a saying from their mouth; . . . Allah's curse be on them.

Clearly the differences between the two faiths are greater than their similarities. Jesus was born of a virgin as angels spoke to the parties involved. But His mission was nothing like that supposed in the Qur'an. In Christianity, He is Savior and reigning King, Whose kingdom will not end. In Islam, He is a human messenger who will go to the dust from which He was created. Indeed, the varying portraits of Jesus' life best demonstrate the vast differences between the two largest religions in the world.

The Miracles of Jesus Christ

One Muslim scholar explains the limited view of Jesus:

All the Prophets of whom we have any detailed knowledge, except one, had wives and children. The exception is Jesus the son of Mary. But his life was incomplete; his ministry barely lasted three years; his mission was limited; and he was not called upon to deal with the many-sided problems that arise in a highly organised society or State. We pay equal respect to him, because he was Allah's Messenger; but that is not to say that his Message covers the same universal ground as that of Al-Mustafa [Muhammad].[7]

With all of the rhetoric by Muslim apologists today, this quotation, found in the commentary of the official English translation of the Holy Qur'an, speaks volumes. Jesus is merely one among many, not the final revelation. Because His mission was limited in time and message to the Israelite people, He is not to be followed universally.

Nonetheless, according to Islam, Jesus was a mighty miracle worker. He performed many supernatural acts, including making a bird out of clay, healing the blind and the lepers, and raising the dead (sura 5:110). Each of these miracles was done "by [Allah's] leave."

Jesus did not perform these acts to point to Himself and His character; rather, the miracles were a "sign from the Lord" (sura 3:49). The son of Mary, like other messengers from Allah, carried out His appointed tasks to direct people to Allah.

Christ's Message According to the Qur'an

Jesus was sent to confirm the gospel (injil), which commanded faith and obedience to Allah. According to Muslim scholars, the Qur'an has preserved what people today need to know about Christ (sura 5:47). The Islamic view of a gospel of works cannot be equated with the inadequate gospel of grace revealed in the four Gospels of the Christian New Testament. Thus, Muslims accept only a vague message given by Jesus Himself, of which only fragments survive in the New Testament and other sources.

Whenever a doctrine conflicts with the Qur'an, it must be rejected as fallacy and fable. The ministry of Jesus is never allowed to contradict the miracle of the Qur'an. Jesus merely worked to prevent false worship. The Qur'an expounds:

And behold! Allah will say: "O Jesus the son of Mary! Did you say to men, 'Take me and my mother for two gods beside Allah'?" He will say: "Glory to You! Never could I say what I had no right [to say]. Had I said such a thing, you would have indeed known it." (sura 5:116)

This statement is clearly Muhammad's reaction to Eastern Christian contemporaries who not only worshiped Christ but gave adoration to Mary. Muhammad wishes to show that Jesus would have had contempt for those who elevated Him above what Allah intended. The Qur'an credits Jesus with saying, "It is Allah who is my Lord and your Lord; Then worship Him. This is a Way that is straight" (sura 3:51).

The Nature and Names of Jesus Christ

In Islam, Jesus is not God. This is the essential difference between the Jesus of Islam and the Jesus of Christianity. The Qur'an argues, "Christ the son of Mary was no more than a Messenger; many were the Messengers that passed away before him" (sura 5:75).

Allah, transcendently separated from creation, cannot have a Son. The Qur'an explains that Allah is far "from having partners they associate [with him]" (sura 9:31). The ramifications of such a doctrine as the sonship of Christ would extinguish Allah's light (sura 5:32). Moreover, the Muslim who links the nature of Allah with the nature of man has committed the ultimate sin (shirk).

Therefore, Jesus is primarily distinguished as "Ibn Maryam" (Son of Mary), a title given twenty-three times in Islamic scriptures to stress His humanity and mortality (see sura 34:45). (The term *Son of Mary* is only mentioned in Mark 6:3 in the Bible.) Second, Jesus is called "Al Masih" (Messiah), designating Him as an "anointed one," but nothing more. *Messiah* was a personal name for One who had a precise mission.

The third most mentioned title of Jesus in the Qur'an is "Rasul" (Apostle or Messenger). As simply the mouthpiece of God, but not in any way connected to the nature of God, Jesus was sent specifically to the Jews, as many others were appointed to go to other people groups. As a messenger, Jesus was a "prophet" since Allah gave revelation through Him: "He has given me Revelation and made me a prophet" (sura 19:30).

In the Bible, no one is found equal with Jesus Christ besides the Creator God Himself, with whom Jesus is identified (John 1:1; Col. 2:9; Heb. 1:5). In the Qur'an, Jesus is likened to a set of human predecessors:

- Adam: The Chosen of God
- Noah: The Preacher of God
- Abraham: The Friend of God
- Jesus: The Word of God
- Muhammad: The Apostle of God

Christ Himself is purported to say, "I am indeed a servant of Allah." Whereas Jesus is seen both as Servant and Savior in the Bible, Jesus is just a servant in Islamic scriptures.

Christ's Death and Ascension

That they said [in boast], "We killed Christ Jesus the son of Mary, the Messenger of Allah"; but they killed him not, nor crucified him. Only a likeness of that was shown to them. And those who differ therein are full of doubts, with no [certain] knowledge. But only conjecture to follow, for a surety they killed him not:—Nay, Allah raised him up unto Himself; and Allah is Exalted in Power, Wise;—And there is none of the People of the Book but must believe in Him before his death; and on the Day of Judgment he will be a witness against them. (sura 4:157–59)

One thing is absolutely certain to Islam—Jesus did not die on the cross. Although they cannot confidently say what did happen, Muslims boldly state what did not happen. Muslim scholars attempt to disprove the Gospels by asserting that His followers were not present at the crucifixion. This is blatantly false, as the apostle John, Mary the mother of Jesus, and other followers clearly were there.

Muslim traditions offer numerous explanations for what happened on the day of the crucifixion. The three most popular follow:

- Jesus hid while one of His companions died in His place.
- God made Judas Iscariot to appear like Jesus and to take His place.
- Simon of Cyrene replaced Jesus before the crucifixion.

Perhaps the oddest story holds that Satan, who attempted to stop the message of Allah from being transmitted, was himself placed on the cross as punishment for his disobedience.

Jesus Is Coming Back

The Qur'an claims that Jesus was born peacefully and will die peacefully. Jesus is credited with saying, "So Peace is on me the day I was born, the day that I die, and the day that I shall be raised up to life (again)" (sura 19:33).

The generally accepted Muslim view affirms that Jesus did not die, but that Allah raised (rafa'u) Him to himself. The Qur'an explains that "People of the Book . . . must believe in Him before his death" (sura 4:159).

According to Islam, since Jesus, a human just like Adam, has not died, His ministry cannot be complete. Tradition explains that He will appear to all just before the final judgment. He then will battle the Antichrist, defeat him, confess Islam, kill all pigs, break all crosses, and establish a thousand years of righteousness. Some expand on this notion and explain that Jesus will subsequently die and be buried beside the prophet Muhammad.[8]

Notes

1. Andy Bannister, "The Quest for the Lost Jesus," http://www.answering-islam.org/Andy/quest1.html.
2. It must be noted that skeptical scholars are prone to use sources not considered trustworthy, such as the Gospel of Thomas. Further, pagan historians have affirmed the crucifixion of Jesus Christ.
3. This quote from Josephus, *Antiquities* 18:63 (written in A.D. 93–94)

is the longest non-Christian reference to Jesus from the first century. It is also repeated in Eusebius's *Ecclesiastical History* (1.11), written some two hundred years later, circa A.D. 300. Some elements of the original quote are probably later interpolations. The authors have removed all elements from Josephus's statement that are considered suspect by scholars in order to demonstrate its authenticity. For further discussion of this important historical reference, see two works by Paul L. Maier that present scholarly support for the authenticity of the statement: *Josephus: The Essential Works* (Grand Rapids: Kregel, 1994) and *Eusebius: The Church History* (Grand Rapids: Kregel, 1999).

4. Babylonian Talmud, *Sanhedrin* 43a.

5. Pliny the Younger, *Letters* 10:96–97.

6. This is inconsistent with Christ's statement in John 8:58, "Before Abraham was, I AM." This verse not only recognizes the preexistence of Jesus before His birth, but affirms His deity as Yahweh (God) Himself is called "I AM" in Exodus 3:14.

7. Mushaf Al-Madinah An-Nabawiyah, ed., *The Holy Qur'an* (Saudi Arabia: King Fahd Printing Complex, 1956), 686.

8. George Braswell, *What You Need To Know About Islam and Muslims* (Nashville: Broadman and Holman, 2000), 120.

16

INSIDE THE MUSLIM: EARNING A HEARING AND WINNING A SOUL

Well-Intentioned and Offensive

A GUY QUOTES Scripture at the top of his lungs in the stands of a basketball game. At a dinner party a man casually tells his wealthy host that he is going to hell, loudly enough that every person at the party hears it. A Christian visits a Jewish household and brings a baked ham for a meal. An urban missionary inadvertently wears warring gang colors to a prison.

We've all heard of these tales wherein a Christian, motivated to share the gospel with a certain people group or culture, negates his or her witness by somehow offending the culture, heritage, or practices of that group. Although the person is well-intentioned, he or she ruins the opportunity by some oversight or misstatement and must begin again by apologizing and rebuilding trust.

To witness to some of the 1.2 billion Muslims on the earth, the Western Christian has many cultural hurdles and potholes to maneuver. The mission field is littered with the carcasses of failed missionary endeavors. Most Christians who have a passion for the Great Commission sincerely desire to reach their Muslim friends, neighbors, and colleagues. At speaking engagements to which the authors of this book are called, we are often approached with this question: "I have friends/neighbors/relatives who are Muslim. How do I begin to share my faith in Jesus Christ with them?"

It is this seminal question that this book hopes to answer. Reaching a lost world is difficult enough, even without making relational offenses (cultural mistakes and personal missteps), and creating misunderstandings in revelation (theological foundation). Some simple prescriptions can help Christians avoid errors and more effectively witness to Muslims.

Relational Land Mines

In a westernized and friendly culture, Christians often commit sins of "familiarity" and oversight, which greatly hamper their efforts of evangelism. The issue of respect looms large in the Islamic culture. To insult Muslims or cause them to lose face before their families will irrevocably hinder further relationship. Cultural sensitivity can allow Christians to earn a hearing from their Muslim friends rather than lose the chance for open communication. All of the following principles are of utmost importance.

Greeting and Approach

In most cultural contexts, and certainly in non-Western areas, one never greets a Muslim by shaking his left hand. The left hand is used for personal hygiene; it is offensive to offer the left hand in greeting.

Calling a Muslim "Brother"

Intelligent Muslims understand the gaping differences between Christianity and Islam. We once heard an evangelist refer to a Muslim he was debating as "my brother." The Muslim, an imam, bristled at this statement and corrected the evangelist immediately. Offense at the term *brother* is more than just a cultural issue, it is a theological one, for brotherhood assumes theological agreement in Muslim (and to some extent in Christian) circles. One may call a Muslim "my friend," which is a positive social statement that does not assume agreement of philosophy or belief.

Accepting Hospitality

Muslims who are not consumed by jihadic warfare freely extend hospitality. To decline such invitations is a personal affront. If offered a meal in the home of a Muslim, the Christian must follow the practices in the home. Family members often remove their shoes immediately upon entering the home, and the Christian guests should follow suit. Eat everything set before you, even if you do not know the nature of the food or its source. Middle Eastern food is delicious and will not harm you. Thanking the Muslim and complimenting on the food will be a great help in eventual witness.

Extending Hospitality

An effective method to build bridges to the Muslim is the offer of hospitality. Certain protocols, however, must be observed. No wine or other alcoholic beverage should be offered at a meal when serving a Muslim. Also, be sure to follow the dietary rules of Islam in preparing the meal—no pork or lard-based cooking, and no shellfish. Explain to your guests that you offer thanks before the meal, and ask them if you may do so. If they are amenable, do not use the prayer as a sermonic event or a deceptive form of evangelism! Simply thank God by using the term *Lord*, and make it short. We the authors are certainly not ashamed of the gospel of Christ, but presenting it during grace abuses the privilege of prayer. Explain the essence of each course, to allay their fears concerning the preparation and to show them that you have taken great pains to respect their culture and beliefs.

Speaking with the Opposite Sex

Most Islamic cultures strongly forbid casual conversation with a member of the opposite sex. To cross this boundary may be viewed as insulting in a Muslim family. For a woman to speak forcefully to a man shows disrespect, and a Christian man who speaks to a Muslim woman without her husband present insults the husband. American Islam tends to be less restrictive, but Christians should observe conversation protocols until they discern that it is safe to do otherwise.

Interruption of Religious Service

If invited to a mosque, a Christian can make great strides in friendship by attending a service. The Christian is not a participant in this worship, so it is not appropriate to "fit in" by assuming the stance and practice of the Muslim. Standing to the side quietly, and asking questions of your host is seen as gracious. Standing on the prayer rug and asking questions loudly during prayer is not.

Sensitivity toward worship practices extends to other arenas. Do not insult the Muslim by insisting on dining out for lunch during the Ramadan fast. On the other hand, do not question the Muslim's motives or depth of faith if you see them eating during the month.

Rushing to Evangelize

Given the historic hostility between Christians and Muslims, one must build bridges and friendships before presenting the gospel. God promises to open doors for witness, if we are faithful to discern what is appropriate in time and place. In Christianity, there is always a right thing to do, a right way to do it, and a right time to do it.

In their eagerness to win Muslims to Jesus Christ, Christians sometimes rush to a gospel presentation within minutes of introduction. And confrontational evangelism may, indeed, be an appropriate and effective means of witness at some point. The authors of this book have been trained in virtually every witnessing method, and we are rarely without a gospel tract. In the Islamic community, however, the Christian must earn the right to be heard. Muslims are immersed in a heritage of enmity against Christians, and care must be taken to establish a connection across the divide. This slow process of building relationship explains why Muslims do not come to Christ as frequently as do those from other faith systems.

Earning a hearing takes time and discernment. The Muslim who develops a friendship with a Christian moves through levels of suspicion to trust. Even trust may not mean openness. That may not occur until the friends have reason to comfort one another over an experience of grief or loss. The sharing of honest comfort and aid may then flow naturally into sharing the reasons that a Christian possesses confidence in the midst of tragedy.

A vast difference exists between using opportunities that God provides to share our faith in Jesus Christ, and forcing a door of opportunity. Particularly in witnessing to a Muslim, one must use discernment in knowing how and when to share one's faith, seasoned with grace. Confrontational evangelism has historically been somewhat effective in time-constrained, high-tech Western culture. But it is ineffective in communicating with a Muslim.

Avoid Political Arguments

Muslims may view a presentation of the gospel as a defense of Israel or a political insult. Whatever one's view toward Israel and the Middle East situation, taking a divergent conversation path into politics pulls the conversation path away from the main issue of Jesus Christ as Savior.

Patriotism vs. Evangelism

Worldwide, Muslims do not distinguish between Christianity and America. Any Westerner who comes into a store where a Muslim is working and spits on him or calls him a name is a "Christian." It does not matter if the bigot has never stepped into a church; in the Muslim's mind, a Christian did this. Therefore, Christians of any nationality must be careful not to confuse Christ with pride of country. The authors are happy to be American citizens, but citizenship saves no one's soul. Defending Christ does not mean defending a national foreign policy.

Be Candid About the Sins of Supposed Christians

Every intelligent Muslim remembers that Pope Urban II called the first crusade into being at the Council of Clermont in 1095. This event remains a dark chapter in history, when ostensible leaders of faith declared a "Christian jihad." No difference exists between Urban's promised forgiveness of Crusaders who died in battle and the same promises made to fighters in Islamic jihad. Do not defend this horrible era or the Muslim will see just another hypocritical Christian.

Remember What Conversion May Mean

In America, a conversion to Christ seldom destroys the new believer's family relationships. Elsewhere, conversion often means rejection by family, expulsion from country, and in some cases facing a possible death sentence. Even while remaining gently firm about the Muslim's need for Christ, Christians must understand a Muslim's hesitation to convert because of the implications. In Islamic culture, the complete rejection of a Christian alters that person's entire life, affecting heritage, inheritance, family connections, and friendship. Christians in Islamic countries may face torture and imprisonment or be destitute without home, job, and land.

The Clear Message

Some people seem unable to communicate faith in Jesus Christ without using theological "church talk." Such terms as *born again*, *atonement*, *saved*, and *lost* become a Christian's natural language. For the Muslim, such words constitute a foreign vocabulary. One minister preached a "crusade" on a mission field, a bad use of promotional terminology in a Muslim country. This preacher repeatedly spoke of "accepting Jesus in your heart." When he asked why so few people had accepted the invitation, he learned that many of his listeners assumed the invitation was to agree to surgery—to place Jesus in the ventricle chamber. Speak in clear terms, without using language that assumes previous knowledge.

The Clear Message: Grace

For most converts from Islam, the finished and atoning work of Jesus Christ on the cross speaks powerfully. They have learned that freedom in Christ means liberation from works and the fear of the scales. Emphasize the forgiveness of Christ of all sin, and the payment of the debt owed. Grace, in all of its elements, is a magnificent doctrine.

The Clear Message: God's Love

Islam does not know an intimate, personal, and loving God. Allah is an impersonal creator and judge. The only term of "intimacy" in the Qur'an refers to a threat of judgment: Allah is as "close as your jugular vein" (sura 50:16). The omnibenevolence of Christ on the cross and His transcendent love overwhelms the Muslim mind.

Revelation: The Crux of All Theological Arguments

A religion is only as stable as the foundation on which it stands. The authenticity of Islam rises and falls on the substantial claim of Muhammad that the Bible is corrupt and the Qur'an is the perfect word of Allah. Denials of the Trinity, the deity of Christ, the crucifixion, the resurrection, and salvation by God's mercy rise or fall on that claim.

Christians in contact with Muslims or any other unbelievers must be prepared to defend Scripture and its sure testimony that Jesus Christ, God incarnate, came to earth to die for the sins of the world so that man may be forgiven of his sins and be reconciled to God. On what basis can anyone claim that God has intervened in history as Christ? The ultimate source is the Bible.

Experience can feel real and yet be wrong. Revelation given by the Creator and Sustainer of the universe provides information that, although questioned, can never be invalidated.

Which Book to Trust?

Islam and Christianity alike claim to hold the inerrant, infallible Word of God. Yet according to Aristotle's law of non-contradiction (e.g., the Word of God cannot *not* be the Word of God) and law of the excluded middle (something is or is not a particular thing) only three conclusions can be reached after carefully viewing the evidence:

- The Qur'an is the Word of God.
- The Bible is the Word of God.
- Neither is the Word of God.

The Qur'an and the Bible cannot both be the Word of God, because God does not teach different and contradictory things at different points in history. The texts are antithetical to each other in essential statements. The tolerant postmodernist asserts that both books are divine because both contain *some* truth. Unless God lies, changes His mind, or make mistakes—in which cases He is less than God—it cannot be that both books are divine. If God is less than God, then discussions of salvation, redemption, heaven, and hell are moot, because no god has spoken concretely.

Introducing Presuppositions

When privileged to speak to a Muslim about faith, the Christian must be prepared to demonstrate that the Bible gives evidence within itself that it is completely trustworthy. Three passages of Scripture present this evidence, and Christians would do well to memorize them:

Jesus himself in His day believed the very words of the Old Testament were inspired by God and could not be corrupted (Matt. 5:17-18).

The apostle Paul believed that the words of the Bible were breathed out of the mouth of God (2 Tim. 3:16).

The apostle Peter believed that the person of the Holy Spirit communicated to the writers of the Bible exactly how it was to be transmitted (2 Peter 1:20-21).

In themselves, these verses will not convince the Muslim of the veracity of the Bible, but they will provide a foundation for discussion. Otherwise, the Christian will be proven ignorant of the Bible's own claims and not worthy of further conversation.

Christians need to defend their faith wisely and biblically (see 1 Peter 3:15). Whether this exercise is at all convincing to the Muslim, it protects the heart of the Christian believer. Those who convert to Islam most often are ignorant of the Christian faith with which they had identified. The Bible is either absolute or it is obsolete. It either insulates the believer against heresy or it isolates people from the will of God.

The Bible from a Muslim Perspective

Christians often read only material by writers who share their beliefs. Much valuable information, however, lies within the English interpretations of the Qur'an. The Qur'an includes many verses that favorably evaluate the Bible. According to the Qur'an, for example, Christians have the knowledge of truth in their Bible:

> You People of the Book! Why reject you the Signs of Allah, of which you are [yourselves] witnesses? You People of the Book! Why do you clothe truth with falsehood, and conceal the Truth, while you have knowledge? (sura 3:70-71)

Muhammad believed that the text of the Bible contained truth but that Christian interpretation had contaminated Bible interpretation:

> There is among them a section who distort The Book with their tongues; [As they read] so that you would think it is a part of the Book, but it is no part of the Book; and they say, "That is from Allah," but it is not from Allah: it is they who tell a lie against Allah, and [well] they know it. (sura 3:78)

Muhammad placed authority on the Scripture, and blamed false teaching on ignorant Jews who did not read the Old Testament.

> And there are among them illiterates, who know not the Book, but [see therein their own] desires, and they do nothing but conjecture. (sura 2:78)

Thus, the Muslim who "honors" the Gospels or the "people of the Book" faces a contradiction: How can the Muslim honor those who have corrupted the very words of God? Is not one who has corrupted the written Word of God the greatest of infidels? The Muslim cannot have it both ways. Either Christians are "people of the Book" who should follow the Bible as it has been passed down for two millennia, or they are "people of the Book" responsible for demolishing the revelation of God, the greatest supernatural catastrophe in world history.

Muhammad and the Purity of the Bible

The most disturbing verse of the Qur'an for the Muslim is sura 10:94, a verse that should be embedded in the mind of every Christian who desires to share his or her faith with the average Muslim. The verse states

> If you were in doubt as to what We have revealed unto you, then ask those who have been reading the Book from before you: the Truth has indeed come to you from your Lord: so be in no wise of those in doubt.

Here Muhammad places the veracity of his words on par with the authenticity of the Bible as it was available in the seventh century. First, if the Bible of the seventh century is the Bible of today, any contention that the Bible is corrupt opposes the words of Muhammad, who represented the final revelation of Allah to the world. Surely Muhammad would not have asked his followers to accept a corrupted version of the New Testament. Second, the New Testament of Muhammad's day is substantially the same as today's Bible and is based on manuscripts that go back centuries before Muhammad.

By the logic of sura 10:94, then, Muslims should accept biblical authenticity and the authenticity of today's Bible.[1]

By knowing the doctrine of revelation, a Christian can challenge the Muslim, using the words of the Qur'an, and then have a basis for discussing a more obscure doctrine, such as the Trinity. Having some familiarity with the Qur'an also is one of the best ways to get a hearing with a Muslim. Most Muslims believe (with good reason) that Christians have never opened, much less read, the Qur'an. The Christian who truly cares about the soul of the Muslim will engage in the mind-set of the Muslim.

Intellectual Honesty and Non-Contradiction

The Law of Non-Contradiction is a simple concept. It states

that something cannot be what it is not. For example, a rose cannot *not* be a rose, or else it would be a self-contradiction. This precept was formulated by the Greek philosopher Aristotle (384–322 B.C.), who tutored world conqueror Alexander the Great, and is highly respected by both Muslims and Christians as one of the greatest minds to ever have existed. Aristotle's works were placed in lofty esteem in Baghdad's unmatched library at the height of its cultural domination in Muslim history.

In religious terms, the law of logic means that the Word of God cannot *not* be the Word of God. Therefore, the Christian can use the Qur'an to demonstrate the validity of the Bible. The Qur'an states that the Bible is the Word of God:

> Can you [O you men of Faith] entertain the hope that they will believe in you?—seeing that a party of them heard the Word of Allah, and perverted it knowingly after they understood it. (sura 2:75)

According to the Qur'an, the Bible cannot not be the Word of God.

> We have, without doubt, sent down the Message; and We will assuredly guard it [from corruption]. (sura 15:9)

The Bible, if the Word of God, cannot have been changed. If it were changed, then it was never the Word of God, something that is anathema in Islamic doctrine. How can the Word of God be corrupted by man? Is man greater than his Creator? Did the Creator allow the corruption for some mystical reason?

The End of Biblical and Religious Illiteracy

For years the average Christian has ignored, neglected, and abstained from the reading and observance of the Bible. New conversations with Muslims may have a positive effect on Christianity and its adherents. In the faithful Muslim who lives and works nearby, the nominal Christian is confronted with a rival who knows his or her holy book and obeys its principles. True, many Muslims merely, like sheep, follow their messenger, but more take their faith and practice seriously.

Being challenged by intelligent people who care about faith in God should awaken Christians from their biblical and theological slumber. Perhaps they will be inspired to open their own Bibles and read what Scripture actually says, instead of relying upon preachers to spoon-feed bits of proof text to them.

If Christians do not stir their souls and search after the truth— the gospel of the resurrected Savior Jesus Christ—then Muslims have every right to point out the vast wasteland that once was religious wisdom. Yet if Christians are concerned with the soul and mind of the Muslim, they will receive of the Muslim a hearing proportional to the Christians' passion. Truth is immortal!

Notes

1. Norman Geisler and Abdul Saleeb, *Answering Islam* (Grand Rapids: Baker, 1993), 212.

17

THAT CAMEL JUST WON'T HUNT: COLLATERAL DAMAGE IN THE CULTURE WARS OVER ISLAM

WHEN *UNVEILING ISLAM* was first published, we simply rejoiced at having our first book in print. As two professors, we had labored for years to get anyone to even care about Islam, much less publish a work explaining Islam to Christians. We would have been happy for a few thousand copies to sell.

Fast-forward a number of years, a few hundred thousand copies, and many opportunities to speak to the larger Christian community. After a few hundred interviews, we began to appear on national radio and television. In the aftermath of September 11, hundreds of books were published on Islam. What made ours any different?

Nothing, except that neither of us would ever take the politically expedient route. We avoided the two extremes of most major works published in our generation. Many authors sounded portentous alarms of global conspiracies, in which world leaders were in secret negotiations to hand over the Western World to Islam. Just as we did not desire to be unnecessarily provocative, neither did we want to allow the Muslim apologists to slide by with easy answers or diversions. Since we were raised as devout Muslims, we were happy to debate them. We refused to accept the "Islam has been hijacked" apologetic, even though it was constantly being pushed on television. We knew historically that this is the face of devout Islam. We knew the Qur'an.

Still, in the years that have followed September 11, 2001, much of the landscape in culture has changed. The initial shock of the bombings on America's shores has given way to the conspiracy theories of left-wing bloggers. America's common resolve has been replaced by splintered political voices. In truth, this is not a surprising development, given the short attention span of our culture. However a few developments have surprised us. We believe it is necessary to revisit a number of these issues for the sake of clarification.

The Response of Surrender by Cultural Elites

In the wake of the clash of the Western and Islamic worlds, a rising tide of capitulation has become strangely popular. In February of 2008, Archbishop of Canterbury Rowan Williams suggested that Britain accept parts of sharia law into practice. Lecturing at the Royal Courts of Law, he put forward his desire to integrate Muslim regulations into the British judicial system.

Though a firestorm ensued, his approach illustrates a central premise: Islam is growing at such a rapid rate that we must be willing to negotiate. Eventually, the argument goes, they will outnumber us. One way to prepare for that eventuality is to concede.

In a classic overcorrection, another parallel tack is to blame the victim, rather than the perpetrator. In October 2003, the pastor of the Trinity United Church of Christ, Rev. Jeremiah Wright, was quoted in the *Trumpet*, his church's own newsletter:

> In the 21st century, white America got a wake-up call after 9/11/01. White America and the Western world came to realize that people of color had not gone away, faded into the woodwork or just "disappeared" as the Great White West kept on its merry way of ignoring Black concerns.

We call this mind-set "Hatriotism."

Similarly, some of the cultural elite sympathize with Islam. Even in the face of the brutality of female circumcision, the death penalty for conversion, and the murder of those who dare to question Muhammad, otherwise reasonable journalists will posit that Islam seeks purity in an impure world, even though the means are questionable.

This is strange in light of the forthrightness of many Muslim leaders. In March of 2006, one of Norway's leading Islamic scholars, Mullah Krekar, granted an interview to *Dagbladet*. After a furor arose over cartoons depicting Islam in a negative light, around the world Muslims rioted. Buildings were burnt, stores were razed, and many died. Instead of lamenting the violence, Krekar said, "Our way of thinking . . . will prove more powerful than yours."[1] Remarkably, he further stated that Osama bin Laden was misunderstood. "'Osama bin Laden is a good person,' Krekar said. He claimed Osama bin Laden is considered a terrorist simply because he lacks his own state."[2]

One of the fundamental conflicts between Islam and the rest of the world is the key point of religious liberty. Even though the authors are passionate Christians, we do not believe faith in Jesus Christ can be coerced. This is intellectually impossible. In December 1948, the United Nations General Assembly adopted resolution 217, entitled the "Universal Declaration of Human Rights." Article Eighteen of the resolution reads:

> Everyone has the right to freedom of thought, conscience and religion; this right includes freedom to change his religion or belief, and freedom, either alone or in community with others and in public or private, to manifest his religion or belief in teaching, practice, worship and observance.[3]

The solution to the societal clash is not capitulation but rather freedom. Since Jesus never forced anyone to believe, Christians can heartily endorse this clarion call. Muslims as well can use the earlier suras of the Qur'an, such as Al-Baqara 2:256, "There shall be no coercion in matters of faith."

The Response of Syncretism by Christian Leaders

Upon the first publication of this book, certainly we expected backlash from the Muslim community. After all, we were coming forth publicly as "apostates" of Islam, two men who had converted to faith in Jesus Christ. Furthermore we had the audacity to publish under our own names, rather than using pseudonyms as others had done. In the ensuing days, as this book gained notoriety, the response from the Muslim community was angry, if not belligerent. Since most Muslim immigrants had lived in countries where such books are illegal, they responded with fury over our words.

We lived with the risk of being interrupted and threatened. In churches around the country, Muslims stood in the middle of our sermons and began to shout. They came forward during invitations to argue. They attempted to shout us down. This continues to this day. Recently I (Ergun) was speaking in a church when a local imam came forward to demand that he be given equal time. The pastor explained to him that he would be happy to allow the imam to speak in his church on a Sunday, provided that he be allowed to preach in the mosque the Friday prior.

Obviously this never happened.

However, our greatest consternation has been not with those outside the faith, but with some evangelical leaders who have accepted a subtle heresy that has the potential of doing immense harm to the gospel witness. Though the movement comes under many names, it is all based on a central premise: Allah is just the Arabic term for God, and is therefore synonymous with the God of the Bible.

Let us be as emphatically clear as possible: Allah is *not* the God of the Bible.

The Wandering Camel

Recently, a revised edition of a book entitled *The Camel: How Muslims Are Coming to Faith in Christ!* was published by evangelical missionary Kevin Greeson. Serving in an Islamic context, he discovered an ancient Muslim proverb that states there are one hundred names for Allah. Ninety-nine were recorded by Muhammad in the

Qur'an, and the final one was whispered to his camel. According to this method, the one-hundredth name of Allah is *Isa al-Masih*, Jesus the Christ.

Within the work, Greeson asserts that the Qur'an can illustrate that Jesus "was much more than a prophet."[4] Ironically, the Qur'anic passage Greeson attempts to use (sura 3:42–55) is strikingly similar to an ancient heresy known as Arianism, a fourth-century deception promulgated by a North African Bishop, Arius, who argued that Jesus was not God but was a created being. Sura 3:47 states, "She said: 'O my Lord! How shall I have a son when no man hath touched me?' He said: 'Even so: God creates what He wills: When He has decreed a plan, He but says to it, "Be," and it is!'" Hence, Greeson actually attempts to use a passage that explicitly denies Jesus' deity to prove that He is more than a prophet. He actually argues that we should use a passage that asserts one of the most notorious heresies in the history of the Church—rejecting the essential character of Christ—to witness to Muslims!

Not only do we find this teaching abhorrent, but we continue to be amazed at the acceptance this method has found among otherwise orthodox Christian scholars. The premise is that Muhammad was seeking the true God of the Universe, and Allah is close. The practitioners of the method say they are using the Qur'an as a bridge to the gospel, and that subsequent followers leave Islam, even though their practices may still mimic some Islamic practices.

Furthermore, missionaries using this model of missions have even taken to recognizing and celebrating Ramadan, praying in the Islamic way, and otherwise identifying themselves in Islamic categories. Greeson himself admits that converts from the CAMEL method call their pastors imams, worship on Fridays, identify themselves as "Jesus Muslims," and perform ablution before prayers.[5] Words cannot express how repugnant this is to those of us who came out of Islam into faith in the only true and living God.[6]

Imagine the methodology applied to other forms of witnessing:

- Would you be *baptized for the dead* in a Mormon Temple ceremony, all the while secretly believing that Jesus is not the twice-sired, half-brother of Lucifer, as Mormonism teaches?

• Would you add a statue of Jesus to a Hindu's home altar, next to Ganesh or Vishnu, in an attempt to show that Jesus is God among the Hindu's 330 million gods?

While the desire to reach Muslims is admirable, the method is fatally flawed. The belief that Muhammad was partially correct, or on the right track, is beyond the scope of logical and biblical consistency. In comparing the biblical proclamation of the triune God to the Qur'an, one must come to three simple conclusions with which no one can argue:

1. Islam denies the intimacy of God the Father in the Trinity.

   Sura Al-Ma'idah 5:73: "Indeed, the truth deny they who say, 'Behold, God is the third of a Trinity'—seeing that there is no deity whatever save the One God. And unless they desist from this their assertion, grievous suffering is bound to befall such of them as are bent on denying the truth."

2. Islam denies the divinity of God the Son.

   Sura Nisa 4:171: "O People of the Book! Commit no excesses in your religion: nor say of Allah anything but the truth. Christ Jesus the son of Mary was no more than a Messenger of Allah. . . . Do not say "Trinity": desist: it will be better for you: for Allah is One God: Glory be to Him: far exalted is He above having a son." (sura 4:171)

3. Islam denies the person of God the Holy Spirit.

   Sura Nahi 16:102: "The Holy Spirit has brought it [the Qur'an] down from your Lord, truthfully, to assure those who believe, and to provide a beacon and good news for the submitters."

> Sura Shu'ara 26:193: "The Honest Spirit [Gabriel] came
> down with it."

In short, Islam completely repudiates how God chose to reveal Himself. And, in so doing, any other similarity of divine attributes suffers a fatal blow and diverges in meaning from the Bible's revelation of God's nature.

This was the fundamental concept of Islam—that the teaching of the Trinity was a manufactured doctrine from the Apostles. On all three Persons of the Trinity, the Qur'an explicitly denies Trinitarian teaching. In fact, Muhammad adamantly argued in Sura Mu'minun that three gods are logically impossible:

> Sura 23:91: "Never did Allah take to Himself a son, and never
> was there with him any other god—in that case would each god
> have certainly taken away what he created, and some of them
> would certainly have overpowered others; glory be to Allah
> above what they describe!"

It Is the Nature of God, Not His Name

The uproar caused by this methodology brought out the defenders of the method, saying that the use of "Allah" is an issue of language and linguistics. *Allah*, they would argue, has the same origins (etymology) as the Hebrew *Elohim* and the Aramaic *Alaaha*. However, simple logic requires that proper communication not only demand the same vocabulary (words) but also the same dictionary (to define those words).

When a Muslim speaks of Allah, he is speaking specifically of the Islamic god as detailed in the Qur'an. He does not believe that the Triune God of the Bible is also revealed in the Qur'an. Muhammad believed that Christianity was a false religion, long gone astray. Muhammad does not allow any Christians into Paradise, unless they leave the alleged false teaching of the Christian God.

Unfortunately, these well-intentioned Christian missionaries miss the issue entirely. This is not about the use of the word but rather the inherent deception of the use of the word. There is a lack of integrity in pretending to be the same when in fact Muhammad's entire religion is based on the rejection of the Christian concept of God. This is not just about God's name, but about the nature of God. As Dr. Malcolm Yarnell aptly noted,

> Deceptive tactics and strategies do not reflect well on the Christian God of truth and integrity. Biblical fidelity cannot be sacrificed on the altar of pragmatism (2 Cor 4:2).[7]

The Response of Service by Christians

If the first two reactions to the Christian-Islam impasse have been negative, this final one is inspiring. Thousands of Christians have become friends and compatriots in reaching Muslim people.

When *Unveiling Islam* first came out, we were a bit worried about our coming out of the closet as former Muslims. Certainly we had never been quiet about our past, but we both wanted to become professors based on our scholarship, rather than the novelty of our heritage. Also, we were a bit worried that Christians would lump us all into one category of terrorists, regardless of our rejection of Islam and acceptance of Jesus Christ as Lord and Savior.

Thankfully, we have never been more wrong.

Instead, among countless churches and conferences, we have been greeted with warmth and overwhelming love. Instead of facing hatred toward our kinsmen, we have found incalculable numbers of Christians who passionately want to reach our Islamic brethren with the gospel. Without a doubt, the most common question we have heard from the thousands of Christians we have encountered has been: How do I reach my Muslim friend?

To those wonderful Christians, we respond with three simple points of engagement. While there are many methods offered and many apologetic methods, we focus on those that have been most effective.

First, we suggest a loving interest in their lives. Especially for immigrants, the Western world can be a lonely place. In every other country in which we lived, we were in the majority. When Muslim immigrants move to a place like America, they are outnumbered. Adding to their fear is the fact that everything they have ever been taught about Christians has been taught in the mosque. They believe the images they see on television. They believe Christians hate them.

Please remember that you may be the first Christian friend that a Muslim has ever had. There are layers of suspicion and doubt that must be cut away, especially for those immigrants who believe in the caricature of Christians as hateful, selfish, and openly sinful. It may take time to bridge that gap. Often, taking an interest in their lives is the best open door. Ask questions. Be genuinely curious. Ask about their clothing, holidays, and dietary restrictions. Once they respond in kind, do not be secretive about your faith, rather be clear. Christianity does not need to borrow from other movements, and neither do we need secret service agents!

Second, we suggest a clear presentation of grace. Though the Qur'an calls Allah gracious, Islam has no concept of grace. Remember, *grace is not the same as mercy*. Mercy is when God chooses not to punish me. The Qur'an is filled with teachings of the prevention of disaster if the person does good.

However the Qur'an has no concept of *grace*. Grace is when God shows favor to the undeserving soul. We do nothing to earn grace. We do not "clean up" in order to receive grace. Grace is given to the sinful person, not because he is good, but precisely because he knows that he is not good. This is the true nature of repentance.

Finally, we suggest a genuine patience. It often takes years for a Muslim to embrace Christ. It is difficult for Muslims to understand why Jesus would save them when they do not merit salvation. Often, salvation is accompanied by the loss of family and friends and sometimes by the loss of everything. Television stations in Islamic countries broadcast the deaths of converts as a deterrent. It is a formidable decision, but with patience your friend will see the Truth of Jesus Christ.

Caveats

Certainly we have had our detractors. Some take issue with our adamant stand with Israel, now that we are evangelical Christians. Once we came to read the Scriptures for ourselves, we lost our hatred for Israel, and saw them as God's chosen Priest Nation.

The "Replacement Theologians" have had a field day in setting an expiration date on God's unconditional covenant (Gen. 12:1–3). We do not apologize for our belief. If God can break the unconditional covenant He has with Israel, then He can also break the unconditional covenant of salvation He has promised to all who believe in Christ (Jer. 31:31–34), which we believe Scripture teaches He would never do.

Another group of evangelicals regularly make fodder of our belief that Jesus Christ died for the world. We believe adamantly that one of the major distinctions between the God of the Bible and all other religions is that God is "not willing that any should perish but that all should come to repentance" (2 Peter 3:9). Those who hold to a belief that God only selectively loves a few have written myriads of articles against our view of general atonement. We stand by our view that God "so loved the world" (John 3:16).

In fact, our most vehement detractors have acted much like the Muslims we have encountered. They respond with fury when we do not ascribe to a God who could hate anyone or receive glory from their damnation. The largest collection of "hate mail" we received has not come from Muslims, but from those of this small theological persuasion. A few years ago, we even noted that many of them were acting worse than Muslims! There is a significant difference, however, in comparing the two—*Christians should know better.* As followers of Jesus Christ, we should know better than to defend theological leaders, denominational founders, churches, or movements. Our faith should stand in Jesus Christ, and on no other foundation.

Christ died so that "whosoever will may come." That includes Muslims. We pray that we will see a coming to faith among our Muslim brothers and sisters, even in our lifetime.

Notes

1. Nina Berglund, "Krekar Claims Islam Will Win," *Aftenposten*, March 13, 2006, http://www.aftenposten.no/english/local/article1247400.ece.
2. Ibid.

3. United Nations, "Universal Declaration of Human Rights," http:// www.un.org/Overview/rights.html.

4. Kevin Greeson, *The Camel: How Muslims Are Coming to Faith in Christ!* (Arkadelphia, AR: WIGTake Resources, 2007), 42. This book is a revision of Greeson's earlier work, *Camel Training Manual: The Secret of the Camel Is Out . . . Muslims Are Coming to Faith in 'Isa* (Bangalore, India: WIGTake Resources, 2004).

5. Ibid., 34, 35, 40, 170.

6. In missiological terms, the CAMEL method is a C5 orientation at best, and often a C6 model, where Christians secretly and superficially practice other religious forms in an attempt to "bridge a gap" into a Christian witness. Often dress, diet, and practice is indistinguishable between the believer in Jesus Christ and the follower of another religion. These categories are seen in Phil Parshall, "Danger! New Directions in Contextualization," *Evangelical Missions Quarterly* 34, no. 4 (October 1998): 404–10.

7. Malcolm Yarnell, *Summary of a Common Evaluation of the Camel Method of Evangelism,* July 6, 2007. Personal correspondence with the authors.

18

FREEDOM AND THE CONSCIENCE OF THE NATION: A NOD TO THE GIPPER

ON THE TENTH anniversary of the Supreme Court decision in *Roe v. Wade*, President Ronald Reagan, affectionately known as "The Gipper" by his closest friends, penned a brief yet profound essay entitled "Abortion and the Conscience of the Nation." This eleven-page pamphlet called our nation to grieve over a decision, which, up to 1983, had "snuffed out" fifteen million lives.[1] Referencing Abraham Lincoln's arduous battle to emancipate millions of African-Americans from the grip of slavery, Reagan related, "Lincoln recognized that we could not survive as a free land when some men could decide that others were not fit to be free. . . . Likewise, we cannot survive as a free nation when some men decide that others are not fit to live."[2] Reagan dreamed that his pursuit for the rights of the unborn would come to fruition during his presidency; yet his hopes were dashed and, indeed, did not even materialize during his lifetime.

Nonetheless, his words have not been forgotten as millions of Americans still hope for a brighter future for the unborn in this country. The battle, seemingly passé to so many, still carries forth although it does not get the regular media attention it did when Reagan held office. This chapter, as the title denotes, is dedicated to the noble efforts of that great president and gleans from his perspective. In many ways, the authors realize that present-day battles in our culture are not greatly disassociated from previous culture wars. Freedom, whether it is for the unborn or for those overseas, is a righteous pursuit worth undertaking.

Reagan's platform overtly demonstrated such, as he not only fought for the freedom of those within the States, but heralded with unbridled optimism that one day men and women behind the Iron Curtain of the Soviet Empire would taste freedom as well. On June 12, 1987, Reagan delivered a speech at the Bradenburg Gate, near the Berlin Wall, and gave the now-famous challenge to the dictator of the Soviet Union, "Mr. Gorbachev, tear down this wall!" Just before that clarion call, Reagan prophetically uttered, "We believe freedom and security go together, that the advance of human liberty could only strengthen the cause of world peace."

Beginning in 1989, what once was deemed impossible by so many—freedom—came to multitudes in Germany, Hungary, Czechoslovakia, Romania, Poland, and many other countries. As Peter Jennings asserted about the era, "It was a magnificent decade for democracy." May the same be said today. May another prophetic voice rise from the ashes of pessimism and confront tyranny, and may people desire such freedom with the passion of their souls.

A Proper Perspective: I Have No Wounds

A belief in freedom cannot be a selfish one, nor can it be an isolated one. Thomas Jefferson recognized the true roots of freedom and equality in the Declaration of Independence by stating, "We hold these truths to be self-evident, that all men are created equal, that they are endowed by their Creator with certain unalienable [inalienable] Rights, that among these are Life, Liberty, and the Pursuit of Happiness."[3]

Hence, freedom is not a right given to men by men; it is an inalienable right given solely and exclusively by God Himself. If the power of freedom were solely placed in the hands of legislators or judges, it could and would be stripped away as easily as it was first given. But if God is the provider of freedom, only He has the right to remove that which He has granted. And, recognizing that God is universal in His sovereignty over all the peoples of the earth, Americans have, from our very inception, acknowledged that freedom is a right everyone in the world should taste equally.

Today, our deeply held belief in freedom is once again being tested, our resolve questioned. The gravity of the wars in Iraq and Afghanistan and the slow pace in which reforms are implemented have taken their toll on the American psyche. But Americans must realize what is at stake during this current, momentous struggle: the very rights we have so fittingly enshrined in our founding documents are now, once again, up for debate. Perhaps no one understands the pressing struggle for our liberties better than Clarence Thomas, one of the nine justices presently serving on the Supreme Court of the United States.

Recently Judge Thomas visited with military personnel at a local hospital. Overwhelmed by the attitudes of our servicemen and women, he humbly recollected, "I had a chance . . . to talk to some wounded veterans from Iraq, these young kids. And they're just, you know, serious wounds . . . amputations, et cetera. And they were thanking me for spending time with them, and I was so ashamed. I spent a few hours with them. They actually had suffered major wounds to uphold what we believe in in this country, the kind of country we have, the Constitution. I've suffered no wounds . . . I have no wounds."[4] The ultimate question this generation will have to answer is simply this: are we willing to sacrifice in order to uphold our liberties and the advancement of freedom around the world?

Will we accept the wounds?

Diminishing Returns: The First Four Freedoms
Perpetually Questioned in the Media

Congress shall make no law respecting an establishment of religion, or prohibiting the free exercise thereof; or abridging the
freedom of speech, or of the press; or the right of the people
peaceably to assemble, and to petition the government for a
redress of grievances.

> First Amendment, Bill of Rights

Sometimes known as the first four freedoms, the Bill of Rights
establishes freedom of religion, speech, press, and assembly. Yet,
these freedoms are the very liberties most fervently under attack
in the world today. These liberties are completely foreign to the
traditions of Islam and are regularly condemned by Muslims worldwide. Many Muslims view these freedoms as the essential reason
the West is so perverted, so innately immoral. Beyond the blatant
falsehoods of such connections,[5] what many fail to realize is that
these freedoms, enshrined in law more than two centuries ago, are
themselves moral standards and, thus, their opposites are immoral.

Even since 9/11 most Muslim-dominated countries receive
a blind pass (or a meaningless slap on the wrist from the United
Nations) for the blatant civil rights abuses within their borders. For
many in the media, however, it is fashionable to blame America for
almost every evil in this world. We are presently condemned for
interfering with Iraq's sovereignty even though in 1991, during
the first Persian Gulf War, the same media criticized the American
government for not doing enough to topple the Hussein dictatorship. Few remember that the last five conflicts that America has
undertaken—Kuwait, Somalia, Bosnia, Afghanistan, and Iraq—were
intended to defend and free not millions of "Christians," but millions of Muslims. And, we have done so.

The once engraved, time-honored belief of advancing freedom
in the world has given way to a new age, the Age of Cynicism.
This new era embarks on ensuring that no one leads and everyone
follows. There should be no superpower, no champion of liberty.

Instead, there should be an acquiescing of divergent beliefs, all of which are equally correct even if they are in complete disagreement with each other. The arrogance of holding one's belief system as virtuous must bow at the altar of Postmodernism. There are no absolute truths, and thus no absolute liberties, and to say so would be utterly immoral. Headlines that once would have grabbed the American heart and tied our stomachs in knots are now acceptable. The cynic simply responds, "That's the world we live in. Get used to it."

Now let's see if these three headlines, typical of the new age, are bothersome to you. Are you an optimist or a pessimist? Can liberty be advanced or has it seen its best days?

"Death Could Await Christian Convert" *(CNN, 2006)*

Consider the first freedom mentioned in the Bill of Rights, freedom of religion, and ask yourself this question: is it moral or immoral to grant someone the right to believe according to his or her conscience? If it is immoral, then the ethic of Jesus also becomes suspect since He, throughout His ministry, allowed men and women to choose to follow or reject Him (Matt. 13:24–20; 22:37). As one expert noted, "As God, he had the power to make people do anything. Nevertheless, he chose a very different approach."[6] And, if religious liberty is a morally based belief, then Muhammad's ethic comes into grave question as he denied this inalienable right (Bukhari hadith 9.57–58). This is especially the case for a person who either is born a Muslim or converts to Islam. Such people have no right to convert to another faith, as they have seen the superior light of Islam and cannot go back to the time of ignorance.

Since 9/11, a plethora of stories have been written about people who have chosen, for whatever reason, to forsake Islam. Their fate, if tied to traditional Islam, is sealed according to the Qur'an and the Hadith. They must die for committing treason against Allah.[7] In one such case, CNN reported of a convert to Christianity in liberated Afghanistan. Abdul Rahman was arrested due to his newfound faith and, under the new Afghan constitution, faced the death penalty for his actions. In actuality, the constitution recognizes both Islamic law and religious freedom. Western forces with troops stationed in the country began demanding Rahman's immediate release. Former Italian President Francesco Cossiga exclaimed, "In a country where soldiers from all faiths, including Christianity, are dying in defense of your government, I find it outrageous that Mr. Rahman is being prosecuted and facing the death penalty for converting to Christianity."[8] International outcry became so boisterous that the national Afghan government, led by Hamid Karzai, buckled under Western pressure, and forced locals to release the religious prisoner. Rahman was granted asylum in Italy later that year.

In the aftermath, Afghan leaders and the public at large were outraged at Western interference. The BBC documented several opinions from Afghans, which include the following:

- "Islam is a religion of peace, tolerance, kindness and integrity. That is why we have told him if he regrets what he did, then we will forgive him" (Ansarullah Mawlafizada, the trial judge for the case).
- "What is wrong with Islam that he should want to convert?" (Abdul Zahid Payman).
- "According to Islamic law he should be sentenced to death because God has clearly stated that Christianity is forbidden in our land" (Mohammed Qadir).[9]

Freedom of religion had won the day even in the midst of an Afghan public that was nearly unanimous in its thirsty desire for execution. But this victory is hollow unless the West, led by the United States, demands religious freedom among all nations. This seemingly impossible task is a noble ideal that will take eternal vigilance. The endeavor must begin with Muslim nations who have already been assisted by the West, nations such as Kuwait. Presently, Kuwait acknowledges Islam as the official religion, forbids Muslims from converting to another religion, and mandates Islamic education in its public schools. As an ally liberated by American and Western forces, Kuwait must be perpetually challenged to fulfill the words of its constitution, which promises "absolute religious freedom."[10]

We stand at the crossroads of history, with countries such as Kazakhstan, a former Soviet Republic, in the balance. This country is nearly split between the number of Christians and Muslims and, currently, is heavily influenced by the rising tide of militant Islam. This delicate population balance is also found in African nations including Nigeria, Tanzania, Chad, and Ethiopia. And militant Islam, when it tightens its grip, becomes ever so oppressing, as has been seen in countries such as Malaysia where Muslims make up nearly 60 percent of the population. Presently, each separate state in Malaysia has a fatwa (religious law) committee that aggressively implements Islamic laws.

Recently, Malaysian Lina Joy, a Muslim-turned-Christian, was denied the right to change her legal status on her identity card. The highest federal court in the country, in a 2-1 split decision, deemed the court's jurisdiction as improper. The decision argued that Islamic courts had sole right to decide whether one could convert from Islam. Chief Justice Ahmad Fairuz Sheikh asserted, "You can't at whim and fancy convert from one religion to another."[11] Malaysia, considered one of the most moderate Islamic countries in the world, has been thrust into a state of flux and instability as Muslims and non-Muslims are increasingly at odds with each other. And one must ask, Where is the moral compass of the West in standing for the right of the freedom of religion?

*"Cartoons of Prophet Met with Outrage" (*Washington Post, 2006)

The next two freedoms listed in the First Amendment, speech and press, are similar liberties that allow for individuals to speak and distribute remarks as they choose. This right was also codified by the United Nations in 1948. In a unanimous vote, the organization passed a thirty-article document, the Universal Declaration of Human Rights.[12] Article 19 asserts, "Everyone has the right to freedom of opinion and expression; this right includes freedom to hold opinions without interference and to seek, receive and impart information and ideas through any media and regardless of frontiers."[13]

These two freedoms took center stage when, in September 2005, the conservative Danish newspaper, *Jyllands-Posten*, published a dozen cartoons of Islam's prophet. These cartoons depicted Muhammad as the instigator of modern-day terrorism. One caricature is of Muhammad with a bomb in his turban while another cartoon portrays Muhammad greeting martyrs in heaven with the statement, "Stop, stop, we have run out of virgins!" Muslim communities throughout the world were infuriated at the depictions and demanded their retraction as well as immediate justice. The various reactions, documented in part by Islamic critic Robert Spencer, are emblematic of the contemporary Muslim worldview:

- Arab interior ministers declared, "We ask the Danish authorities to take the necessary measures to punish those responsible of this harm and to take action to avoid its repeat."
- Two employees of the Danish corporation Aria Foods were beaten in Saudi Arabia.
- In the Gaza strip, Palestinian gunmen seized the European Union office and demanded an apology from Denmark. The next day at another protest, one jihadist explicated, "We demand that the Danish government make a clear and public apology for the wrongful crime."[14]

The Danish public coalesced around the freedom of expression. The Danish prime minister, Anders Fogh Rasmussen, has doggedly refused to apologize, calling freedom of speech an "absolute." The newspaper itself articulated, "We are sorry if Muslims have been offended . . . [but Denmark] is not a dictatorship like Saudi Arabia that is going to dictate our editorial line here in Denmark."[15]

World reaction included re-publication of the cartoons in much of Western Europe, including Germany, France, and Belgium. The vast majority of papers in the United States and Canada cowered from the controversy and did not republish the prints. Danish embassies in Iran, Lebanon, and Syria were set afire. In the end, tens of thousands protested across the world and dozens were killed in the wake of the more violent protests.[16]

Where Christian images have been treated with contempt, there has been a much different reaction. Andres Serrano's well-publicized art piece entitled "Piss Christ," which pictures a crucifix dipped in urine, is almost universally offensive to Christians. Except for the offensiveness of the Muhammad cartoons and Serrano's art, however, these two examples could not be farther apart. First, the Danish cartoons were published independently while Serrano's "art" was funded with a government endowment. Second, the Danish cartoons portrayed a provocative image of Muhammad in order to arouse discussion on the merits of Islam as a peaceful religion. The portrait of Christ was purely profane in its meaning. Finally, the reaction from the Christian community was utter disgust but never violence. Protestors may have demanded the removal of taxpayer dollars from such reprehensible images, but they did not demand that the American government prosecute Serrano as a criminal deserving of prison or worse. Entire Islamic governments led in the demands for swift and severe justice against the Danish cartoonist. Muslims demonstrated the "peacefulness" of Islam by setting Danish embassies ablaze, beating Danes in Muslim countries, and calling for the death of the cartoonist. No Christians, however, called for Serrano's execution.

A picture is worth a thousand words, and the lessons learned from these cartoons are worth far more. Westerners must remember that many Muslim countries are laden with illiteracy and, therefore, depictions may elicit a harsher reaction than an article. Furthermore, Muslims would have been angry at any published portrait of Muhammad, regardless of its meaning. This form of freedom of speech is unquestionably denounced in Islam and has been throughout Islam's history. While minority religious groups have fought for their basic human rights to worship freely for years, this marks the first concerted effort that media outlets have had in a generation to fight for their sacred tenet on an international basis.

"First Catholic Church Opens in Qatar, Sparking Fear of Backlash Against Christians" (Fox News, 2008)

The fourth liberty given by the Bill of Rights, the freedom of assembly, is in direct opposition to one of the founding documents of Islam, the Pact of Umar. Named after the second leader of Islam after Muhammad's death, the seventh-century document demanded that after a region was conquered by Islam, it was not to build, rebuild, or remodel churches. Thus, the above headline from Fox News is stunning in light of the history of Islam. To not cause a stir, Catholic leadership decided to build Our Lady of the Rosary fifteen minutes "into the barren desert." Additionally, the facilities have no markings of a normal Roman Catholic church. There are no crosses, no bells, no steeple, no sign. Still, Qatar citizens are calling for a referendum on the church to close its doors. As one Qatari stated, "[Christians should] worship their God in their homes."[17]

But the emir (prince) of Qatar is attempting to reform the country, even though the vast majority of Qataris follow the strict form of Islam known as Wahhabism (see p. 167). He is an ardent ally of the United States and desires to demonstrate such. When the church opens, Saudi Arabia will be the sole Gulf State not to allow any churches on its territory. But that may change within a short time. *Time* magazine is reporting that the Roman Catholic Church is in discussions with Saudi royalty to open a church there as well.[18]

These small steps of progress cannot be overemphasized in their importance. It may be the case that the new church in Qatar opens the floodgates for other churches to begin worship services. More likely, this church will find itself in a generational battle between Muslims who struggle with an expansion of Christianity on a territory that has been declared a House of Islam. The situation is bound to get far worse, especially if a Qatari converts to Catholicism and desires to visit the facility. In countries such as Egypt, it is illegal for Christian churches to open their arms to former Muslims. Additionally, while some in the Middle East attempt to open their borders ever so slightly, other nations, such as Nigeria, are implementing forms of Islamic law that call for the closure of Christian assemblies. Other countries, including Pakistan and Indonesia, turn a blind eye to the destruction of churches or readily assist in church closures.[19] Local pastors are regularly kidnapped and/or murdered by local militants. Furthermore, while some Islamic leaders may recognize Catholicism to some extent, the recognition of smaller Protestant denominations such as Pentecostal and Baptist, will not come easily. They are lesser understood and, due to their independence, less protected by any international body.

In the twenty-first century, the underground church will gain its greatest prominence. With a belief that the freedom of assembly is a divine right and therefore cannot be removed by man-made laws, Christianity will continue to expand in Muslim-dominated countries in much the same way as it did during the first century. Christians will risk their own freedom and safety in order to demonstrate their faith and their belief in the freedom of assembly. For Christians, the gathering with fellow believers is not a suggestion or an option, it is a command. Like the millions who meet in underground churches in China, Christians in Islamic-led countries may lead in the next expansive revolution in Christianity.

The Clash of Civilizations: Democracy or Theocracy

In February 2008, Archbishop of Canterbury Rowan Williams triggered significant debate over remarks he made about the inevitability of Islamic law coming to Great Britain. Great Britain is home to more than two million Muslims, the majority of which live in the London area. Speaking to a crowd of more than 800 at the Great Hall for the Royal Courts of Justice, Williams articulated, "It's not as if we're bringing in an alien and rival system; we already have in this country a number of situations in which the internal law of religious communities is recognized by the law of the land. . . . There is a place for finding what would be a constructive accommodation with some aspects of Muslim law as we already do with some kinds of aspects of other religious law."[20] He further clarified in subsequent interviews that only the moderate forms of Islamic laws, such as are found in divorce law, would be welcome. Harsher laws, like those found in Saudi Arabia, were not to be considered. Williams was purportedly stunned by much of the nation's backlash.

Many political and religious leaders called for his resignation, but to no avail. Instead, he simply reiterated his support for English law and his desire to discuss the issue further in the future.

The vision of Archbishop Williams is in complete contradistinction to that of former president Reagan. Williams's hopes are based on the supposedly realistic notion that Islam is an unstoppable force that must be given its proper place within the West. Reagan, with his eternal optimism, believed freedom could convince even the hardest critic to abandon old philosophies (or theologies) for those of a divine order. To the naysayer who mocks this optimism, one can look to Turkey for a glimmer of hope. Consider the following:

- Before the reforms by Turkish President Mustafa Ataturk, Turkey was the leader of Islam and home of the caliphate (Islamic Council).
- Before the inauguration of democracy, Turkey was the most noted persecutor of Christians in the early twentieth century. Between 1915 to 1918, two million Armenian Christians were killed by Turks.
- Turkey was the first Islamic nation to implement democracy in a significant way.

Here is a nation that at its core was an Islamic superpower which, for more than four centuries, ruled much of the civilized world. Yet, two major events transformed the country. First, the nation was brought to its knees after World War I as Turkey sided with the Central Powers against the Allies. Ataturk returned to an Istanbul that was occupied by British and French forces. Second, Turkey was guilty of some of the worst persecution of Christians in the history of the world.

The aftermath of such tragedies brought the Turkish people toward a new day and a new mind-set. The lessons learned by the Turks are still as applicable today. First, where bloodshed is greatest may be where freedom finds its next home. Second, for freedom to flourish, it needs an indigenous face such as Ataturk.

Third, democracy is possible even in places where it has never gained a footing. Finally, freedom, when captured by people, is a powerful force that can change a country. No one would have ever guessed that the nation which conquered the greatest Christian city outside of Rome—Constantinople, now known as Istanbul—could be transformed into a secular democracy. And, yet, it happened.

In the wake of today's rising Islamic militancy, the greatest irony may be that if America does not awake and stand against the tyranny of Islamic law, Turkey may gradually move toward its former roots. As more than a dozen countries have already implemented Islamic laws within the past twenty years, the tide presently is in favor of Islamic theocracy. All of this has occurred while much of the West has slumbered. When free countries are unwilling to stand up for the inalienable rights of all, other countries are the first to suffer the consequences. Freedom can only survive if it is believed in, defended, and expanded. Otherwise, freedom will be overthrown by tryanny.

Truth is Immortal!

Notes

1. President Ronald W. Reagan, "Abortion and the Conscience of the Nation" (Washington, D.C.: The White House, 1983), 1.
2. Ibid., 11.
3. To view the Declaration of Independence in its entirety, see http://www.archives.gov/exhibits/charters/declaration.html.
4. Clarence Thomas, interview by Rush Limbaugh, *The Rush Limbaugh Show*, October 1, 2007, http://www.rushlimbaugh.com/home/daily/site_100107/content/01125106.guest.html.
5. See Robert Spencer, *Religion of Peace: Why Christianity Is and Islam Isn't* (Washington, D.C.: Regnery Publishing, 2007). For example, one report notes that Indonesia, the world's most populous Islamic nation, has nearly twice as many abortions as America even though America has 25 percent more population.
6. Barrett Duke, "The Christian Doctrine of Religious Liberty," in *First Freedom: The Baptist Perspective on Religious Liberty*, ed. Thomas

White, Jason G. Duesing, and Malcolm B. Yarnell III (Nashville: Broadman and Holman, 2007), 21.

7. See Samuel Zwemer, *The Law of Apostasy in Islam* (London: Marshall Brothers, 1924).

8. "Death Could Await Christian Convert," *CNN.com*, March 22, 2006, http://www.cnn.com/2006/WORLD/meast/03/21/afghan .christian/index.html.

9. Sanjoy Majumder, "Mood Hardens Against Afghan Convert," *BBCNews.com*, March 24, 2008, http://news.bbc.co.uk/1/hi/ world/south_asia/4841334.stm.

10. U.S. Department of State, "Kuwait International Religious Freedom Report 2007," http://www.state.gov/g/drl/rls/irf/2007/90214 .htm.

11. Jalil Hamid and Syed Azman, "Malaysia's Lina Joy Loses Islam Conversion Case," Reuters.com, May 30, 2007, http://www.reuters .com/article/worldNews/idUSSP20856820070530.

12. Eight countries, including Saudi Arabia, abstained from the vote.

13. Department of Public Information, United Nations, "Universal Declaration of Human Rights," http://www.un.org/Overview/ rights.html.

14. Robert Spencer, "Spencer: Cartoon Rage vs. Freedom of Speech," *FrontPage*, February 2, 2006, www.jihadwatch.org/archives/010009 .php.

15. John Ward Anderson, "Cartoons of Prophet Met with Outrage," *Washington Post*, January 30, 2006, http://www.washingtonpost.com/ wp-dyn/content/article/2006/01/30/AR2006013001316.html.

16. "Jyllands-Posten Muhammad cartoons controversy," http:// en.wikipedia.org/wiki/Danish_cartoons (accessed February 6, 2009).

17. Sonia Verma, "First Catholic Church Opens in Qatar, Sparking Fear of Backlash Against Christians," Fox News, March 14, 2008, http:// www.foxnews.com/story/0,2933,338014,00.html.

18. Jeff Israely, "A Church in Saudi Arabia?" *Time*, March 19, 2008, http:// www.time.com/time/world/article/0,8599,1723715,00.html.

19. "Indonesia: 110 Churches Closed in Three Years," Compass Direct News, April 2, 2008, http://www.compassdirect.org/en/display.php ?page=news&lang=en&length=long&idelement=5315.

20. Riazat Butt, "Archbishop Backs Sharia Law for British Muslims," *Guardian*, February 7, 2008, http://www.guardian.co.uk/uk/2008/feb/07/religion.world.

Appendix A

Topical Index to the Qur'an

Animals

apes 2:65; 5:60
camel 5:103; 7:73–77; 11:64–66; 17:59;
 22:28; 26:155; 54:27; 81:4; 88:17;
 91:13
cow 2:67–71; 12:43, 46
dog 18:18–22
donkey 2:259; 16:8; 31:19; 62:5; 74:50
elephant 105:1–5
goat 6:143
horse 3:14; 16:8; 59:6; 71:1
in ark 11:37–50
mule 16:8
sheep 6:143–46; 21:79; 38:23–24; 54:31
swine 5:60

Belief

Allah knows 4:25
angels and 40:7
at judgment 6:158; 22:18; 22:56; 30:56
everlasting life and 6:113; 17:10
examining 3:141
example of 66:11
guidance in 4:175; 6:82; 7:203; 9:23; 42:52;
 45:20; 49:17
heart's 49:7, 14
recanting 3:177; 4:137; 7:89; 9:66; 16:106
reward for 2:25–26; 10:9; 52:21
striving toward 9:88; 49:15
supplication and 3:193

Charity

amount of 2:219
believers' gifts of 3:16–17; 32:15–16;
 35:32
command to give 16:90
covenant with Allah for 9:75
for show 4:38
manners in 2:262–64, 271; 22:36
promotion of 4:114
purification through 9:103
recipients of 2:215, 271, 273; 9:60
repentance by 9:104
reward for 2:272, 274; 3:92; 3:133–34;
 4:162; 12:88; 30:39; 57:7, 18
toward debtors 2:280
unbelievers' 3:117; 4:38; 41:7

Christians

at judgment 2:113; 22:18
claim of 5:18
covenant with 5:14
death of 4:159
dialog with 29:46
fancies of 2:111
guidance of 2:120
invitation to 3:64; 5:15
Messiah and 9:30
monasticism of 57:27
nearest to Muslims 5:82
question to 3:70–71, 98

Appendix B

Free Will, Fatalism, and the Qur'an

Free Will

Sura 76:29:
This is an admonition: Whosoever will, let him take a (straight) Path to his Lord.

Context of Sura 76:29:
This passage is explained by the following verse, "But you will not except as Allah wills." Man doing wrong is thereby doing Allah's will.

Sura 3:108:
These are the Signs of Allah: We rehearse them to thee in Truth: and Allah means no injustice to any of His creatures.

Context of Sura 3:108:
Here injustice is not the equivalent of free will. Allah does want hell for those creatures who are "black" (3:106).

Sura 4:26:
Allah does wish to make clear to you and to guide you into the ways of those before you; and (He does wish to) turn to you (In Mercy): and Allah is All-knowing, All-wise.

Context of Sura 4:26:
This promise of guidance is for believers in Allah, and not to "those who follow their lusts" (4:27). Once again, the kindness of Allah is selective, not universal as seen in Christianity (John 3:16).

Sura 5:6
Allah does not wish to place you in a difficulty, but to make you clean, and to complete His favour to you, that you may be grateful.

Context of Sura 5:6
This is another promise to "you who believe" (5:6) and not to all. His favor is only upon those he selects and wills, and not upon all humankind.

Sura 33:33
And Allah only wishes to remove all abomination from you, your Members of the Family, and to make you pure and spotless.

Context of Sura 33:33
The passage is referring to the household of the Prophet (Members) and is not a universal promise for all Muslims, much less the entire world.

Fatalism

Sura 6:35:
If it were Allah's Will, he could gather them together unto true guidance: So be not you among those who are swayed by ignorance and impatience!

Context of Sura 6:35:
In Islamic theology, Allah is all-powerful and all-knowing. Yet, he chooses not to gather all people into true guidance. This is the key passage in understanding the will and work of Allah.

Sura 10:25:
But Allah does call to the Home of Peace: He does guide whom He pleases to a Way that is straight.

Context of Sura 10:25:
Fatalism becomes even more dangerous since works determine part of Allah's mercy. Allah does not desire to turn those who do wicked things to a straight path. In regards to this "Home of Peace," the Hadith expounds, "An angel is sent to him [in the womb] and given four commands with reference to his sustenance, the duration of life, and whether he is to be wretched or happy. . . ."

Sura 6:125:
Those whom Allah wills to guide,—He opens their breast to Islam; those whom He wills to leave straying,—He makes their breast close and constricted, as if they had to climb up to the skies: thus does Allah lay abomination on those who refuse to believe.

Context of Sura 6:125:
Although the Muslim scholar reminds the reader of the Qur'an over and over about human responsibility, this passage clearly demonstrates that Allah desires to leave some straying, although he has no obligation to do so. In Christianity, God desires all, although they are wicked, to be saved (2 Peter 3:9). One early Muslim scholar, Ibn Hazn, wrote, "Nothing is good but Allah has made it so, and nothing is evil, but by His doing."

APPENDIX C

CHRISTIANITY AND ISLAM: A COMPARISON OF BELIEFS

Yahweh and Allah: The Being of God

Yahweh is eternal and changeless.
Every good gift and every perfect gift is from above, and cometh down from the Father of lights, with whom is no variableness, neither shadow of turning. (James 1:17; all Scripture text in this appendix is KJV)

Allah changes.
If we supersede any verse or cause it to be forgotten, We bring a better one or one similar. Do you not know that Allah has power over all things! (sura 2:106)

Yahweh loves utterly.
For God so loved the world that he gave his only begotten Son. (John 3:16)

Allah changes in affections.
If we so willed, we could have brought every soul its true guidance, but the word from me will come true: "I will fill Hell with demons and men all together." (sura 32:13)

Yahweh cannot lie.
In hope of eternal life, which God, that cannot lie, promised before the world began. (Titus 1:2)

Allah deceives.
They plot and plan, and Allah, too plans, but the best of planners [in context meaning "deceivers"] is Allah. (sura 8:30)

Yahweh is one God in three persons.
Jesus answered, If I honor myself, my honor is nothing: it is my Father that honoreth me; of whom ye say, that he is your God. (John 8:54)

Allah can be no God but one.
The Trinity is blasphemous.
They do blaspheme who say God is one of three . . . for there is no Allah except one Allah. (sura 5:73)

For in him dwelleth all the fulness of the Godhead bodily. (Col. 2:9; cf. John 1; 8:58)

But Peter said, Ananias, why hath Satan filled thine heart to lie to the Holy Ghost. . . . Thou hast not lied unto men, but unto God. (Acts 5:3–4)

In the one God of the Trinity are the persons of the Father, the Son, and the Holy Spirit.	*The Christian Trinity is three Gods—the Father, Mother (Mary), and Son (Jesus).*
Go ye therefore, and teach all nations, baptizing them in the name of the Father, and of the Son, and of the Holy Ghost. (Matt. 28:19)	And behold! God will say: O Jesus the son of Mary didst say unto men, "worship me and my mother as gods" in derogation of Allah? (sura 5:116)

Jesus (Yeshua) in the Bible and Isa (Jesus) in the Qur'an

He is eternally the uncreated God.	*Isa is a created human being.*
And he [Christ] is before all things, and by him all things consist. (Col. 1:17)	The similitude of Isa before God is as that of Adam; He created him from dust. (sura 3:59)
He is Lord—the only way to God.	*He is one of Allah's apostles.*
Jesus saith unto him, I am the way, the truth, and the life: no man cometh unto the Father, but by me. (John 14:6)	O people of the book, commit no excess of your religion: nor say of Allah aught but truth, Christ Isa the son of Mary was an apostle of Allah. (sura 4:171)
His crucifixion was a sacrificial death to remove sin's penalty.	*Isa only appeared to be crucified.*
For I determined not to know any thing among you, save Jesus Christ, and him crucified. (1 Cor. 2:2)	That they said in boast "we killed Christ Isa, the son of Mary" . . . but they killed him not, nor crucified him. (sura 4:157)
In whom [Christ] we have redemption through his blood, the forgiveness of sins, according to the riches of his grace. (Eph. 1:7)	
Jesus is the eternal Son of God.	*Isa is a created human being.*
And the Word was made flesh, and dwelt among us, (and we beheld his glory, the glory as of the only begotten of the Father,) full of grace and truth. (John 1:14)	And it (the Qur'an) warns those who say: "Allah has taken a son." Surely, of this they have no knowledge, neither they nor their fathers; it is a monstrous word that comes from their mouths, they say nothing but a lie. (sura 18:4–5)

Jesus and Muhammad

Jesus knows the thoughts of others.
And all the churches shall know that I am he which searcheth the reins and hearts. (Rev. 2:23)

Muhammad did not know the thoughts of others.
I do not say to you that I possess the treasuries of Allah, and I do not know the unseen. (sura 11:31)

Jesus is our Advocate before the Father.
My little children, these things write I unto you, that ye sin not. And if any man sin, we have an advocate with the Father, Jesus Christ the righteous: And he is the propitiation for our sins: and not for ours only, but also for the sins of the whole world. (1 John 2:1–2)

Muhammad is not an advocate.
(It is the same) whether or not you beg forgiveness for them. If you beg forgiveness for them seventy times Allah will not forgive them, for they have disbelieved in Allah and His Messenger. Allah does not guide the evildoers. (sura 9:80)

Jesus forbade using the sword in His defense.
Then said Jesus unto him, Put up again thy sword into his place: for all they that take the sword shall perish with the sword. (Matt. 26:52)

Muhammad urged use of the sword.
O Prophet, urge the believers to fight. If there are twenty patient men among you, you shall overcome two hundred, and if there are a hundred, they shall overcome a thousand unbelievers, for they are a nation who do not understand. (sura 8:65)

Jesus taught forgiveness.
Ye have heard that it hath been said, An eye for an eye, and a tooth for a tooth: But I say unto you, That ye resist not evil: but whosoever shall smite thee on thy right cheek, turn to him the other also. (Matt. 5:38–39)

Muhammad taught revenge.
The sacred month for the sacred month, prohibitions are (subject to) retaliation. If any one aggresses against you, so aggress against him with the likeness of that which he has aggressed against. (sura 2:194)

Jesus was sinless.
For even hereunto were ye called: because Christ also suffered for us, leaving us an example, that ye should follow his steps: Who did no sin, neither was guile found in his mouth. (1 Peter 2:21–22)

Muhammad was sinful.
Say: "I am only a human like you, revealed to me is that your God is One God. Let him who hopes for the encounter with his Lord do good work, and not associate anyone with the worship of his Lord." (sura 18:110)

Salvation

Humankind is radically fallen into a state of sin and misery.
For all have sinned, and come short of the glory of God. (Rom. 3:23).

Wherefore, as by one man sin entered into the world, and death by sin; and so death passed upon all men, for that all have sinned. (Rom. 5:12)

Human beings are not born fallen, and sin only through their personal misdeeds.

Jesus is the only way to salvation.
Being justified freely by his grace through the redemption that is in Christ Jesus: Whom God hath set forth to be a propitiation through faith in his blood, to declare his righteousness for the remission of sins that are past, through the forbearance of God; . . . that he might be just, and the justifier of him which believeth in Jesus. (Rom. 3:24–26)

Jesus was simply a worshiper of Allah.
He (the baby) said: "I am the worshiper of Allah. Allah has given me the Book and made me a Prophet." (sura 19:30)

Salvation is offered to all.
For whosoever shall call upon the name of the Lord shall be saved. (Rom. 10:13)

Who is saved is strictly the decision of Allah.
Allah forgives whom He pleases, and punishes whom He pleases, for Allah has power over all things. (sura 2:284)

Salvation is a gift of God's grace.
For by grace are ye saved through faith; and that not of yourselves: it is the gift of God: Not of works, lest any man should boast. (Eph. 2:8–9)

Salvation is based in works.
For those things that are good remove those that are evil. (sura 11:114)

One can have confidence that salvation is irrevocable.
And I give unto them eternal life; and they shall never perish, neither shall any man pluck them out of my hand. (John 10:28)

Jihad is the only eternal security.
And if you are slain, or die in the way of Allah, forgiveness and mercy from Allah are far better than all they could amass. (sura 3:157)

Salvation is never forced.
Come unto me, all ye that labor and are heavy laden, and I will give you rest. Take my yoke upon you, and learn of me; for I am meek and lowly in heart: and ye shall find rest unto your souls. For my yoke is easy, and my burden is light. (Matt. 11:28–30)

Allah forces worship.
Fight against them until there is no dissension, and the religion is for Allah. (sura 2:193)

Fight those who neither believe in Allah nor the Last Day, who do not forbid what Allah and His Messenger have forbidden, and do not embrace the religion of the truth, being among those who have been given the Book (Bible and the Torah), until they pay tribute out of hand and have been humiliated. (sura 9:29)

Appendix D

Glossary of Arabic Islamic Terms

Abu Bakr	Rich merchant among the first converts to Islam. First Muslim caliph.
A.H.	"After Hijra," denoting solar or lunar years on Islamic calendar.
Aishah	The daughter of Abu Bakr, and Muhammad's wife at age six.
Al-Faraa'id	Laws of inheritance.
Ali	Son-in-law and cousin of the prophet Muhammed; the fourth caliph and the first caliph recognized by the Shiite Muslims.
Al-Janaa'iz	Funeral.
Allah	God's name of essential being in Islam.
"Allahu Akbar"	"God is great." A direct praise to Allah.
Aulema	A scholar or theologian.
Aya	A verse in the Qur'an.
Ayatollah	"Sign of God." The highest rank of Shiite Muslims.
Baraka	A blessing.
Behesht	Paradise.
"Bismillah"	"In the Name of Allah." Beginning of prayer recitation.
Caliph/Kaliph	Title of Islamic leaders after Muhammad's death.

Deen	Muslim religious practice, as in ethic.
Dhul-Hijjah	Holiday, the "Day of Arafat."
'Eid-ul-Adha	One of the two major holidays—"Feast of Sacrifice."
'Eid-ul-Fitr	Feast breaking Ramadan fast. One of the two major holidays.
Fana	Sufi term for the "passing away" of the self.
Fatima	The daughter of Muhammad.
Fatwa	Religious decree.
Fiqh	Jurisprudence.
Ghair Muqarribat	Remote wife.
Ghusl	Bathing before prayer.
Hadith	"Story." Collection of sayings and examples of Muhammad; highest authority after the Qur'an.
Hafiz	One who memorizes the Qur'an.
Hajj	Pilgrimage to Mecca and one of five pillars. Every Muslim must make this journey once.
Hijra	Muhammed's migration from Mecca to Medina in 622. The beginning of Islam, and the starting date for the Islamic calendar.
Ibadat	Duty or obligation.
Iblis	Qur'anic name for Satan.
Iftar	Evening meal during Ramadan.
Ijma	Consensus of legal scholars.
Ijtihad	Private opinion of law and ethic.
Imam	Spiritual leader in the local mosque.
Injil	The New Testament Gospels, as revised in the Qur'an.
Isa	Arabic for "Jesus."
Ishmael	Son of Abraham through Hagar, Sarah's maidservant. Muslims believe Allah has a covenant with Ishmael, not Issac (c.f., Gen. 16:1–17:27).
Islam	"Submission" to the will of Allah.
Istisqaa	Prayer for rain.
Jihad	Holy fighting.
Jinn	Angels of Allah.
Kaaba	The "House of Allah," a square building in Mecca toward

	which Muslims turn for prayer. It is believed to have been given to Gabriel and built by Abraham and Ishmael.
Kafir	Infidel.
Khadija	Muhammed's first wife.
Kismet/Qadar	Fatalism which teaches Allah decrees everything.
Lailat ul-Qadr	"Night of Power," the twenty-seventh night of Ramadan, when Muhammed received first verses of Qurʾan.
MʾAmalat:	Ethics.
Mahabbah	"Love of Allah."
Mahdi	A coming world leader in Islamic eschatology.
Madrassah	Islamic religious school.
Mecca	Birthplace of Muhammad in Saudi Arabia, considered the holiest of cities. Site of the hajj.
Medina	The second most holy city, to which Muhammad fled in 622.
Mihama	New Year's Day on Islamic calendar.
Minaret	Mosque prayer tower from which the muezzin calls to *rakats*.
Mosque	Place of worship.
Muezzin	Leader who calls worshipers to prayer five times daily.
Muhammad	Allah's final and greatest prophet.
Mujahidin	Muslims who fight in the holy wars.
Muqarribat	Intimate wife.
Muslim	"One who submits to Allah." Follower of Islam.
Nikaah	Marriage.
PBUH	Acronym for "Peace be upon him." Always used in references to a prophet.
Qurʾan	The collected texts of Allah's revelation, corresponding with an original in Allah's heaven.
Ramadan	Ninth month in lunar calendar, commemorating the giving of the Qurʾan to Muhammad.
Rasul/Nabi	"God's messenger." A collective term for the prophets, including Adam, Noah, Abraham, Moses, Jesus, and Muhammad.
Salam	Greeting of peace.
Salat	The five prescribed daily prayers.

Sawm	Fasting during Ramadan. One of the five pillars.
Shahada/Kalimah	"To bear witness." The creed of Islam, "There is only one God, Allah, and Muhammad is his Prophet."
Sharia	Law and jurisprudence.
Shiite	"Followers of Ali." Those who believe Ali was the true successor to Muhammad.
Shirk	Idolatry or blasphemy against Allah.
Suhoor	During Ramadan, the meal before sunrise.
Sunnah	Written tradition, following the examples of Muhammad.
Sunni	"People of the Way." Followers of Abu Bakr and Umar as successors of Muhammad.
Sura	A chapter in the Qur'an.
Tafsir	A commentary on the Qur'an.
Tahajud	Evening prayers.
Tahrif	Teaching that the Bible is corrupted.
Tariqa	The Sufi inner way of meditation in Allah.
Tawhid	Allah's complete and total unity. A denial of the Trinity.
Tayammum	In absence of water, rubbing hands and feet with dust as an ablution before prayer.
Umar	The second Caliph, who burned all variations of the Qur'an.
Uthman	Third Muslim Caliph.
Wudu	Ablution before Islamic prayer.
Zakat	Almsgiving. Muslims must give one-fortieth of their worth in alms.

INDEX

EMIR FETHI CANER
ERGUN MEHMET CANER

More Than
a Prophet

An
Insider's Response
to Muslim Beliefs About
Jesus & Christianity

ISBN: 978-0-8254-2401-4

ALSO AVAILABLE FROM
KREGEL PUBLICATIONS

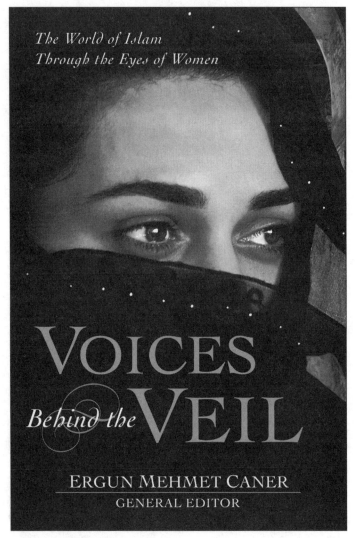

The World of Islam
Through the Eyes of Women

VOICES
Behind the VEIL

ERGUN MEHMET CANER
GENERAL EDITOR

ISBN: 978-0-8254-2402-1

Available wherever books are sold

ALSO AVAILABLE FROM KREGEL PUBLICATIONS

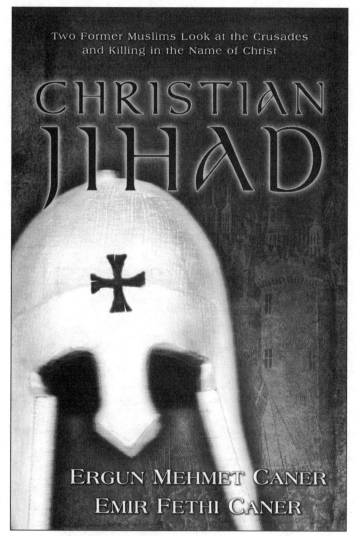

Two Former Muslims Look at the Crusades
and Killing in the Name of Christ

CHRISTIAN JIHAD

ERGUN MEHMET CANER
EMIR FETHI CANER

ISBN: 978-0-8254-2403-8

Available wherever books are sold

ALSO AVAILABLE FROM
KREGEL PUBLICATIONS

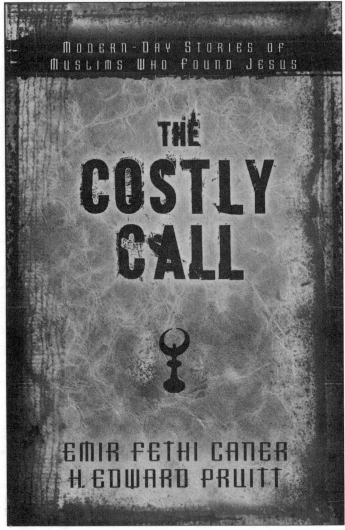

ISBN: 978-0-8254-3555-3

Available wherever books are sold